EXCEL 5
FOR WINDOWS

in easy steps

ROY ROACH

COMPUTER
STEP

First published October 1994

Computer Step
5c Southfield Road
Southam
Warwickshire CV33 OJH
England

Tel. 01926 817999
Fax. 01926 817005

British Library Cataloguing in Publication Data
A catalogue record for this book is available from the British Library.

Printed in England

ISBN 1 874029 15 6

About the Author

Roy Roach was formerly a Senior Lecturer in the Department of Graphics Technology at Manchester Metropolitan University (Manchester Polytechnic), where he lectured on information technology and ran a Departmental network of personal computers. Originally he taught spreadsheets using Multiplan but switched to Excel when Windows 2 was introduced. He used Excel extensively as an invaluable aid for administration and research, especially for graphical work.

Roy has a B.Sc(Hons) in Special Physics from London University and an M.Sc in Computation from UMIST (University of Manchester Institute of Science and Technology). He is a member of the British Computer Society.

Presently he still lectures part-time at Manchester Metropolitan University but offers consultancy and training services, specialising in computer aided design.

Dedication

To James, Ben and Sam

Acknowledgements

I wish to thank my wife, Barbara, for her encouragement and patient support during the writing of this book and my daughter, Pam, for all her help.

Also I would like to record my grateful thanks to all my former students on the B.Sc(Hons) in Printing and Photographic Technology and the Higher National Diploma Courses in Printing and in Photographic Technology, who enabled me to test my ideas on the practical teaching of Excel.

Table of Contents

13. Macros and Customizing......327

Index 337

CHAPTER

1

Getting Started

in easy steps

Introduction to the Screen

It is assumed that Excel 5 has been installed. Double click on the Excel icon to start it.

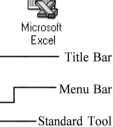

Microsoft
Excel

On *first installing* Excel 5, the opening screen will appear as shown below.

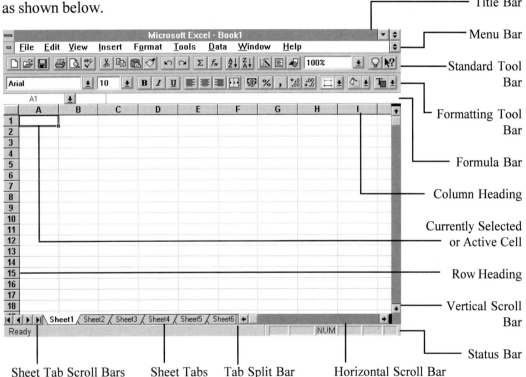

This busy complicated screen most probably will appear daunting to all but the most experienced of computer users. Some comfort may be gained if you have experience of Microsoft Word in that, although the application is quite different, the format of the various bars will look very familiar. Also, there will be some similarity to other Microsoft Windows and Apple Macintosh applications software.

If the screen does not appear exactly like this, do not worry. It has probably arisen because Excel has already been used and the previous user has adjusted its format. Any such discrepancies can be corrected by using the techniques shown in the following sections.

Elements of the Screen

Refer to the opening screen shown on the previous page:

The Spreadsheet
This is the large central rectangular area which is subdivided into a grid of **Cells**, used to store the spreadsheet data.

The Title Bar
This contains the title of the program and the name of the file which contains the spreadsheets and any associated charts, etc.. It also contains at the left-hand end the button for the pull-down control menu. Remember that the easiest way to exit from Excel is to double click this button with the mouse left button.

The Menu Bar
This contains the menu names for all the commands used to build, format and control the spreadsheet. Clicking any menu name with the mouse left button will display a pull-down menu from which may be selected various options.

The Standard Toolbar
This contains a selection of 'buttons' representing the most commonly used commands required for standard tasks. These provide a more convenient and quicker way of accessing these commands, compared to using the menu bar.

The Formatting Toolbar
This contains a selection of 'buttons' representing the most commonly used commands required for formatting the contents of the spreadsheet. These again are usually faster although less comprehensive than using the menu bar.

The Formula Bar
This displays the location and the content of the currently selected cell.

The Column Heading
This gives the horizontal location of each cell, the columns being labelled A, B, C...etc..

The Row Heading
This gives the vertical location of each cell, the rows being numbered 1, 2, 3...etc..

The Vertical Scroll Bar
This enables you to move the window vertically up and down the spreadsheet, under the control of the mouse.

The Horizontal Scroll Bar
This enables you to move the window horizontally to left or right across the spreadsheet.

The Sheet Tab Scroll Bars
These enable you to control which sheet tabs are displayed just to the right.

The Sheet Tabs
These enable you to select which spreadsheet should be displayed.

The Tab Split Bar
This allows you to adjust the horizontal subdivision of space between the sheet tabs and the horizontal scroll bar.

Note
Try to remember these terms, since they will be used throughout the book. The resulting screen appears packed and complex. Is it easy to simplify it? The answer is yes and for this reason it is possible that previous users may have changed the elements displayed to suit their personal preferences. In fact all these parts are optional except for the title bar and the menu bar and, of course, the spreadsheet itself. The following sections will demonstrate this and, should it be necessary, will enable you to restore the screen to its full complement of graphic bars.

Control of Window Options

The elements which appear in the Excel window are controlled by two commands:

The **Options...** command from the **Tools** menu and
The **Toolbars...** command from the **View** menu.

The procedure is as follows:

1   Point with the mouse to the keyword '**Tools**' on the Menu Bar.

Tip
Always keep your eye on the status bar for an indication of the use of commands.

2   Read the message which appears in the status bar:

"Provides auditing and analysis tools,
        records and runs macros,
            changes general options"

It is this last facility that we require.

3   Click with the mouse left button so that the Tools pull-down menu is displayed:

Various keywords are available on this menu. Some have a keyword and others a keyword followed by a right pointing triangle or ellipses (...).

Tools

Spelling...	F7
Auditing	▶
Goal Seek...	
Scenarios...	
Solver...	
Protection	▶
Add-Ins...	
Macro...	
Record Macro	▶
Assign Macro...	
Options...	

Keyword alone   means command will be executed immediately.

Keyword + triangle   means a sub-menu will be displayed.

Keyword + ellipses   means a dialogue box will be displayed.

4   Click **Options...** to display the dialogue box on the next page.

▷

5   The 'View' window should be displayed as below. If this is not so, then click the **View tab**.

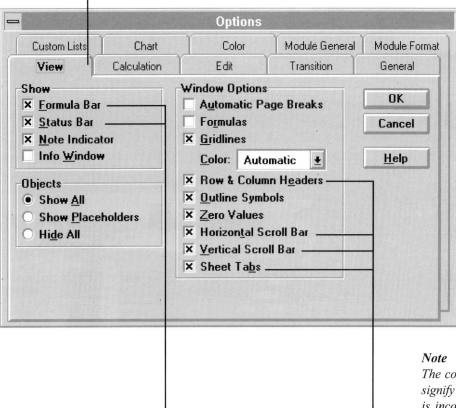

6   By clicking with the mouse, make sure that the following are *checked*, i.e. the respective check boxes contain crosses:

Show	**Window Options**
Formula Bar	Row and Column Headings
Status Bar	Horizontal Scroll Bar
	Vertical Scroll Bar
	Sheet Tabs

Note
*The convention to signify **checking** is inconsistent. Here in a check box, it is a **cross**. On the menu bar, as on the next page, it is a **tick**. Option buttons are filled with a **black dot**.*

View
√ Formula Bar
√ Status Bar
Toolbars...

Full Screen

Zoom...
View Manager...

7   Correspondingly point to the **View** menu on the Menu Bar.
The status bar will display the following description:
"Changes display settings
        toolbars,
        or document views"
Click with the mouse to display the menu.

8   Point to the **Toolbars...** command and the status bar
will display:-"Shows, hides, or customizes toolbars."
Click to display the dialogue box.

9   Make sure that the 'Standard' and 'Formatting' options
are *Checked.*

Tip
*Make sure the **Large***
***Buttons** option is*
***unchecked** as here.*
Otherwise the screen
may not display the
full complement of
buttons on toolbars.

Tip
*Make sure the **Tool***
***Tips** is **checked** as*
here to display the
descriptions of the
buttons on the tool
bars.

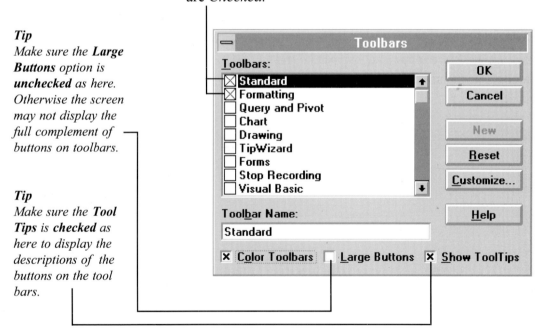

10   Click the '**OK**' button and the screen should appear as
shown at the beginning of this chapter. On quitting Excel,
these settings will be retained for future use.

Working with 'Full' Screen

By *Unchecking* all the options listed in the previous section under the Options... and Toolbars... dialogue boxes, it would be possible to strip the screen so that it contained only the Title Bar, the Menu Bar and the worksheet. This implies that it is possible to use Excel 5 with only the Menu Bar, which is the case provided greater reliance is placed on the keyboard instead of the mouse. However to do so would ignore the many graphic features which Excel 5 has provided to aid you and to speed up the process of learning the software. The point to be emphasised is that these graphic features, such as the toolbars, scroll bars and status bar are optional and that you should choose whichever technique you find easier to use.

Should such a simplified screen be required, there is a command to temporarily hide everything but the Title and Menu bars together with the Row and Column Headings. Since this maximises the size of the worksheet, it is referred to as the 'Full' screen.

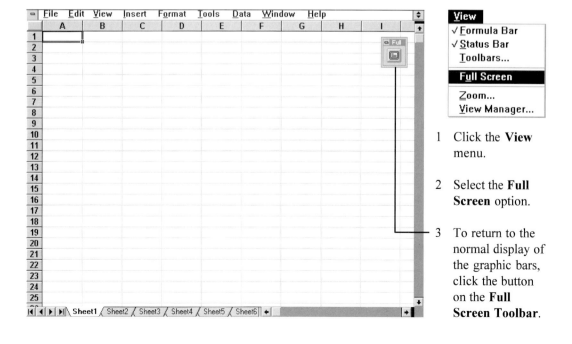

1   Click the **View** menu.

2   Select the **Full Screen** option.

3   To return to the normal display of the graphic bars, click the button on the **Full Screen Toolbar**.

The Window on Worksheet

What is a Workbook?

A Workbook is a file which holds together a collection of Worksheets (spreadsheets) and possibly Chart Sheets. You will see in later chapters that it is usual to have several spreadsheets linked together and often convenient to summarise the data on these spreadsheets in the form of charts or graphs. The Workbook is the most convenient way of holding together this collection of linked files. This feature is new to Excel 5.

What is a Worksheet (Spreadsheet)?

It was seen earlier that a Worksheet or Spreadsheet is an array of cells used to store data. This often involves simple arithmetic calculations linking the cells together in tables, usually for some kind of analysis.

The Window on a Worksheet

The opening Excel window displays initially:

typically 9 columns	labelled A to I
typically 18 rows	labelled 1 to 18

the exact number of rows and columns depending on the monitor screen and driver.

It must be appreciated that this is only the extreme top left hand corner of the full worksheet which extends to:

256 columns	labelled A to Z, AA to IV
16384 rows	labelled 1 to 16384

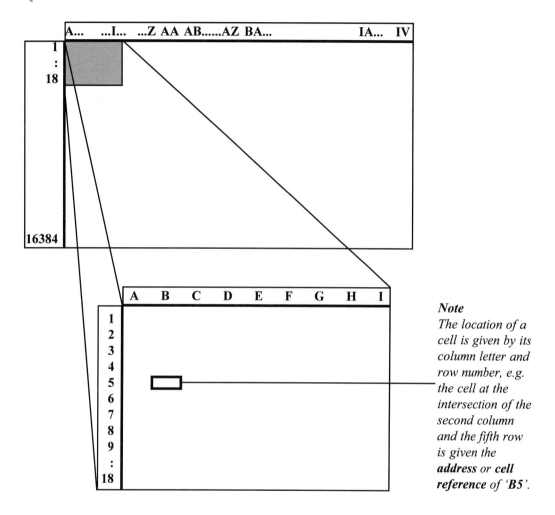

Note
*The location of a cell is given by its column letter and row number, e.g. the cell at the intersection of the second column and the fifth row is given the **address** or **cell reference** of 'B5'.*

The Excel screen displays only a tiny window of the available worksheet.

Note that after labelling the first 26 columns A to Z, it is necessary to resort to double letters:

           AA to AZ
           BA to BZ etc...

resulting in cell references such as 'AB25'.

Keying in Text

The technique for inserting text is quite simple:

1   In the Worksheet the mouse pointer is shaped like a cross.
     Position it over the destination cell and click the mouse left
     button to make the cell active. A border will appear around
     the cell, and the cell address or reference will be displayed
     on the Formula Bar.

2   Simply key in the text required. The characters will appear
     simultaneously in the cell and on the formula bar.

3   To terminate the input, it is possible to use many different
     keyboard control keys, for example the Enter key or the
     Arrow keys. This does not affect the content of the cell,
     but it does control the direction in which the next active
     cell is selected. Whereas the Enter key normally moves
     down to the next cell, the arrow keys move in their
     respective directions.

4   To locate the next cell the appropriate key is repeatedly
     pressed. Since you are using the keyboard to input text, it
     is more convenient to use these keys rather than to move
     your hands away from the keyboard to reach out for the
     mouse.

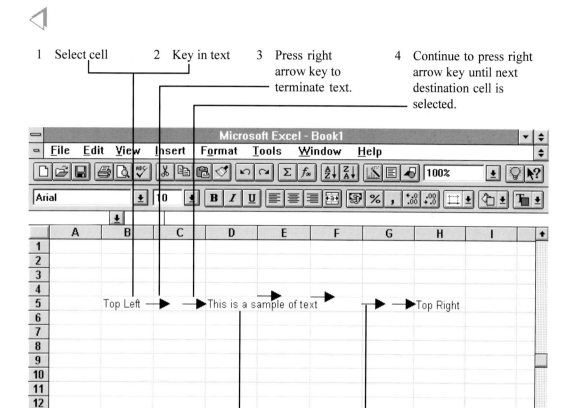

1 Select cell 2 Key in text 3 Press right arrow key to terminate text. 4 Continue to press right arrow key until next destination cell is selected.

5 The text, "This is a sample of text", is too long to be accommodated by the width of the cell's column. However, you'll see that the text bleeds to the right into the two adjacent cells. Such overflow text will be displayed provided the adjacent cells are empty as in this case.

6 Pressing the right arrow key four times will locate next cell.

7 The rest of the cells are selected by moving with arrow keys or by clicking with the mouse pointer, and the text is keyed in as shown.

Moving using the Mouse

It is easy to scroll the window around the worksheet using the mouse on the scrollbars.

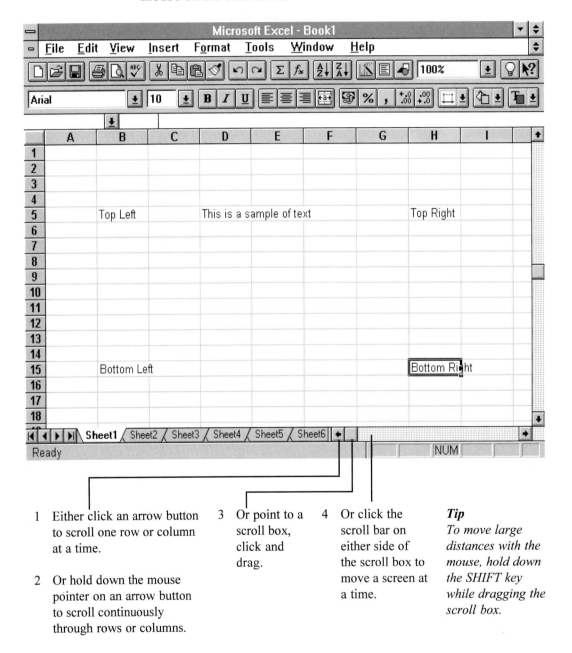

1 Either click an arrow button to scroll one row or column at a time.

2 Or hold down the mouse pointer on an arrow button to scroll continuously through rows or columns.

3 Or point to a scroll box, click and drag.

4 Or click the scroll bar on either side of the scroll box to move a screen at a time.

Tip

To move large distances with the mouse, hold down the SHIFT key while dragging the scroll box.

Moving using the Keyboard

Generally, it is more positive and faster to move around a worksheet using the keyboard, rather than the mouse. The problem is that it is necessary to remember a few control keys, which are listed in the table on the next page.

1 From cell H15, pressing Control + Home will make A1 the Active Cell.

2 From cell A1, pressing Control + End will return to H15, since this is the bottom right hand corner of filled cells.

3 From cell B5, pressing Control + Right Arrow twice will move across to D5 and then to H5.

4 From H5 pressing Control + Left Arrow twice will return to B5, jumping to next filled cells each time.

5 From B15, pressing End followed by Enter will move active cell to end of line at H15. This switches on the 'End' mode, which is shown on status bar.

6 From H15, pressing Home will move to beginning of line at B15

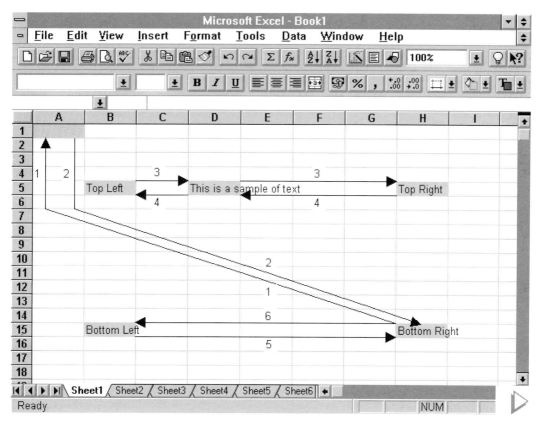

Why is so much emphasis being placed on using these keyboard techniques and learning these control keys? If you try moving within a spreadsheet, which is either wider or deeper than the window, then you will find that they give you more positive control and faster response than the mouse.

Keyboard Control Keys

Key(s)	Alone	In Combination With...
		CONTROL
Up Arrow	Up one row	Up...)to next filled
		)
Down Arrow	Down one row	Down...)region or to
		)
		)
Left Arrow	Left one column	Left...)furthest row
		)
Right Arrow	Right one column	Right...)or column
		CONTROL
HOME	To beginning of row	To top left - Cell A1
END	[Sets END mode]	Bottom right hand corner of filled spreadsheet
END, ENTER	Last cell in row [END followed by ENTER]	
		ALT
PAGE UP	Up one screen (typically 18 rows)	Left one screen (typically 9 columns)
PAGE DOWN	Down one screen (typically 18 rows)	Right one screen (typically 9 columns)

Moving using Edit Goto

An alternative technique of relocating the active cell is by means
of the Go To command.

1   Suppose the active cell is
     H15. From the **Edit** menu
     select the **GoTo...** option
     to display the Go To
     dialogue box.

2   Key in the cell reference,
     e.g. B5.

3   Click the '**OK**' button.

4   The active cell will
     change to B5.

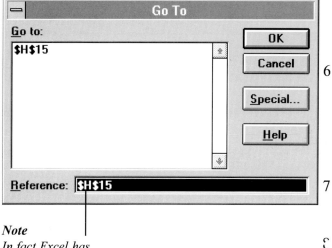

5   Suppose the Go To
     dialogue box was again
     displayed by using the
     command **Edit GoTo...**

6   The dialogue box would
     generally display a list of
     previous locations, but in
     this case it will show only
     'H15'.

7   This may be accepted by
     clicking the '**OK**' key.

8   The active cell will
     change to H15 again.

Note
*In fact Excel has
used the reference
'$H$15'. This is
the absolute
reference, which
will be explained
later.*

It must be evident that such moves would be easier using the
mouse or the keyboard. The Go To dialogue box is more
appropriate for off-screen locations.

Moving using the Formula Bar

A final method is to use the formula bar.

1   Move the pointer to the left end of formula bar, and click
     the reference to the current cell, e.g. B5.

2   It will be highlighted in reverse video.

3   Key in the address of the cell required, e.g. AH15, and
     press Enter.

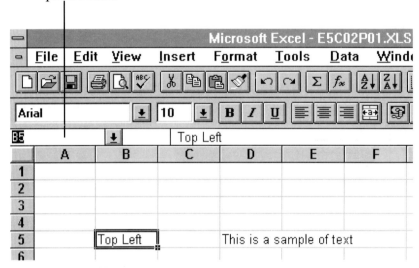

4   The active cell will change to AH15.

As with the Go To dialogue box, using the formula bar for
changing the active cell is more appropriate for off-screen
locations.

Moving between Worksheets

It is easy to switch between worksheets in the current workbook by using either the mouse or the keyboard.

1   Using the mouse simply click on the required worksheet tab at the bottom of the display, e.g. 'Sheet 5'.

2   A completely blank worksheet will be displayed.

3   To display undisclosed worksheet tabs, use the tab scrollbars as shown below.

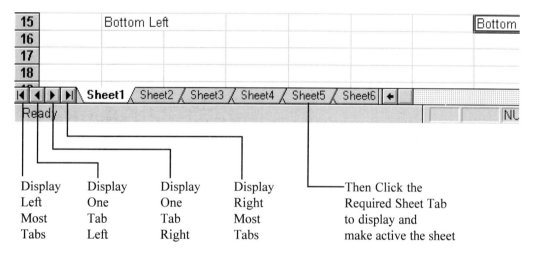

| Display Left Most Tabs | Display One Tab Left | Display One Tab Right | Display Right Most Tabs | Then Click the Required Sheet Tab to display and make active the sheet |

4   The keyboard code for changing the worksheet is to hold down the **Control** key and press **Page Up** or **Page Down** for left or right respectively.

5   Finally, if it is not necessary to display so many worksheets, the Tab Split Bar can be dragged with the mouse:

Warning
*It is almost inevitable that these keyboard commands will be confused with **Alt** plus **Page Up** or **Page Down** for moving the active cell horizontally by one screen!*

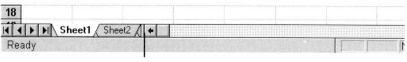

Drag with mouse

Selecting Cells with the Mouse

Tip
Always use the technique which is most efficient, either mouse or keyboard as appropriate but do not ignore the keyboard!

Cells can be selected with the keyboard or the mouse.

Generally keyboard selection is obtained by using the keyboard move codes, while holding down the Shift key additionally.

However, it must be admitted that the codes seem involved and in this case it is much easier to use the mouse.

Selection	Technique With Mouse
Single Cell	Point to cell and click mouse left button.
Multiple Adjacent Cells	Point to one extreme corner, hold down the mouse left button, and drag to opposite extreme cell.
Multiple Separated Cells	Hold down the Control key while making the selections above.
Row(s)	Click a single row heading or a selection of row headings.
Column(s)	Click a single column heading or a selection of column headings.
Entire Worksheet	Click the intersection of the row and column headings in the top left hand corner of worksheet.

To select the whole worksheet, click the intersection of the row and column headings, i.e. the '**Select All**' button.

To select a row or a column click the appropriate row or column heading.

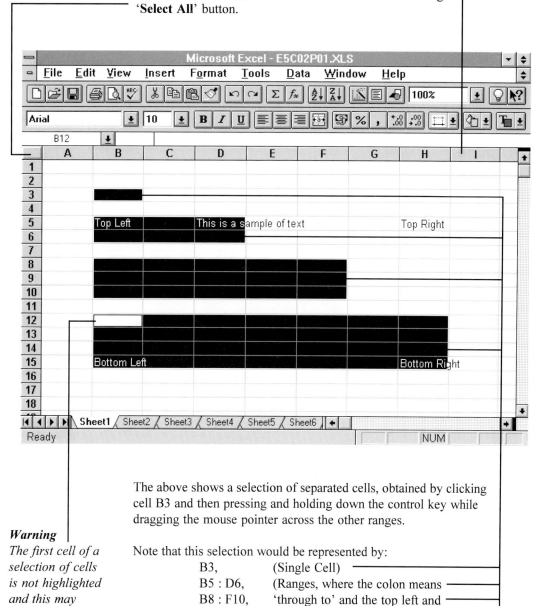

The above shows a selection of separated cells, obtained by clicking cell B3 and then pressing and holding down the control key while dragging the mouse pointer across the other ranges.

Warning
The first cell of a
selection of cells
is not highlighted
and this may
confuse new users.

Note that this selection would be represented by:

B3,   (Single Cell)

B5 : D6,   (Ranges, where the colon means

B8 : F10,   'through to' and the top left and

B12 : H15   bottom right cells of blocks are given)

Zooming using the Menu Bar

Zooming a Worksheet Using the Menu Bar

A very useful facility is that of enlarging or reducing (zooming in and out) the screen display of a worksheet or a chart.

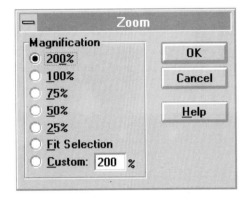

1   From the **View** menu select the **Zoom...** option.

2   In the **Zoom** dialogue box, click the **200%** button and the OK button to increase the size of the cells, restricting the display to show fewer cells.

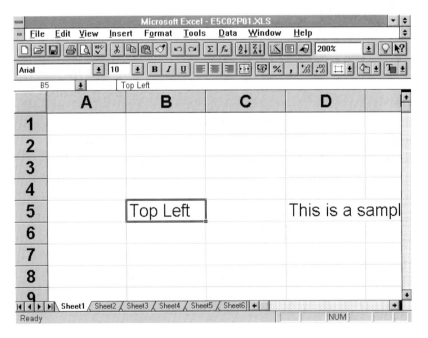

This is useful to view finer detail. Unfortunately, not all of the cell contents are displayed. The method of correction will be shown in a later section.

Using the Toolbars 'Tool Tips'

So far neither the Standard Toolbar nor the Formatting Toolbar have received the attention they deserve. Remember that these provide access to the more commonly used commands and are designed to be more convenient than accessing commands via the menu bar.

The problem with the menu bar for a new user is that the user does not know under which menu a particular command is accessed. It is for this reason that on selecting a particular menu, the status bar gives an overall description of the commands available.

The problem with the toolbars for a new user is that the icons on the buttons may have less than obvious meanings. Therefore to help, Excel also gives a description of the command on the status bar.

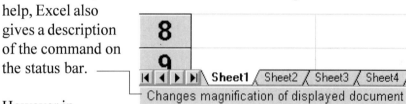

However in addition to this Excel provides a facility called 'Tool Tips'. By pointing at one of the buttons with the mouse, e.g. on the Standard Toolbar (the upper one of the two) there is a drop

down list box at the right hand side, a small (yellow) box should appear which contains the description, "Zoom Control".

Pointing at other buttons will display similar description boxes.

Should Tool Tips not be enabled, then refer to a previous section, 'Control of Window Options', to see how to restore it.

Taking Advice from the 'Tip Wizard'

So far the 'Tip Wizard' on the Standard Toolbar has been ignored. The icon which represents this is an electric light bulb at the right end of the toolbar. At this stage it should be illuminated (yellow on a colour monitor) to indicate that the Tip Wizard has a tip for you. To read it, follow this procedure.

1   Click the Tip Wizard button. ─────────────────

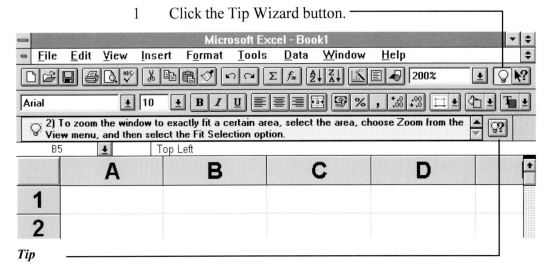

Tip
Click this icon for further help - see following sections.

2   The Tip Wizard box will appear between the Formatting Toolbar and the Formula Bar.

3   The message is "2) To zoom the window to exactly fit a certain area, select the area, choose Zoom from the View menu, and then select the Fit Selection option.".

Tip: Resetting the Tip Wizard
If Excel is not newly installed, it may be necessary to reset the Tip Wizard to obtain the full range of its advice. The reason is that it will have already issued tips to a previous user and it will not give these tips again, unless it is reset. The procedure is as follows:
*From the **Tools** menu, select the **Options...** option to display the **Options** dialogue box. Click the **General** tab. Check the **Reset Tip Wizard** box and click OK.*

Note: *The Reset Tip Wizard box will be automatically unchecked after resetting.*

4   Click the scroll button on the pull-down list of Tip Wizard
     box to display the earlier message.

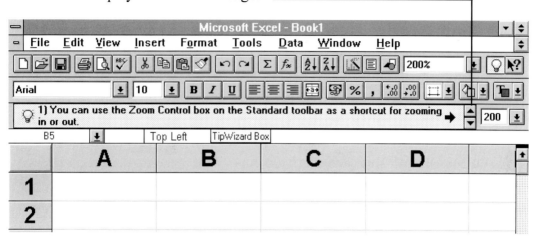

5   The earlier message was "1) You can use the Zoom
     Control box on the Standard toolbar as a short-cut for
     zooming in and out.". This also gives the icon of the
     appropriate button to the right. Also to the right of this (if
     not off screen) is the icon to press for further help.

6   The first message is recommending to the user the use of
     the Standard Toolbar. The second message is giving more
     general advice, which is helpful for magnifying the display.
     All such tips are stored in this list for reference during the
     current session.

7   To remove the Tip Wizard Box click the Tip Wizard
     button. The lamp will now appear switched off. It will only
     light up when the Tip Wizard has additional advice to add
     to its list of tips.

Warning: *The Tip Wizard may suggest the use of toolbar buttons which are
not available on the standard toolbars - see chapter 13, 'Macros and
Customizing'.*

Tip
*Keep your eye on
the tip wizard icon
- the advice given
is very useful,
since it is linked
to your actions.*

Warning
*The 'Tip of the
Day' is a tip given
at the beginning
of each Excel
session. Since it
appears to be
selected at
random, it is less
useful and may
even distract a
new user!*

Zooming using the Standard Toolbar

The tips issued by the Tip Wizard to zoom using the standard toolbar can be used as shown.

1 Point to the Zoom Control button on the Standard Toolbar and click the mouse left button to display the pull-down list.

2 Select 100% and the display will be restored to the default magnification.

3 Use the mouse to select the rectangular area of cells lying between the top left hand corner at cell B5 and the bottom right hand corner at cell H15, usually abbreviated to 'B5 : H15'.

4 Click the Zoom Control button again to display the pull-down list and select the word 'Selection'. The display will zoom in on the selected area, as suggested by the second tip. Note magnification of 131%.

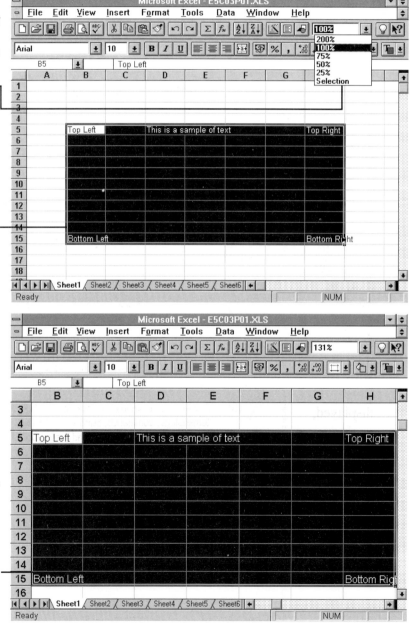

General use of Help

Like most other software packages, Excel has a comprehensive Help system. Theoretically, it should be possible to locate all necessary information via this system. It can be started at various levels.

Starting Help Contents from Menu Bar or from Keyboard

1   *Either*:   from **Help** menu select the **Contents** option.
    Or: press the function key **F1**.

2   The following Help Contents will be displayed.

3   Click the **Search** button to search for required topic.

4   The Help Search window is displayed, as shown on the next page.

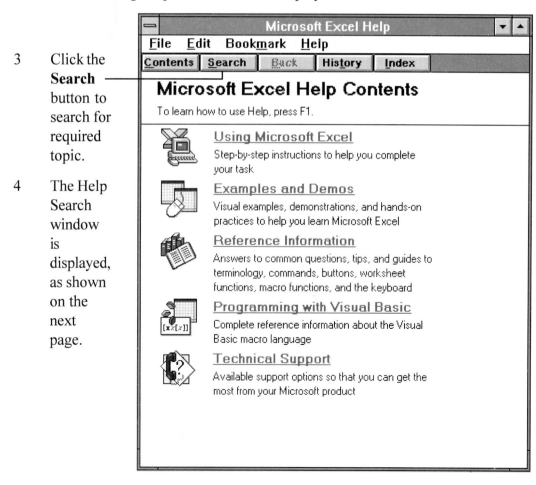

Searching for Help Topics

Starting Help Search from Help Button

1   *Double click* the Help Button at the far right end of the
     Standard ToolBar. ——————————————————————————

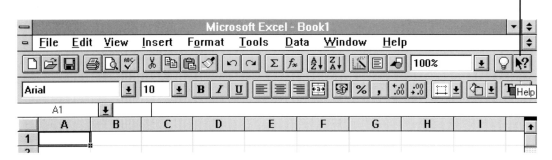

2   The Help Search window is displayed.

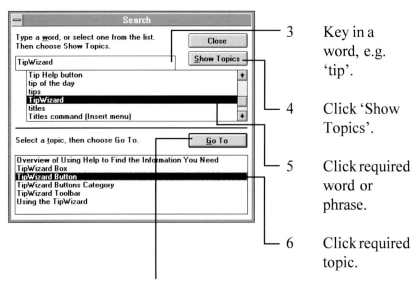

3   Key in a
     word, e.g.
     'tip'.

4   Click 'Show
     Topics'.

5   Click required
     word or
     phrase.

6   Click required
     topic.

7   Click GoTo button.

8   The help screen specifically on the 'Tip Wizard Button' is
     displayed as shown in the next section.

Specific Help

The Help Button at the far right end of the Standard ToolBar is particularly useful for learning about Excel 5.

1   *Click* the Help Button (just a *single click* with mouse left button). ───

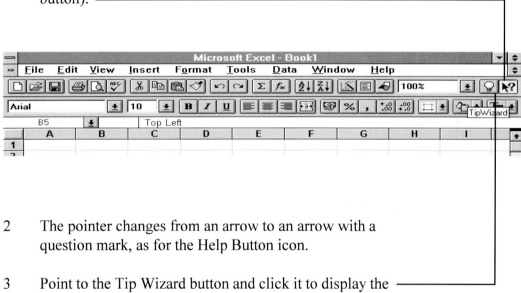

2   The pointer changes from an arrow to an arrow with a question mark, as for the Help Button icon.

3   Point to the Tip Wizard button and click it to display the ─── Help screen on the next page.

Such help can be obtained about most aspects of Excel. Simply single click the Help Button, so that the pointer has the question mark attached. Then point and click at an item on the screen or execute some keyboard action.

This technique is more positive than the previous two methods of obtaining help, since it takes you directly to the topic about which you wish to learn, without having to navigate a complex sequence of windows.

Tip
The Help Button is a powerful facility, which is invaluable for learning the system.

Click for overview of HELP contents.　　Click for search window - key in a word or select a topic from list.　　Click to revert to previous HELP window.　　Click to display list of HELP topics used in this session.　　Click to display alphabetic list of HELP topics.

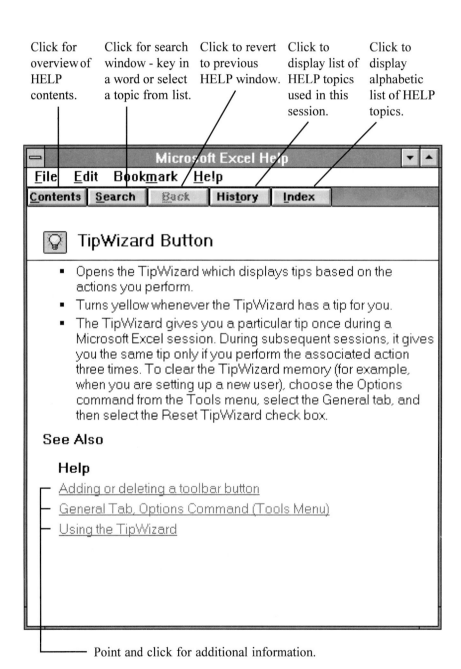

Point and click for additional information.

CHAPTER 2

Creating and Editing a Simple Spreadsheet

in easy Steps

The Differences between Text, Numbers and Formulas

When text or numbers are keyed into a cell, Excel must analyse the sequence of characters to determine whether they represent a number. It does this by applying the rules we use normally to represent numbers, i.e. a combination of digits, optionally a full stop to represent a decimal point somewhere within the digits, and possibly a plus or a minus sign at the beginning. Excel will also recognise a '£' sign at the beginning or a '%' sign at the end. Provided the type of characters and their sequence follow the logic to represent a number, Excel will store the value of this number in the cell. Otherwise, it retains the sequence as a string of characters and stores it as text.

In the case of a formula, Excel must be alerted initially to expect a formula by the first character, which must be an equals sign, '='.

Consider in each case the difference in what is stored and what is displayed:

In the case of *text*, a string of characters is stored as in a word processing program. Provided the cell is sufficiently wide or sufficient adjacent cells are empty, the whole of the text will be displayed up to a limit of 256 characters.

In the case of a *number*, the string of characters is converted to the equivalent numeric value, and this value is stored. What is displayed will depend on the format to which the cell is set, the number of decimal places, and possibly '£' sign for currency or '%' sign for percentage.

In the case of a *formula*, the formula is stored and the result of evaluating the formula is displayed according to the format of the cell.

This chapter covers the input and editing of such data and its arrangement and formatting to produce a simple spreadsheet.

Keying in Data

Tip
To convert numbers to text:
Select the cell(s).
Use menu option
Format Cells...
Select the
Number *tab.*
For the **Category**
select **Text**.
Click OK.

Introduction

Assume that Excel 5 is running and that the opening screen contains a full complement of graphic bars as shown in Chapter 1, and that 'Workbook 1' is open and empty.

Keying In Data

Suppose the following data was entered as shown on the opposite page:

Tip
To convert text to numbers:
Select the cell(s).
Use menu option
Format Cells...
Select the
Number *tab.*
For the **Category**
select **Number**.
Select appropriate
Format Code.
Click OK.

1   The first block of cells, B5 : C8, are filled with descriptive text simply by typing the text and terminating each cell by pressing the Enter or an Arrow key.

2   Cell C10 is selected and the digit 1 is input followed by the latter capital O, followed by the Enter key. This is the deliberate repeat of a common mistake, the misuse of capital O instead of the digit 0. As a result the text, "1O", will be displayed, normally aligned to the left as shown.

3   If in cell C12 the sequence of digit 1 followed by digit zero is terminated by Enter, this will be displayed as the number, "10", normally aligned to the right.

Tip
Sometimes errors in calculations occur as a result of wrongly keyed numbers which Excel interprets as text.
Such mistakes are more easily spotted if you remember that the **alignment** *in such cells will usually be* **left** *rather than right.*

4   Finally if in cell C14, the equals sign was keyed in, followed by the simple arithmetic calculation, "6 + 4", terminated by Enter, this will be evaluated and the resulting value, "10", will be displayed also aligned to the right of the cell. Note that the formula is always displayed on the formula bar and its result is normally displayed on the worksheet.

The alignment for text is usually to the left as is normal for text whereas the alignment for numbers or numbers resulting from evaluating formulas is usually to the right, often being formatted to produce decimal point alignment.

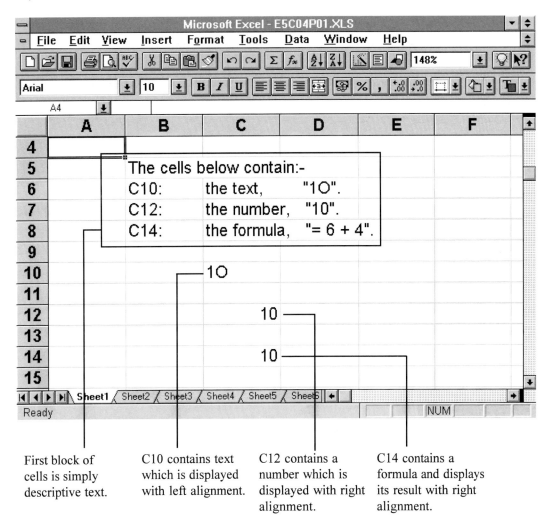

First block of cells is simply descriptive text.

C10 contains text which is displayed with left alignment.

C12 contains a number which is displayed with right alignment.

C14 contains a formula and displays its result with right alignment.

Tip
To force a sequence of digits to be input as text, precede the digits by a single quote, e.g. as for a reference number **'001234**.

Displaying Formulas instead of Results

Whereas text and numbers are displayed largely in the form in
which they are keyed, it is the results of evaluating formulas
which are displayed. This is the normal default for spreadsheets.
However to view the formulas stored, the default can be changed
as follows:

1   From the **Tools** menu select the **Options...** command to
       display the options dialogue box.

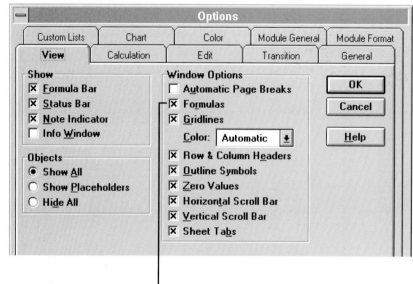

Tip
*A much quicker
way of switching
between the
display of
formulas and
results is to hold
down the Control
key and press the
open quote key (`)
at the top left of
the keyboard.*

2   On the **View** tab check the **Formulas** option box.

3   Click OK button and the display will show formulas.

Note
*It is normal
practice to display
the results of
calculating
formulas and this
is how worksheets
should be set up.*

*Cell C14
displays formula
instead of result.*

Editing on the Formula Bar

If mistakes are made in keying in text, numbers or formulas and, if subsequently minor changes are needed, then editing can be done on the formula bar. The procedure is quite simple:

1   Select the cell for editing, e.g. B5.

2   The formula bar will display
     the current cell reference and its contents.

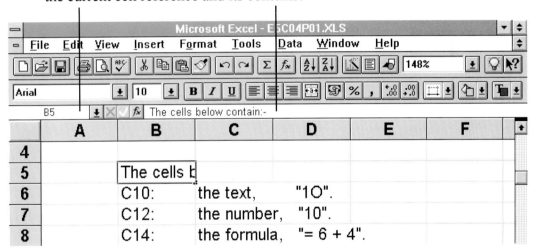

3   Move the mouse pointer to the cell's contents on the
     formula bar, where the pointer will change to the familiar
     I-beam, as used in word processing and desktop
     publishing programs.

4   Adjust the I-beam so that it is near the character(s) to be
     changed.

5   Click the mouse button so that the insertion point is placed
     as a flashing vertical line.

6   Edit the cell contents using the keyboard control keys
     given in the next section.

Keys for Editing Data

While Keying Data into Cells

While text, numbers or formulae are being keyed in, the editing which is supported is very limited. All that can be used is the **Backspace** key to delete characters to the left of the insertion point. If a control key, such as Left Arrow, is used then the entry of data will be terminated, as shown in the table below.

Control Keys for Data Entry

Key	Effect of Key Alone
Backspace	Delete character to left of insertion point.
Left Arrow	Terminate data entry and select cell to left.
Right Arrow or Tab Key	Terminate data entry and select cell to right.
Up Arrow	Terminate data entry and select cell above.
Down Arrow or ENTER	Terminate data entry and select cell below.
ESCAPE	Cancels data entry.

Tip
If you wish to stop the Enter key reselecting a cell, then from the **Tools** *menu select the* **Options...** *command, click the* **Edit** *tab and uncheck the* **Move Selection after Entry** *box.*

For Subsequent Editing on Formula Bar or at Cell

The control keys used for editing for later corrections, either on the formula bar or at the cell, are more comprehensive and are the same as those used for most word processing programs. These are summarised next.

As usual, by keying in extra text at the insertion point, it will be placed either between the existing characters or over the top of them. This depends on whether the keying is being done in *insertion* or in *overtype* mode. This mode is toggled by pressing the '**Insert**' key. When *overtype* mode is on, 'OVR' appears on the right of the Status Bar. When *insert mode* is on, 'OVR' is removed from the Status Bar.

Editing is terminated by pressing the 'Enter' key. At any stage before Enter is pressed, editing can be abandoned and the cell restored to its original contents by pressing the Escape key.

Control Keys for Editing on Formula Bar or at Cell

Key	Effect of Key Alone	Effect of Key in Combination With...
		CONTROL KEY (CTRL)
Left Arrow	Move insertion point one character left.	Move insertion point one word left.
Right Arrow	Move insertion point one character right.	Move insertion point one word right.
HOME	Move insertion point to beginning of line.	
END	Move insertion point to end of line.	
Backspace	Delete character to left of insertion point.	
DELETE	Delete character to right of insertion point.	
ESCAPE	Abandon editing and restore cell.	
ENTER	Terminate editing	

Note
The arrow keys work normally in this case and do not terminate data entry.

Editing at the Cell

An alternative technique to editing on the formula bar is to edit the contents of a cell at the cell itself. The procedure is:

1   Place the pointer over the cell to be edited, e.g. C14, and double click the mouse left button.

C14		↓ X ✓	*fx* = 6 + 4	
	A	**B**	**C**	**D**
13				
14			= 6 + 4	
15				

2   The contents, whether text, numbers or formulas, will be displayed in the cell, extended if necessary to accommodate the contents with the insertion point located at the end, ready for editing:

C14		↓ X ✓	*fx* = (6 + 4) * 5 / 3				**C**
	A	**B**	**C**	**D**			
13							
14			= (6 + 4) * 5 / 3				16.66667
15							

3   Using the editing techniques summarised in the previous section, the formula could be changed to:
$$= (6 + 4) * 5 / 3$$
where the asterisk represents the multiplication sign and the oblique stroke represents the division sign.

4   On pressing Enter, the resulting value 16.66667 will be displayed.

Changing Cell Contents

Overtyping Cell Contents

Text, numbers or formulas can all be changed by simply typing a new entry over an existing one. The procedure is simple:

1   Select the cell to be changed.

2   Key in the new value or formula.

3   Press the Enter key and the new value will be displayed.

Clearing Cell Contents

There are several ways to clear a cell , i.e. to remove any previous entries and leave it blank. The easiest way is to select it and press the keyboard **Delete** key.

Clearing versus Deleting Cells

Tip
In the case of numbers stored in cells, it is almost always easier to rekey them rather than edit them. It may be easier to edit formulas and text.

Warning
Note the confusion between the keyboard control key 'Delete' and the Edit menu command Delete!

Clearing Cell Contents:

Select the cells and from the **Edit** menu **Clear** sub-menu select the option required. **All** is equivalent to the keyboard *Delete* key.

Deleting Cells (and Contents) **from Worksheet**:

Select the cells and from the **Edit** menu select the **Delete...** option and complete the Delete dialogue box.

Using Undo and Repeat:

In case you clear or delete cells inadvertently you can rectify your mistake by using the **Undo** command from the **Edit** menu or from the **Standard Toolbar**. Undo and Repeat can be applied to most other commands.

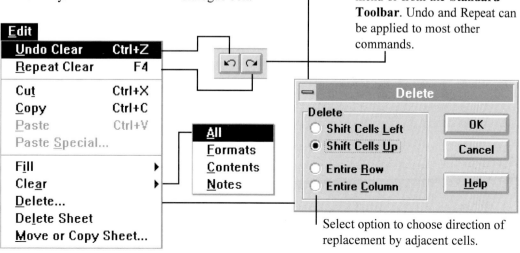

Select option to choose direction of replacement by adjacent cells.

Rules for Arithmetic Operations

It may be appropriate at this stage to remind you of the symbols used generally in information technology to represent simple arithmetic operations:

Arithmetic Operators

Symbol	Meaning	Examples
+ (plus)	Addition	6 + 4 = 10
- (minus or hyphen)	Subtraction or negation	6 - 4 = 2 or -4
* (asterisk)	Multiplication	6 * 4 = 24
/ (oblique stroke)	Division	6 / 4 = 1.5
^ (caret)	Exponentiation	6 ^ 4 = 1296 (6 multiplied by itself 4 times)

The order of precedence for the evaluation of these operations is:

First	( )	Brackets
Second	^	Exponentiation
Third	* /	Multiplication and Division
Fourth	+ -	Addition and Subtraction

Note
Brackets can be used to override the priority order of any other symbols.

Note
Where equal priority applies, the order taken is left to right.

Note
It is necessary that you are able to handle at least simple arithmetic and rules such as these.

Consider two examples to illustrate how brackets alter the order of priority:

$$4 + 6 / 4 - 2 \qquad = 4 + 1.5 - 2 \qquad = 3.5$$
$$(4 + 6) / (4 - 2) \qquad = 10 / 2 \qquad = 5$$

Planning a Simple Spreadsheet Layout

The Worksheet below shows the text outline of part of a monthly business plan for a fictitious business. This plan is grossly oversimplified, but it is sufficiently realistic for you to learn the basics of Worksheets and Charts. The business is a photographic colour processing laboratory situated in a rented shop. It restricts itself to one service, the developing and printing of 24 exposure 35mm colour negative films. It aims at top quality with a fast turn-around, preferably the same day but certainly within 24 hours, weekends included. Don't worry if the figures used in these calculations are somewhat unrealistic. The main purpose is to have a simple model for demonstrating aspects of Excel 5. This business plan will be extended and developed through the rest of the book.

When starting a new spreadsheet, it is necessary to decide on a strategy for the layout. In this example the text which forms the headings and labels occupies far more space than the numbers and formulas. You need to decide how to store this information:

> *Widen Column* - In some cases it may be better to allocate one column to store all such text and adjust its width accordingly. This technique will be explained later. The problem with this is that subsequent lines in this column cannot be subdivided into further columns.

	A	B	C	D	E	F
1			FastPrint	24 LTD		
2				24 Exposure Colour Nega		
3				24 Hours Maximum Proce		
4			MONTHLY BUSINESS PLAN			
5						
6	SALES INCOME					
7		Developing & Printing Price Including VAT =				
8		Developing & Printing Price Excluding VAT =				
9						
10		Average Number of Films per Day =				
11		Average Number of Days per Month =				
12		Average Number of Films per Month =				
13						
14		Average Sales per Month =				
15						

Tip
*It is more flexible
to allow wide
headings and
labels to straddle
several cells.*

Allow Text to Straddle Columns - In other cases it is easier to allow the wide headings and labels to straddle several columns. This is the strategy chosen here, as shown below.

Warning
You must leave sufficient empty adjacent cells to fully display such text.

If later you change your mind about the layout, then Excel is sufficiently flexible to accommodate changes, but a little thought at the start can save subsequent work.

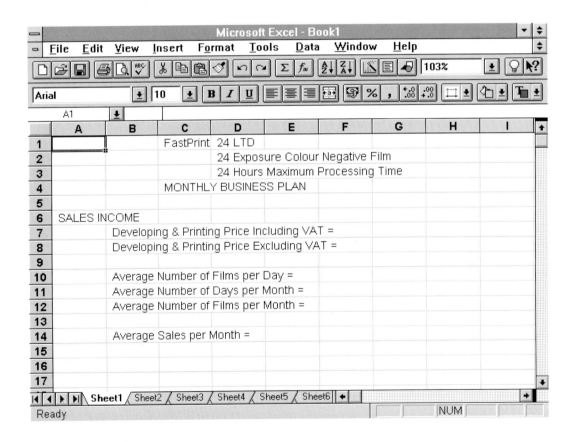

Inputting and Formatting Numbers

The following is a typical sequence for keying in and formatting the numbers on a spreadsheet.

1   The three numbers are keyed in as shown below.

2   Since these calculations will be mainly financial, it is easier to display all figures in pounds (Sterling) and pence. To save time it is easier to format *all* the cells in the worksheet as financial.

(a) Select a sufficient columns of worksheet to accommodate spreadsheet, e.g. A:J.

(b) Click the **Currency Style Button** on the **Formatting ToolBar**.

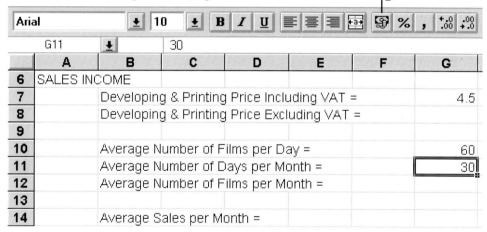

3   All the numbers on the sheet will be displayed in pounds and pence, with decimal point alignment.

4   Unfortunately, the whole numbers in cells G10:G12 will now be wrongly formatted as pounds and pence.

5   Fortunately, it is easy to correct the exceptions like these
        as follows:

        (a) Select the cells to be reformatted, e.g. G10:G12.

        (b) From the **Format** menu, select the **Cells...** option.

        (c) Complete the Format Cells dialogue box Number tab...
            Category: Select **Number**
            Format Codes: Select **0**
            and click the **OK** button.

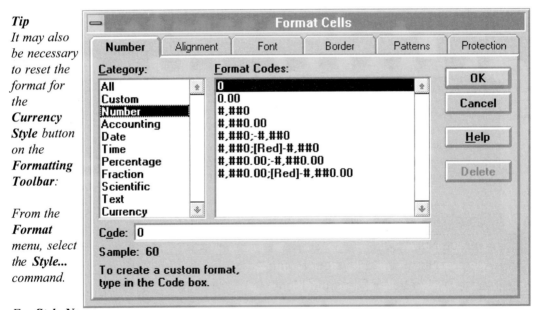

Tip
It may also be necessary to reset the format for the **Currency** *Style button on the* **Formatting** *Toolbar:*

From the **Format** *menu, select the* **Style...** *command.*

For Style Name select **Currency**. *Click the* **Modify...** *button.*

For **Category** *select* **Currency**. *For* **Format** *select* *'£#,##0.00;* *[RED]-£#,##0.00'*

6   The numbers will now be displayed with the
        correct format.

Note
Where possible the Formatting ToolBar should be used for speed, but for more complex formatting it may be necessary to use the option Format Cells... Formatting will be covered in more detail in Chapter 10, 'Formatting Worksheets'.

G
£4.50
60
30

Inputting Formulas

Formulas must be keyed in for three cells. Each of these formulas form calculations based on numerical values in other cells, or on the results of calculating formulas in other cells. The technique of inputting a formula is demonstrated on the calculation of the 'average number of films per month'. This is simply calculated by multiplying the 'average number of films per day' by the 'average number of days per month'. The procedure is as follows:

1   Select the cell which is to contain the formula, e.g. G12.

2   Press the equals key to alert Excel that a formula is being keyed in.

	B	C	D	E	F	G	H
10	Average Number of Films per Day =					60	
11	Average Number of Days per Month =					30	
12	Average Number of Films per Month =					=	

3   Select the cell containing the 'average number of films per day', G10, either by pointing and clicking with the mouse or by using the arrow keys.

	B	C	D	E	F	G	H
10	Average Number of Films per Day =					60	
11	Average Number of Days per Month =					30	
12	Average Number of Films per Month =					=G10	

The selected cell will be identified by a dotted line round its boundary.

The selected cell's reference will appear automatically in the formula.

4   The asterisk key is pressed, where the asterisk represents the multiplication operator.

Asterisk inserted for multiplication.

	B	C	D	E	F	G	H
10	Average Number of Films per Day =					60	
11	Average Number of Days per Month =					30	
12	Average Number of Films per Month =				=G10 *		

5   Select the cell containing the 'average number of days per month', G11.

	B	C	D	E	F	G	H
10	Average Number of Films per Day =					60	
11	Average Number of Days per Month =					30	
12	Average Number of Films per Month =				=G10 * G11		

6   The formula is now complete. It means "Take the content of G10 and multiply it by the content of G11".

7   Press the Enter key to complete it and to display the result.

	B	C	D	E	F	G	H
10	Average Number of Films per Day =					60	
11	Average Number of Days per Month =					30	
12	Average Number of Films per Month =					1800	
13							

It may be quicker, in the case of a simple formula like this, for touch typists to simply key in the formula, "=G10*G11", directly. However, it must be pointed out that this technique of selecting the cell required in a formula by pointing and clicking the mouse is extended to blocks of cells and an error is less likely to occur with this automatic facility. Do what you find easier.

The other two formulas would be completed as shown below.

The formula used in G8 converts the value in G7 from the retail price including VAT of 17.5% to the amount due to the business.

The formula used in I14 is simply the product of the 'average number of films per month' and the 'price excluding VAT'.

	G	H	I
7	4.5		
8	=G7 / 1.175		
9			
10	60		
11	30		
12	=G10 * G11		
13			
14			=G12 * G8

The above display was obtained by displaying formulas in cells. On switching back to displaying results (Control + open quote), the results will be displayed as below. The only problem is that an error message appears in cell I14 (see the next section).

	A	B	C	D	E	F	G	H	I
1			FastPrint 24 LTD						
2				24 Exposure Colour Negative Film					
3				24 Hours Maximum Processing Time					
4			MONTHLY BUSINESS PLAN						
5									
6	SALES INCOME								
7			Developing & Printing Price Including VAT =				£4.50		
8			Developing & Printing Price Excluding VAT =				£3.83		
9									
10			Average Number of Films per Day =				60		
11			Average Number of Days per Month =				30		
12			Average Number of Films per Month =				1800		
13									
14			Average Sales per Month =						######

Adjusting Column Widths

The error message, "#####", indicates that the cell width is insufficient to display the cell contents or the result of evaluating a formula, to the format specified for the cell. In such a case the containing column width must be increased. As usual there are several alternative methods for doing this.

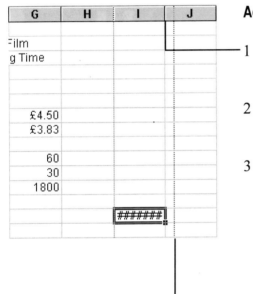

Adjusting Column Width using Mouse

1 Point to the right hand margin of column heading.

2 The pointer will change to a double headed arrow.

3 *Either* double click the mouse button so that the column width is automatically adjusted so that it accommodates the contents of all cells in that column.

Note
This will include text as well as numbers and the results of calculating formulas.

Or better still, drag with the mouse button depressed to increase the column width, as required. The exact width will be displayed on the formula bar as you drag. Adjust it to 10.

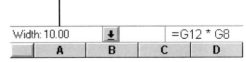

4 The value will be displayed as required.

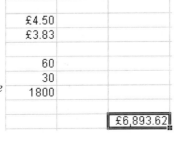

Tip
For speed, use the mouse to control the column width.

Adjusting Column Width using Format Column Width... option

1   Select the column or columns by clicking the respective headings. Remember that separated columns can be selected by holding down the Control key (CTRL) while the headings are clicked.

2   From the **Format** menu select the **Column** sub-menu.

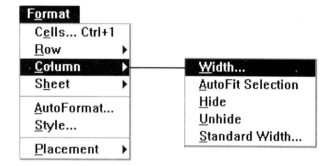

3   From the **Column** sub-menu select the **Width...** option.

4   In the **Column Width** dialogue box key in the width required. Some experimentation may be required to get this right.

5   Click the **OK** button.

6   The value will be displayed as required.

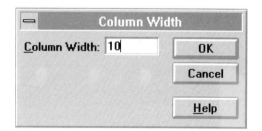

Tip
For a consistent layout, use the **Format Column Width...** *command - this enables you to specify the same width for several columns by selecting them first.*

Inserting Extra Columns or Rows

Suppose that after setting up your spreadsheet, you discover that you have omitted a central part of it or that you wish to add extra information in the middle of it. Fortunately this is not a problem. Excel provides an easy method of inserting extra columns or extra rows wherever you require them.

To demonstrate this the business calculation will be made more general by allowing the VAT rate to be increased, should the Chancellor decree this! This requires three additional rows between Row 7 and Row 8.

Locate New Rows

1   To show where the new rows are to be, select rows 8 to 10, i.e. '**8 : 10**', by pointing at the row headings and dragging with the mouse.

	A	B	C	D	E	F	G	H	I
1			FastPrint	24 LTD					
2				24 Exposure Colour Negative Film					
3				24 Hours Maximum Processing Time					
4			MONTHLY BUSINESS PLAN						
5									
6	SALES INCOME								
7			Developing & Printing Price Including VAT =				£4.50		
8			Developing & Printing Price Excluding VAT =				£3.83		
9									
10			Average Number of Films per Day =				60		
11			Average Number of Days per Month =				30		
12			Average Number of Films per Month =				1800		
13									
14			Average Sales per Month =						£6,893.62

Either Use Command Menu

2   From the **Insert** menu select the **Rows** option.

3   The cells below Row 7 will be displaced downwards by 3 rows to leave three new blank rows, as shown on the next page.

Tip
Don't worry about cell reference changes when inserting extra rows or columns. Excel will adjust them automatically.

Or Use Short-cut Menu

2   This is an alternative way of accessing commands which is faster than the command menu bar. Click the selected rows with the mouse **Right** button.

6	SALES INCOME			
7	Developing & Printing Price Including VAT =		£4.50	
8	Developing & Printing Price	**Cut**	£3.83	
9		**Copy**		
10	Average Number of Films		60	
11	Average Number of Days p	Paste	30	
12	Average Number of Films	Paste Special...	1800	
13				
14	Average Sales per Month =	**Insert**		£6,893.62
15		**Delete**		
16		**Clear Contents**		
17				
18		**Format Cells...**		
19		**Row Height...**		
20		**Hide**		
21		**Unhide**		

Sheet1 / Sheet2 / Sheet3 /   t6

Inserts row, column, or selected cells

Warning
If you delete rows or columns, be careful that you do not delete cells which are still needed and especially those referred to in formulas!

3   A short menu is displayed, giving a selection of the most commonly used commands for the type of selection made.

4   Click the **Insert** option and the three extra rows will be inserted as shown on the next page.

Not only does Excel displace the existing cells to insert three new rows, it also adjusts the formulas used so that the cell references reflect their new positions.

◁

Note
*The three new
blank rows.*

For example the formula for the 'average sales per month' was
previously "= G12 * G8". Reference to the formula bar below
shows that this has been changed to "= G15 * G11".

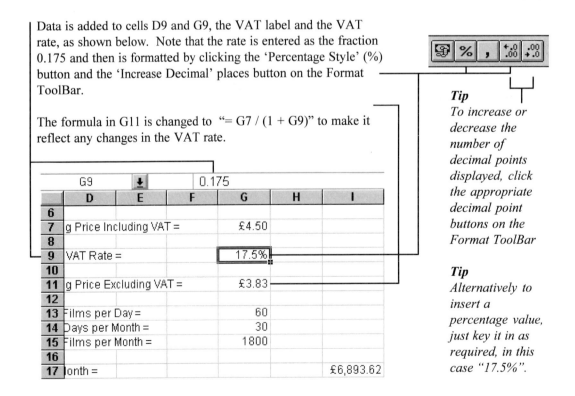

I17			=G15 * G11					
	A	**B**	**C**	**D**	**E**	**F**	**G**	**H**	**I**
6	SALES INCOME								
7		Developing & Printing Price Including VAT =					£4.50		
8									
9									
10									
11		Developing & Printing Price Excluding VAT =					£3.83		
12									
13		Average Number of Films per Day =					60		
14		Average Number of Days per Month =					30		
15		Average Number of Films per Month =					1800		
16									
17		Average Sales per Month =							£6,893.62

Data is added to cells D9 and G9, the VAT label and the VAT
rate, as shown below. Note that the rate is entered as the fraction
0.175 and then is formatted by clicking the 'Percentage Style' (%)
button and the 'Increase Decimal' places button on the Format
ToolBar.

The formula in G11 is changed to "= G7 / (1 + G9)" to make it
reflect any changes in the VAT rate.

G9			0.175		
	D	**E**	**F**	**G**	**H**	**I**
6						
7	g Price Including VAT =			£4.50		
8						
9	VAT Rate =			17.5%		
10						
11	g Price Excluding VAT =			£3.83		
12						
13	Films per Day =			60		
14	Days per Month =			30		
15	Films per Month =			1800		
16						
17	Month =				£6,893.62	

Tip
*To increase or
decrease the
number of
decimal points
displayed, click
the appropriate
decimal point
buttons on the
Format ToolBar*

Tip
*Alternatively to
insert a
percentage value,
just key it in as
required, in this
case "17.5%".*

Renaming a Worksheet

Rather than accepting the default names, it is better to give Worksheets and Charts more meaningful names. As usual there is a choice of procedure:

Using the Command Menu

1   From the **Format** menu select the **Sheet** sub-menu.

2   From the **Sheet** sub-menu, select the **Rename...** option.

3   The **Rename Sheet** dialogue box will be displayed.

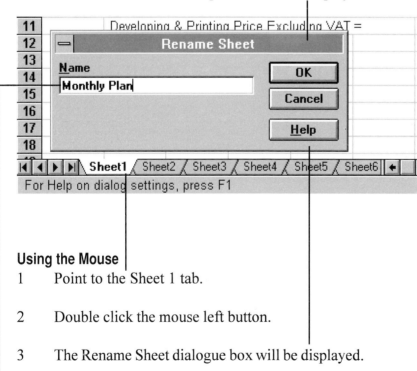

Using the Mouse

1   Point to the Sheet 1 tab.

2   Double click the mouse left button.

3   The Rename Sheet dialogue box will be displayed.

Using Either

4   Key in the new name.

5   Press Enter or click the OK button.

Moving, Inserting and Deleting Sheets

Moving Sheets Within a Workbook

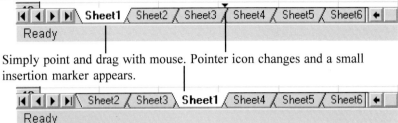

Simply point and drag with mouse. Pointer icon changes and a small insertion marker appears.

Moving Sheets Between Workbooks

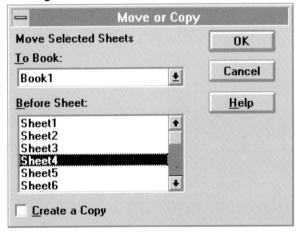

1   From the **Edit** menu, select the **Move or Copy Sheet...** option.

2   Complete the **Move or Copy** dialogue box.

To Book: Select the destination Workbook, which must be open.

Before Sheet: Select the new location within the Workbook.

Create a Copy: *Check* box to *copy*, *uncheck* it to *move* sheet.

Inserting a Worksheet

1   Select the sheet occupying the position for new sheet.

2   From **Insert** menu, select the **Worksheet** option.

3   Change sheet default name if required.

Deleting a Worksheet

1   Select the sheet to be deleted.

2   From **Edit** menu, select the **Delete Sheet** option.

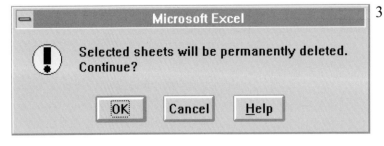

3   In the warning dialogue box, click OK only if you are absolutely sure. You cannot undo this command!

Simple What-If Tests

The power of a spreadsheet is only really appreciated when you carry out 'What-If' tests. This consists of adjusting the numbers in selected cells in order to observe the effect on formulas throughout the worksheet. Any such changes rapidly ripple through the spreadsheet. Even for a comparatively simple business plan, this advantage is apparent.

	A	B	C	D	E	F	G	H	I
1			FastPrint	24 LTD					
2				24 Exposure Colour Negative Film					
3				24 Hours Maximum Processing Time					
4			MONTHLY BUSINESS PLAN						
5									
6	SALES INCOME								
7			Developing & Printing Price Including VAT =				£4.50		
8									
9				VAT Rate =			17.5%		
10									
11			Developing & Printing Price Excluding VAT =				£3.83		
12									
13			Average Number of Films per Day =				60		
14			Average Number of Days per Month =				30		
15			Average Number of Films per Month =				1800		
16									
17			Average Sales per Month =						£6,893.62
18									
19									

I◄ ◄ ► ►I \ **Monthly Plan** / Sheet2 / Sheet3 / Sheet4 / Sheet5 / 9 ◆

Ready   NUM

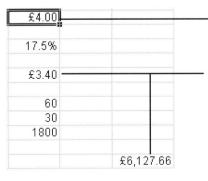

Reduce the retail price to £4.00 and this will affect the calculations of the values displayed in these two cells, which contain formulas which are dependent on the retail price.

Similar tests could be made by adjusting the average numbers of films per day or the VAT rate.

Tip
Such changes should occur immediately. If not, from the **Tools** *menu select the* **Options...** *command, click the* **Calculation** *tab and* **uncheck** *the* **Manual**

Value Stored versus Value Displayed

A warning must be given at this stage about apparent
discrepancies which can arise due to the differences between the
values stored and displayed by formulas or numbers.

Consider the 'FastPrint 24' example. Multiply the 'average
number of films per month' by the 'price excluding VAT'
(1800 times £3.83), which equals £6,894.00. There is apparently
a small error between this and the £6,893.62 which appears on
the spreadsheet. The reason for this is that the value calculated
and stored in the cell giving the ex VAT price is £3.82979...,
which when displayed is rounded to £3.83.

It is normal practice to do all calculations to the accuracy of the
computer and this is the default, but should you choose, you can
reset this to calculate to the accuracy of the display:

Tip
You are advised to
leave this
Unchecked as
shown for the
default.

1   From the **Tools** menu select the **Options...** command.

2   Click the **Calculation** tab and Check (X) the **Precision as
     Displayed** box.

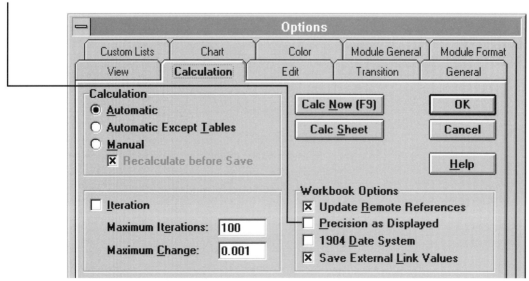

CHAPTER

3

Copying and Moving Cells

in easy Steps

Overview

Introduction

You should by now appreciate that Excel 5 usually offers more than one technique of carrying out a command. For example, the Command Menu can sometimes be circumvented by using a Toolbar. Alternatively some even more direct graphic technique may be available at the cell itself, e.g. a Short-cut Menu.

You should not be surprised that there is a multiplicity of techniques for copying and moving cells, but you may be surprised at the number. In part the reason is historic, in that Excel must support the techniques which were introduced in earlier versions, but in the main this reflects the importance of moving and copying. The copying of formulas in particular make it much more efficient to create rows, columns and tables of numeric values. Since it is not essential to be able to use all the techniques, it is advisable to concentrate on what you find easier.

This chapter will summarise all the techniques, but can only illustrate in detail a sample of them. It is helpful initially to distinguish a few terms...

Copy versus Move

Copy means to reproduce the contents of cell(s) in another location, leaving the original cell(s) intact.

Move means to delete the contents of cell(s) in the original location, and to reproduce them in a new location.

Copying Generally versus Copying to Adjacent Cells

General techniques of *copying* can be applied to cells which are either separated from or linked to the original cell(s).

Techniques of *copying to adjacent* cells apply only to cells which are linked to the original, forming continuous rows, columns or blocks with them.

Copying Within and Between Worksheets

Some techniques of copying are restricted to use within a particular worksheet, whereas others can be used also for copying data between worksheets. The latter case employs the Windows Clipboard as an intermediate store for the data.

General Techniques for Moving Cells

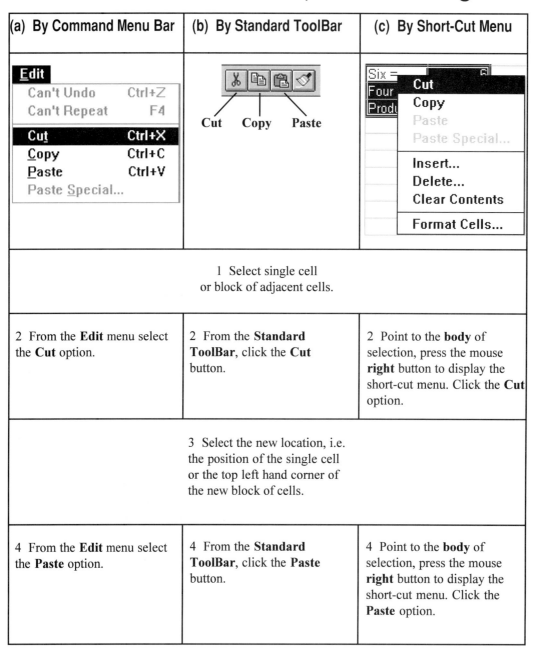

(a) By Command Menu Bar	(b) By Standard ToolBar	(c) By Short-Cut Menu
Edit Can't Undo Ctrl+Z Can't Repeat F4 **Cut** Ctrl+X Copy Ctrl+C Paste Ctrl+V Paste Special...	Cut Copy Paste	Six = Four **Cut** Prod **Copy** Paste Paste Special... **Insert...** **Delete...** **Clear Contents** **Format Cells...**
1 Select single cell or block of adjacent cells.		
2 From the **Edit** menu select the **Cut** option.	2 From the **Standard ToolBar**, click the **Cut** button.	2 Point to the **body** of selection, press the mouse **right** button to display the short-cut menu. Click the **Cut** option.
	3 Select the new location, i.e. the position of the single cell or the top left hand corner of the new block of cells.	
4 From the **Edit** menu select the **Paste** option.	4 From the **Standard ToolBar**, click the **Paste** button.	4 Point to the **body** of selection, press the mouse **right** button to display the short-cut menu. Click the **Paste** option.

(d) By Dragging Border and Short-Cut Menu	(e) By Dragging Border
Fo **Copy** **Move** **Copy Formats** **Copy Values** **Shift Down and Copy** **Shift Right and Copy** **Shift Down and Move** **Shift Right and Move**	Six = 6 Four = 4 Product = 24 Border of Selection
1 Select single cell or block of adjacent cells.	
2 Point to the border of the selected cell(s).	
3 When the border is located the pointer changes from a cross to an arrow.	3 When the border is located the pointer changes from a cross to an arrow.
4 Drag the selection to the new location with the mouse **right** button. Release button and short-cut menu will be displayed. Select **Move** option.	4 Drag the selection to the new location with the mouse **left** button. Release button.

Note
*Techniques **(a), (b), (c) and (d)** can each be applied to moving data **between Worksheets or Workbooks** since they use the Windows Clipboard.*

*Technique **(e)** is restricted to use **within a particular Worksheet**.*

Tip
If dragging the cell by border or fill box does not work, it may need enabling:
*From the **Tools** menu, select the **Options...** command.*
*Click the **Edit** tab.*
*Check the **Allow Cell Drag and Drop box**.*

Tip
The problem with the pull-down menus and sub-menus on the menu bar is the time taken to display them. For a beginner the response seems good; for a regular user it can be frustratingly slow. To speed this up, use the keyboard short-cut control keys:
*While holding down the **ALT** key press e for **Edit**
then press...   t   for **Cut**
                c   for **Copy**
                p   for **Paste**
                as appropriate.*
Normal typing speed omits the menu displays and executes the commands rapidly. The letters to press are underlined as shown.

General Techniques for Copying Cells

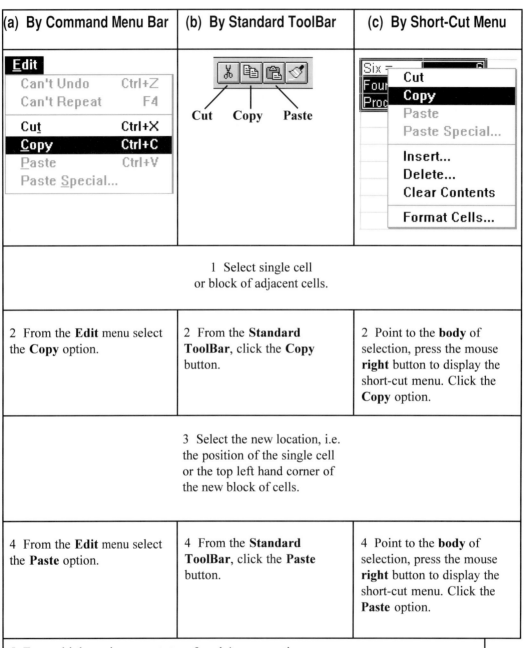

(a) By Command Menu Bar	(b) By Standard ToolBar	(c) By Short-Cut Menu
1 Select single cell or block of adjacent cells.		
2 From the **Edit** menu select the **Copy** option.	2 From the **Standard ToolBar**, click the **Copy** button.	2 Point to the **body** of selection, press the mouse **right** button to display the short-cut menu. Click the **Copy** option.
3 Select the new location, i.e. the position of the single cell or the top left hand corner of the new block of cells.		
4 From the **Edit** menu select the **Paste** option.	4 From the **Standard ToolBar**, click the **Paste** button.	4 Point to the **body** of selection, press the mouse **right** button to display the short-cut menu. Click the **Paste** option.

5 For multiple copies, repeat steps 3 and 4 as many times as necessary. (See Tip on opposite page.) Press **Enter** to terminate pasting.

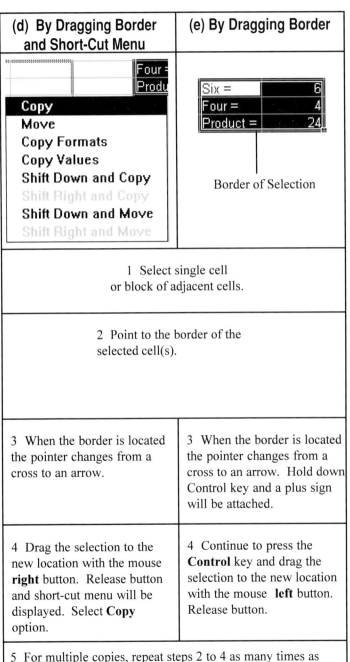

(d) By Dragging Border and Short-Cut Menu	(e) By Dragging Border

Border of Selection

1 Select single cell or block of adjacent cells.	
2 Point to the border of the selected cell(s).	

3 When the border is located the pointer changes from a cross to an arrow.	3 When the border is located the pointer changes from a cross to an arrow. Hold down Control key and a plus sign will be attached.

4 Drag the selection to the new location with the mouse **right** button. Release button and short-cut menu will be displayed. Select **Copy** option.	4 Continue to press the **Control** key and drag the selection to the new location with the mouse **left** button. Release button.

5 For multiple copies, repeat steps 2 to 4 as many times as necessary.

Note
*Techniques (a), (b), (c) and (d) can each be applied to copying data **between Worksheets or Workbooks** since they use the Windows Clipboard.*

*Technique (e) is restricted to use **within a particular Worksheet**.*

Tip
If dragging the cell by border or fill box does not work, it may need enabling:-
*From the **Tools** menu, select the **Options...** command. Click the **Edit** tab. Check the **Allow Cell Drag and Drop box**.*

Tip
For more efficient multiple pasting for techniques (a), (b) and (c) try the following in place of step 3:
*Hold down the **Control** key. Select **all** the new locations by clicking each new position for single cells or the top left hand corners of blocks. Finally execute step 4.*

Example of Copying Cells

Since there are five methods of copying cells, only one will be illustrated in detail. To show that the technique applies to any data, a group of cells have been filled with text, numbers and a simple formula, as shown below.

C5	↓		=C3*C4				
	A	B	C	D	E	F	G
1							
2							
3		Six =	6				
4		Four =	4				
5		Product =	24				
6							

To copy the six cells to another location using the technique of dragging the border, follow the procedure:

1   Select the block of cells.

B3	↓		Six =				
	A	B	C	D	E	F	G
1							
2							
3		Six =	6				
4		Four =	4				
5		Product =	24				
6							

2   Point to the border of the selected cells and press the mouse **left** button.

3   The pointer changes from a cross to an arrow. Press the Control key and a small plus sign is attached to the arrow.

◁

4   While continuing to hold down the Control key, drag the
    selection to the new location. Another border will appear
    and move with the mouse, indicating the new location.
    When in position, release the mouse button, and the copied
    block will appear as shown below.

E3	↓		Six =				
A	**B**	**C**	**D**	**E**	**F**	**G**	
1							
2							
3	Six =	6		Six =	6		
4	Four =	4		Four =	4		
5	Product =	24		Product =	24		
6							

You should note that as well as moving the text, numbers and
the formula, Excel also adjusts the formula so that it gives the
correct cell references for its new location. In the original
location the formula bar showed that the formula in cell C5 was
"=C3 * C4". In the new location, it has been changed to
"=F3 * F4".

F5	↓		=F3*F4				
A	**B**	**C**	**D**	**E**	**F**	**G**	
1							
2							
3	Six =	6		Six =	6		
4	Four =	4		Four =	4		
5	Product =	24		Product =	24		
6							

The reason for this is the use of 'relative references' for the
formulas. This will be dealt with in Chapter 5, 'Cell Referencing'.

Techniques for Copying to Adjacent Cells

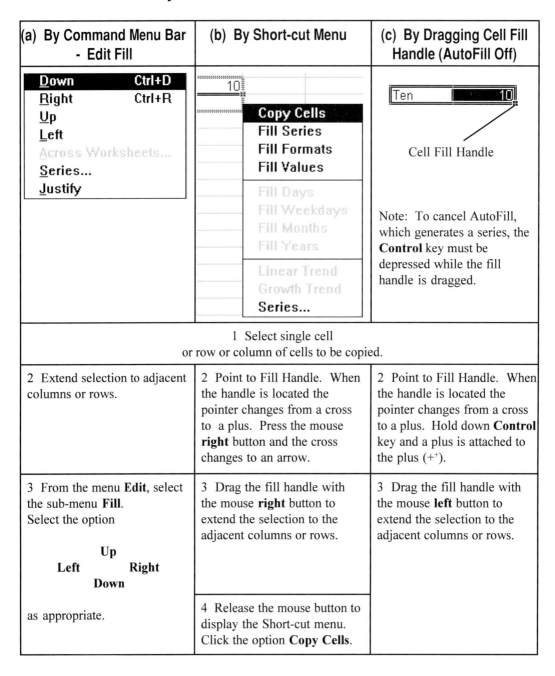

(a) By Command Menu Bar - Edit Fill	(b) By Short-cut Menu	(c) By Dragging Cell Fill Handle (AutoFill Off)
Down Ctrl+D **Right** Ctrl+R **Up** **Left** Across Worksheets... **Series...** **Justify**	10 **Copy Cells** **Fill Series** **Fill Formats** **Fill Values** Fill Days Fill Weekdays Fill Months Fill Years Linear Trend Growth Trend **Series...**	Ten 10 Cell Fill Handle Note: To cancel AutoFill, which generates a series, the **Control** key must be depressed while the fill handle is dragged.
1 Select single cell or row or column of cells to be copied.		
2 Extend selection to adjacent columns or rows.	2 Point to Fill Handle. When the handle is located the pointer changes from a cross to a plus. Press the mouse **right** button and the cross changes to an arrow.	2 Point to Fill Handle. When the handle is located the pointer changes from a cross to a plus. Hold down **Control** key and a plus is attached to the plus ($+^+$).

3 From the menu **Edit**, select the sub-menu **Fill**. Select the option
 	
    Up
Left   **Right**
    Down
 	
as appropriate.
	3 Drag the fill handle with the mouse **right** button to extend the selection to the adjacent columns or rows.
	
	4 Release the mouse button to display the Short-cut menu. Click the option **Copy Cells**.
		3 Drag the fill handle with the mouse **left** button to extend the selection to the adjacent columns or rows.

Techniques for Generating Series

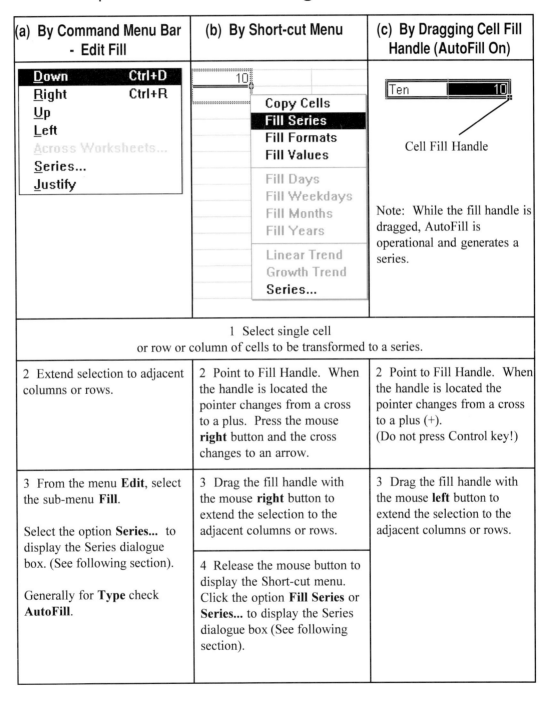

(a) **By Command Menu Bar - Edit Fill**	(b) **By Short-cut Menu**	(c) **By Dragging Cell Fill Handle (AutoFill On)**
Down **Ctrl+D** **Right** **Ctrl+R** **Up** **Left** Across Worksheets... **Series...** **Justify**	10 Copy Cells **Fill Series** **Fill Formats** **Fill Values** Fill Days Fill Weekdays Fill Months Fill Years Linear Trend Growth Trend **Series...**	Ten 10 Cell Fill Handle Note: While the fill handle is dragged, AutoFill is operational and generates a series.
1 Select single cell or row or column of cells to be transformed to a series.		
2 Extend selection to adjacent columns or rows.	2 Point to Fill Handle. When the handle is located the pointer changes from a cross to a plus. Press the mouse **right** button and the cross changes to an arrow.	2 Point to Fill Handle. When the handle is located the pointer changes from a cross to a plus (+). (Do not press Control key!)
3 From the menu **Edit**, select the sub-menu **Fill**. Select the option **Series...** to display the Series dialogue box. (See following section). Generally for **Type** check **AutoFill**.	3 Drag the fill handle with the mouse **right** button to extend the selection to the adjacent columns or rows. 4 Release the mouse button to display the Short-cut menu. Click the option **Fill Series** or **Series...** to display the Series dialogue box (See following section).	3 Drag the fill handle with the mouse **left** button to extend the selection to the adjacent columns or rows.

Comparison of Copying to Adjacent Cells and Generating Series

Copying to Adjacent Cells versus Generating Series

Copying to Adjacent Cells and Generating Series are so similar and bound up that the two sections have been compared on the previous two facing pages.

The main purpose of copying to adjacent cells is to reproduce formulas when building tables. This will be demonstrated in later chapters.

The reason for series is twofold. Either simple arithmetic series can be generated very easily or series on time or dates, which are cyclic and built into Excel, can be called up.

Arithmetic Series

Examples of series are:

Linear:	10, 11, 12	step value = +1
Linear:	10, 7.5, 5.0	step value = -2.5
Growth:	10, 20, 40	step value = (times) 2
Growth:	10, 5, 2.5	step value = (times) 0.5

Time/ Series

The built in series are:

Time:	2:00 PM, 2:30 PM...
Day:	Monday, Tuesday... Sunday.
Month:	January, February... December.
Quarter:	Quarter 1, Quarter 2, Quarter 3, Quarter 4.
Year:	1994, 1995...
Date:	03-Jan-94, 04-Jan-95...

Since time and date are formatted in time or date styles but are stored as numbers, they can be incremented by amounts such as days(+ 1 day) and weeks (+7 days), providing a powerful and useful facility.

Example of Copying to Adjacent Cells and Generating Series

Suppose a spreadsheet was set up with the data shown below. The left hand group of data consists of three cells containing text, a number and a simple formula. This formula simply doubles the value in the cell to its left:

> In D5 it is "= C5 * 2" and
> in D14 it is "= C14 * 2".

The right hand group of data contains cells which store two items of text and a number formatted as a date. These three each form part of a series stored by Excel for days, months and dates.

To copy the data on row 5 to the adjacent rows below, using the drag fill button technique, follow the procedure:

> 1   Select the cells to be copied.

	B5	▼		Ten					
	A	B	C	D	E	F	G	H	▲
1									
2		Copying to Adjacent Cells With AutoFill Off...							
3		Normal Data				Existing Series			
4		Text	Number	Formula		Day	Month	Date	
5		Ten	10	20		Monday	January	03-Jan-94	
6									
7									
8									
9									
10									
11		Copying to Adjacent Cells With AutoFill On...							
12		Normal Data				Existing Series			
13		Text	Number	Formula		Day	Month	Date	
14		Ten	10	20		Monday	January	03-Jan-94	
15									
16									
17									
18									▼

◄◄ ◄ ► ►◄ \ **Sheet1** / Sheet2 / Sheet3 / Sheet4 / Sheet5 / Sheet6 || ◄ |

> 2   Point to the fill handle so that the pointer changes from a cross to a plus sign (+).

▷

3 Press and hold down the **Control** key to suppress AutoFill. The pointer will respond by showing an additional smaller plus sign ($+^+$).

4 Drag the selection, as indicated by the enlarged border, down to the cells shown below.

	B5	↓	Ten						
	A	B	C	D	E	F	G	H	↑
1									
2		Copying to Adjacent Cells With AutoFill Off...							
3		Normal Data				Existing Series			
4		Text	Number	Formula		Day	Month	Date	
5		Ten	10	20		Monday	January	03-Jan-94	
6		Ten	10	20		Monday	January	03-Jan-94	
7		Ten	10	20		Monday	January	03-Jan-94	
8		Ten	10	20		Monday	January	03-Jan-94	
9		Ten	10	20		Monday	January	03-Jan-94	
10									
11		Copying to Adjacent Cells With AutoFill On...							
12		Normal Data				Existing Series			
13		Text	Number	Formula		Day	Month	Date	
14		Ten	10	20		Monday	January	03-Jan-94	
15									
16									
17									
18									↓

Sheet1 / Sheet2 / Sheet3 / Sheet4 / Sheet5 / Sheet6 ←

5 On releasing the mouse button, all the cells will be copied as shown above, so that they are all identical to the cells in the top row of the selection.

6 Select the next row of cells, which in this case will be converted to series by using the AutoFill facility as shown on the next page.

7 Point to the fill handle so that the pointer changes from a cross to a plus sign (+). Do *not* press Control this time.

8   Drag the selection, as indicated by the enlarged border, down to the cells shown below.

	B14	↓		Ten						↑
	A	B	C	D	E	F	G	H	
1									
2		Copying to Adjacent Cells With AutoFill Off...							
3		Normal Data				Existing Series			
4		Text	Number	Formula		Day	Month	Date	
5		Ten	10	20		Monday	January	03-Jan-94	
6		Ten	10	20		Monday	January	03-Jan-94	
7		Ten	10	20		Monday	January	03-Jan-94	
8		Ten	10	20		Monday	January	03-Jan-94	
9		Ten	10	20		Monday	January	03-Jan-94	
10									
11		Copying to Adjacent Cells With AutoFill On...							
12		Normal Data				Existing Series			
13		Text	Number	Formula		Day	Month	Date	
14		Ten	10	20		Monday	January	03-Jan-94	
15		Ten	11	22		Tuesday	February	04-Jan-94	
16		Ten	12	24		Wednesday	March	05-Jan-94	
17		Ten	13	26		Thursday	April	06-Jan-94	
18		Ten	14	28		Friday	May	07-Jan-94	

Sheet1 \ Sheet2 / Sheet3 / Sheet4 / Sheet5 / Sheet6

9   In this case AutoFill has copied the text and the formula in the first group, leaving them the same as before. However the remainder of the cells, including the number from the first group and the whole of the second group, have been converted to series.

To summarise:

The top half of the above spreadsheet has been produced by *copying to adjacent cells*.

The bottom half has been produced partly by *copying to adjacent cells* (the first and third columns) and partly by *generating series* (the remainder of the columns).

Creating your own Autofill Lists

Note
*The cyclic
property of the
new list may or
may not be
relevant to your
application.*

If your application frequently uses lists of text, then it will pay you to make it into a custom list for use under Autofill. Take as an example a list of sales costs used by 'FastPrint 24 Ltd':

1   *Either* select the list on worksheet.

2   From the **Tools** menu, select the **Options...** command and click the **Custom Lists** tab. This will show already the lists for days of the week and months of the year.

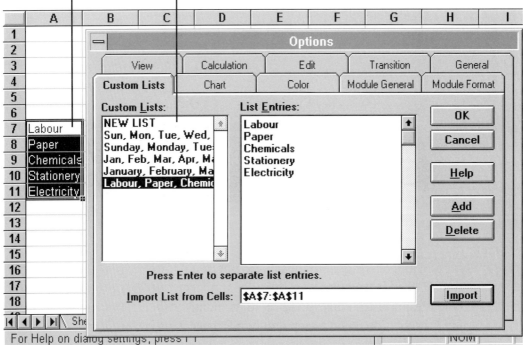

3   Click the '**Import**' button and the list will appear under '**List Entries**'. *Alternatively* you may type a list in this box directly.

4   Click the '**Add**' key, so that the new list appears under 'Custom Lists' and click the OK button to finish.

5   To use your list simply apply Autofill to any single word.

Using the Series Dialogue Box

Either from the **Edit** menu, select the **Fill** sub-menu, from which the **Series...** option can be selected.

Or when dragging the **fill handle** of a cell selection with the mouse **Right** button which displays the short-cut menu, from which the **Series...** option can be selected.

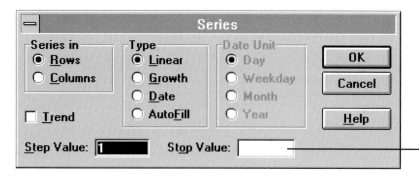

The Series dialogue box gives a much greater degree of control than the methods previously described. To illustrate this a few examples are given on the next page.

Tip
If you are uncertain of the number of items in a series, key in the stop value to terminate the series.

(a) For the 15 minute intervals the step value needed accurate calculation as a fraction of 15 in 60 minutes in a 24 hour day, i.e. 1 / 96 = 0.10416...

(b) To generate the dates corresponding to Mondays only required the first date and a step value of 7 days. This is much easier than copying from a diary.

(c) Remember that fractions are stored as fractions so that the step value had to be -0.2.

(d) In this case each percentage value was 0.5 times the previous one.

(e) Here an existing series, which approximated to a linear trend, was changed to a linear series of step value 20.

(f) In this case the trend was growth, and the existing series was changed to a factor of just over 2.

Starting Cell(s)	Starting Value(s)	Series In	Trend	Type	Date Unit	Step Value	Stop Value
(a) B2	2.00 PM	Columns	Uncheck	Date	Day	0.01042 (15 /60 /24)	
(b) D2	06-Jan-94	Columns	Uncheck	Date	Day	7	
(c) F2	100%	Columns	Uncheck	Linear		-0.2	
(d) H2	100%	Columns	Uncheck	Growth		0.5	
(e) D9 : D13	18 - 98	Columns	Check	Linear			
(f) H9 : H13	18 - 318	Columns	Check	Growth			

	A	B	C	D	E	F	G	H
1		(a) Quarter Hour Intervals		(b) Week Beginning		(c) "Linear" Percentage		(d)"Growth" Percentage
2	Starting Values:	2:00 PM		06-Jan-94		100%		100.00%
3		2:15 PM		13-Jan-94		80%		50.00%
4		2:30 PM		20-Jan-94		60%		25.00%
5		2:45 PM		27-Jan-94		40%		12.50%
6		3:00 PM		03-Feb-94		20%		6.25%
7								
8		Starting Values		(e) After Linear Trend		Starting Values		(f) After Growth Trend
9		18		19.6		18		19.1
10		42		39.6		42		38.8
11		58		59.6		78		78.8
12		82		79.6		162		160.2
13		98		99.6		318		325.6

4

Managing Workbook Files

in easy steps

Overview

When working with any application software, an important consideration is the facility to store your work in files, so that it can be retrieved for future use. In this respect, Excel operates like most other application packages and many users can manage quite adequately with three options from the **File** menu:

> **File   Save As...**
> **File   Save**
> **File   Open...**

However, Excel 5 provides an extensive range of features in addition to these standard options. The purpose of this chapter is to cover all these features. If you are new to such applications, this may prove a little overfacing. If this is the case, it is suggested that you concentrate initially on learning the above options, and return to this chapter at a later date for the more advanced features, when you have more experience and confidence. The initial sections are still pitched at new users.

The order of this chapter will follow the logical sequence in which you would normally require the various features and options:

- Firstly, it will summarise the options for file storage and retrieval.

- Then it will deal with initialising Excel specifically for such file management.

- It will continue the logical sequence of Save As, Save, Close, Exit and Open options and their associated dialogue boxes. After these sections, you may have sufficient information to proceed to the next chapter.

- It will then progress to more advanced features, such as searching for files, opening several Workbooks, and saving the Workspace.

Summary of File Commands

File Menu Commands	Summary of Command	Standard Toolbar
	New opens a new empty Workbook.	New Workbook
File **New** Ctrl+N **O**pen... Ctrl+O **C**lose	**Open...** displays the Open dialogue box, which enables the drive and directory to be selected, and the required existing Workbook filename located.	Open
Save Ctrl+S Save **A**s... Save **W**orkspace...	**Close** closes the active Workbook. If this has not been saved since the last change, a warning message will be issued.	
Find File... Summary **I**nfo...		
Page Set**u**p... Print Pre**v**iew **P**rint... Ctrl+P Print **R**eport...	**Save** saves the current Workbook. If this hasn't been saved previously, then the Save As dialogue box will be displayed.	Save
1 E5C06P01.XLS **2** E5C03P01.XLS **3** E5C04P01.XLS **4** E5C05P01.XLS	**Save As...** displays the Save As dialogue box, enabling the drive and directory to be selected, and a new workbook file name to be entered.	
E**x**it		
Tip *Remember that the keyboard control keys are very efficient. If keyed in quick sequence, the option will be executed without the menu being displayed.*	**Save Workspace...** displays the Save Workspace dialogue box, enabling the drive and directory to be selected, and a workspace file name to be entered. This file records the Workbooks which are current and their locations, size and positions on the screen.	

▷

◁

File Menu Commands	Summary of Command	Standard Toolbar
File **New** Ctrl+N **Open...** Ctrl+O **Close** **Save** Ctrl+S **Save As...** **Save Workspace...** **Find File...** **Summary Info...** **Page Setup...** **Print Preview** **Print...** Ctrl+P **Print Report...** **1 E5C06P01.XLS** **2 E5C03P01.XLS** **3 E5C04P01.XLS** **4 E5C05P01.XLS** **Exit**	**Find File...** displays the Find File dialogue box, which is a powerful tool for searching for files by various techniques including previewing their contents.	*Note* *The only file commands which can be accessed via the Standard Toolbar are* **New**, **Open** *and* **Save**. *This should indicate that most file management can be done with these commands.*
	Summary Info... displays the Summary Information dialogue box, which enables details of the Workbook, such as title and author, to be entered.	

	Page Setup...) These
	                               ) all relate
	Print Preview) to printing
	                               ) and are
	Print...) not relevant
	                               ) to this
	Print Report...) chapter.	

	The File List is a list of the four most recently opened Workbooks, which Excel records and displays at this section of the Edit menu.	
Tip *Remember that the keyboard control keys are the same for many applications:* *New* **ALT + F, N** *Open* **ALT + F, O** *Close* **ALT + F, C** *Save* **ALT + F, S** *Save As* **ALT + F, A**	**Exit** closes all the active Workbooks and quits Excel. If there are changes in any Workbook, which have been made since it was last saved, then Excel gives you the chance of saving it.	

Preparing Excel for File Management

You can make your file management more efficient by a few
initialisation procedures:

1   From the **Tools** menu, select the **Options...** command.

2   On the Options dialogue box click the **General** Tab.

3   Check the **Recently Used File List** box so that the File
     menu will contain a list of the most recently used files.

4   Check the **Prompt for Summary Info** box if you wish
     Excel to request you to update the file summary
     information, when you use the command File Save As.

5   When the File New command is used, the default for the
     number of blank worksheets is 16. You can if you wish
     adjust this, e.g. reducing it to 6 as shown below.

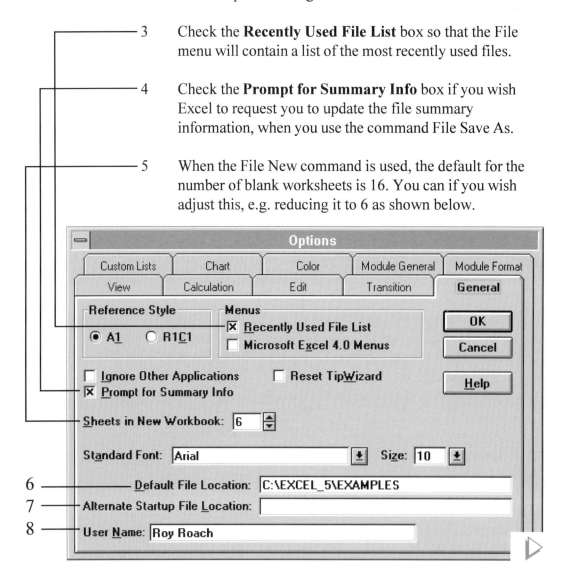

6   You can save yourself substantial time at later stages, by keying into the **Default File Location** the **path** which gives the **directory** in which you propose to store your Excel files. On using the commands File Open or Save As, this path will be supplied automatically which saves having to keep selecting it. Note that the directory which I used has been specified here.

7   You can, if you wish, have Excel automatically open a set of files at start-up. *Either* store these files in the default directory **XLSTART**, which might have the path, "C:\EXCEL5\XLSTART".
        Or specify an alternative path in the **Alternate Startup File Location**.
        Warning: **All** files in the startup directory will be opened!

8   Finally you may key in your name, so that this will be supplied automatically for the file summary information.

DOS Conventions for Directory and File Names

It might be appropriate at this stage to give a brief reminder of the rules which DOS and Windows applies to the names for directories and files:

1   The name may have up to **8 characters**.

2   Use any sequence of the following characters...
        The letters **A...Z** which are not distinguished from **a...z**.
        The digits **0...9**.
        Certain other characters - it is simpler to keep to '-' or '_'.

3   Do **not** use the characters used for the path specification...
        Space( ), slashes(\ /), colon(:), full stop(.), and comma(,).

Additionally the file name may have a three character extension. For Excel these are usually '.XLS' and '.XLW', resulting in filenames such as '**Book1.XLS**' and '**RESUME.XLW**'.

The File Save As Command

Tip
Be careful with your choice of **filename**. *Eight characters are a little restrictive, but try to choose something that will remind you of the contents in a few weeks time!*

Purpose

The File Save As command has two uses:

(a)   Normally to save a Workbook for the first time in a permanent file on a disk drive. The file is usually given a name which describes its contents.

(b)   Sometimes to duplicate a Workbook - perhaps to create a backup in case you wish to return to the original version, or to create another permanent copy from which to develop a similar Workbook.

Method of Use

When Excel is started, it automatically opens a Workbook entitled 'Book1'. Correspondingly, its Worksheets will be called 'Sheet1', 'Sheet2', etc..

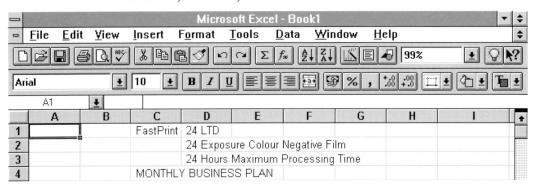

Returning to our example on 'FastPrint24 Ltd', it can be seen that although the Worksheet was renamed 'Monthly Plan', the containing Workbook was still called 'Book1'. The procedure for renaming the Workbook and storing it permanently on a disk drive is as follows:

1   From the **Edit** menu, select the option **Save As**...
        or on the **Standard Toolbar** click the **Save** button.

2   The **Save As** dialogue box will be displayed.

3   Select the disk drive required, normally C for the hard disk or A for the floppy. Note that it is more efficient to operate Excel on files on the hard disk, but it is good practice to back up files to the floppy disk. Here the drive offered is that specified in the previous section.

4   Select the path required, showing the directories and sub-directories. Time can be saved if this is already specified as in the previous section, since they will be displayed already.

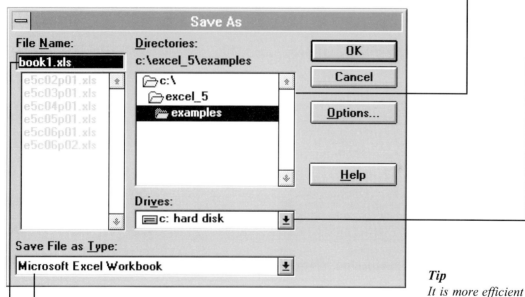

Tip
*It is more efficient to use the normal Excel file name extensions such as **XLS** and **XLW** since Excel automatically displays such files when using the commands File Open and Save As.*

5   Key in the **filename** required. Excel will offer the default Workbook name 'Book1.xls'. It is strongly recommended that you keep the extension, '**.XLS**'. For PastPrint24, the filename 'FP24PLAN.XLS' will be used. You must keep to **DOS Conventions** for these names.

6   Accept **Microsoft Excel Workbook** as the File Type.

7   Consider the options by clicking the **Options...** button. See the next page.

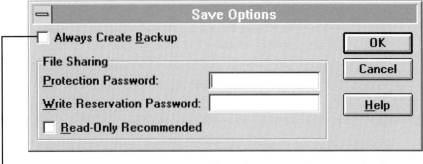

8   If you require a Backup file to be created automatically, then click the option box. See the next page for detail.

9   The rest of the options concern file security, which will be covered in Chapter 7, 'Workbook and Worksheet Security'.

10   Click the OK button in the Save Options dialogue box and OK in the Save As dialogue box.

11   The Summary Information dialogue box will appear.

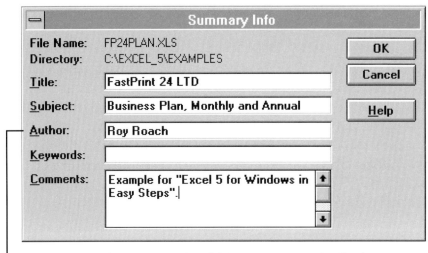

12   The author's name should appear automatically, but you may fill in additional information if required, as shown.

◁

13 On clicking the OK button, your worksheet will now be
    saved permanently in a file on the disk drive and its new
    name will appear on the title bar. ————————┐

	A	B	C	D	E	F	G	H	I
1			FastPrint	24 LTD					
2				24 Exposure Colour Negative Film					
3				24 Hours Maximum Processing Time					
4			MONTHLY BUSINESS PLAN						

Automatic Creation of Backups

It was seen on the previous page that Excel can be set so that it
automatically creates a backup copy when saving a file by
Checking the **Always Create Backup** box in the **Save Options**
dialogue box. This applies to the file which is created when using
the File Save As command. Subsequently when the **Save**
command is used on this file, Excel will maintain a copy of the
previous version of the file in a file of the same name, with the
file extension '.BAK'. The newly saved version will retain the
normal extension '.XLS'. When further changes are made and
the file is saved again, the old backup file will be overwritten.

Exporting Files in Other File Formats

It is possible to convert Excel 5 files to other popular
spreadsheet or database formats by selecting the required format
in the **Save File As Type** list in the **Save As** dialogue box.
Examples are:

     (a) Earlier versions of Excel.
     (b) Multiplan
     (c) Various Lotus 1-2-3 versions
     (d) Various dBASE versions.

The File Save Command

Purpose

The reason for File Save is to transfer any changes made to the Workbook during the current Excel session to the permanent file on a disk drive.

Importance of Regularly Saving File

Until the Save command has been used, there is a danger that the latest updates to the Workbook could be lost. Personal computers and the software they use have become extremely reliable. However, there is still the possibility of the accidental switching off of your machine, whether this is due to a mains power failure or a colleague throwing the wrong switch or removing the wrong plug! Accordingly, it is advisable to save your work at regular short intervals of time. It is foolish to do several hours work and risk its loss.

If you prefer, you can set up Excel to remind you at regular intervals to save your work. See below.

Method of Use

1   *Either* from the **Edit** menu select the **Save** option
       or click the **Save** button on the **Standard Toolbar**.

2   If the file had not been previously saved in a permanent file
       on a disk drive, then the **Save As** dialogue box will be
       displayed. See the previous section.

3   Otherwise there will be a short delay, indicated by the
       pointer changing to the Timer Icon, after which you may
       resume your work.

Installing the AutoSave Command.

The AutoSave command is an **Add-in** command. Add-ins are commands or functions which add special capabilities to Excel. Since these are extra features, they may need installing.

▷

If Excel is newly installed, the AutoSave function may not be installed. If AutoSave doesn't appear in the Tools menu, then follow the procedure:-

1   From the **Tools** menu, select the **Add-Ins...** command.

2   The **Add-Ins** dialogue box will be displayed.

3   Check **AutoSave** and click the OK button.

```
┌──────────────────────────────────────────────────┐
│ ═                    Add-Ins                       │
├──────────────────────────────────────────────────┤
│ Add-Ins Available:                                 │
│ ┌──────────────────────────────┐  ┌────────────┐  │
│ │⊠ AutoSave                  ▒│  │     OK     │  │
│ │☐ Crosstab sheet function    │  └────────────┘  │
│ │⊠ Report Manager             │  ┌────────────┐  │
│ │⊠ Solver Add-In              │  │   Cancel   │  │
│ │☐ Update Add-in Links        │  └────────────┘  │
│ │⊠ View Manager               │  ┌────────────┐  │
│ │                             │  │  Browse... │  │
│ │                             │  └────────────┘  │
│ │                           ▒│  ┌────────────┐  │
│ └──────────────────────────────┘  │    Help    │  │
│                                    └────────────┘  │
│ ┌─AutoSave──────────────────────────────────────┐ │
│ │  Automatically saves your workbook at a time   │ │
│ │           interval you specify.                │ │
│ └────────────────────────────────────────────────┘ │
└──────────────────────────────────────────────────┘
```

4   The checked **AutoSave...** command will now appear in the Tools menu.

Using the AutoSave Command

1   From the **Tools** menu, select the **AutoSave...** option.

2   The **AutoSave** dialogue box will be displayed, as shown on the next page.

Tip
*The interval
between AutoSave
prompts/saves
must be a
compromise
between how often
you can tolerate
being disturbed
and how much
time you can
afford to waste
should an
accidental loss
occur.*

3 Switch on AutoSave by checking the **Automatic Save** box.

4 Key in the **interval in minutes** between automatic saves.

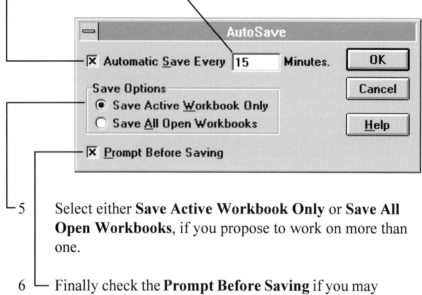

5 Select either **Save Active Workbook Only** or **Save All Open Workbooks**, if you propose to work on more than one.

6 Finally check the **Prompt Before Saving** if you may require to override such saves.

7 Click the **OK** button.

8 Subsequently if you have requested prompts, the following dialogue box will be displayed. Click the **Save** or **Skip** button, as required.

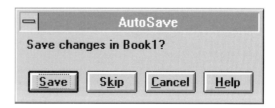

Otherwise, the file will be saved without reference to you at your specified intervals.

The Commands File Close and File Exit

These two commands are so similar that it is appropriate to cover them together.

File Close

1　　This closes the **active** Workbook.

2　　If any changes have been made since it was last saved, then Excel will issue the dialogue box below, which gives you a **warning**.

3　　Excel is left running, either with the remainder of the open Workbooks or with no Workbooks open.

File Exit

1　　This closes **all active** Workbooks.

2　　If any changes have been made to any Workbook since it was last saved, then Excel will issue the dialogue box below, which gives you a **warning**.

3　　Excel is **quit**.

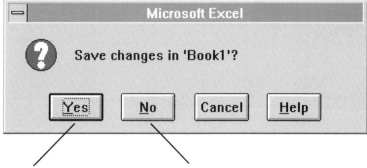

If Yes is pressed, the Workbook is saved, or if it hasn't been saved previously, then the Save As dialogue box will be displayed.

If No is pressed, any changes to the Workbook made since it was last saved will be lost!

The File Open Command

Purpose

The purpose of the File Open command is to retrieve from a disk drive a file, which contains a permanent copy of an existing Excel Workbook, and load it into Excel, ready for use or for changes.

File	
New	Ctrl+N
Open...	Ctrl+O
Close	
Save	Ctrl+S
Save As...	
Save Workspace...	
Find File...	
Summary Info...	
Page Setup...	
Print Preview	
Print...	Ctrl+P
Print Report...	
1 FP24PLAN.XLS	
2 E5C06P01.XLS	
3 E5C03P01.XLS	
4 E5C04P01.XLS	
Exit	

Three Ways of Opening a File

There are actually three ways of opening a file:

(a)   The most direct is to click the file required if it appears in the **Recently Used File List**, which should be displayed in the File Menu.

(b)   The next method is to use the option **Open...** from the **File** menu or to click the **Open** button on the **Standard Toolbar**. Both these will display the Open dialogue box, which is shown below. It is easier to use this dialogue box if you know the drive, directory and filename.

(c)   The third method is to use the **Find File...** option, which is covered in the next section. This is a technique which enables you to search for your file, if for example you have forgotten its name or location.

Method of Use of File Open Command

1   From the **File** menu, select the **Open...** option *or* on the **Standard Toolbar** click the **Open** button.

2   The **Open** dialogue box will be displayed.

3   It should display the disk drive and path to the directory where your files are stored, as set up on the **General** tab which was accessed from the **Tools Options...** option.

4   If you need to change the disk drive, select the new one
     from the drop down list. ─────────────────────────────────────┐

5   If you need to change the directory, select the new path by
     clicking the directories and sub-directories. ──────────────┐

6 ┌─Select the file required from the list displayed.

7 │ Alternatively key in the file name and extension required.

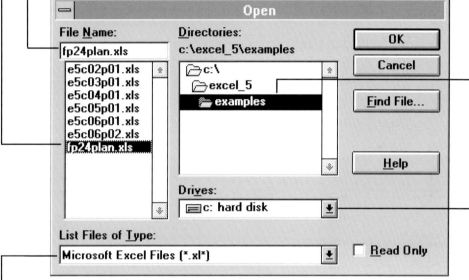

8 └─Accept the default File Type.

9   Click the OK button and the file will be loaded into memory
     and the file name will appear on the title bar

Importing Files in other File Formats

It is possible to convert other popular spreadsheet or database
files to Excel 5 format by selecting the required format in the **List
Files of Type** list in the **Open** dialogue box.

Tip
*If you have
difficulty locating
your file, you can
call the Find File
dialogue box by
clicking the Find
File button.*

The Find File Command

Purpose

The main purpose of the Find File command is to enable you to
search for a file, whose name or location you have forgotten.
This is done by searching specified drives and directories for
information given in the file summary or for the date of the file.
Alternatively you can look at a preview of the file contents,
without opening the file. The second purpose is to provide a file
management facility, which enables you to create new
directories, delete and copy files, without leaving Excel. This
new command is so extensive and useful that several pages will
be devoted to it, illustrating a typical sequence for using it.

Method of Use

1   From the **File** menu select the **Find File...** option. The
      Find File dialogue box will be displayed, possibly showing
      a preview of an existing file as below.

Tree showing location of selected file   Preview of selected file, showing top left hand
corner of the worksheet.

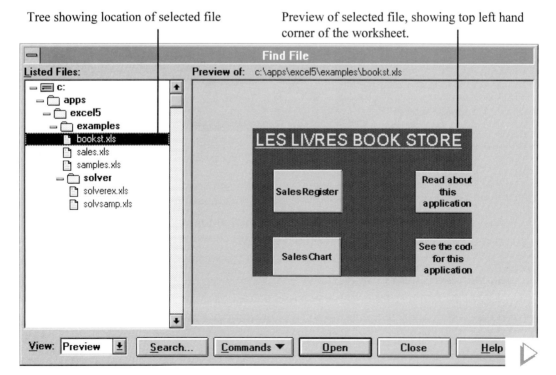

2   The **Find File** dialogue box has several features, to which
     we will return later.

3   To start your own search, click the **Search...** button. This
     will display the Search dialogue box.

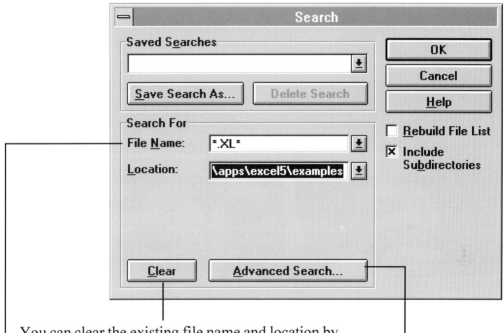

4 │ You can clear the existing file name and location by
     clicking the **Clear** button.

5 └─ You can at this stage specify the form of the file name,
     using 'wildcard characters', i.e. an asterisk (*) for any
     number of characters or a question mark (?) for a single
     character. Therefore the wildcard specification of a general
     filename with an Excel file extension is '**.XL***' or
     '**.XL?**'.

6   Elect to supply the criteria for a more specific and faster
     search by clicking the **Advanced Search...** button. ─────

7   The **Advanced Search** dialogue box will be displayed.

8   Click the **Location Tab** and complete the dialogue box as
     below.

To **remove** search paths: To **add** search paths:

Either   Repeat the following as many times as
    Highlight each path in turn.   necessary:

    Click the **Remove** button. ———   Select the required drive. ———

Or   Select the required path. ———

    Click the **Remove All** button. ——

                                                Click the **Add** button.

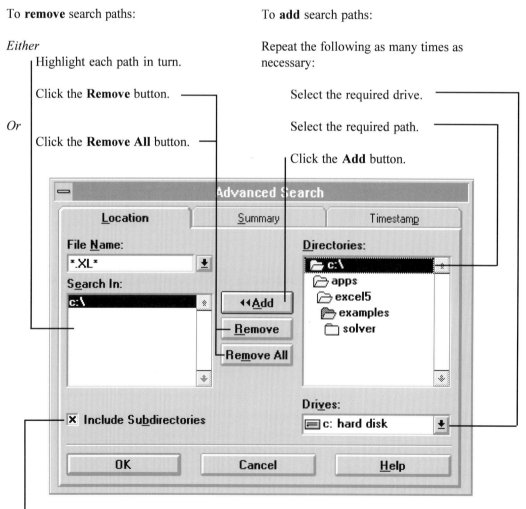

If you wish to extend the search to   ***Note***: *Here for demonstration purposes, the*
subdirectories of the specified paths, check   *search path has been made to cover the whole of*
the **Include Subdirectories** box.   *the hard disk. Normally, it would be narrowed*
                                               down to specific directories.

9   Click the **Summary Tab** and complete the dialogue box as
      below.

Summary Information - Key in the text for any of the following:
   Title
   Author
   Keywords
   Subject
Note that special characters, such as wildcard characters, may be used to specify approximate wording. ──────

──**Containing Text** applies to text which appears in the Worksheet and not in the Summary. Checking **Use Pattern Match** indicates that special search operators are to be used and **Special** selects the operators to be used.

Match Case requires exact match for text.

Options - This applies to everything in the search, i.e. location and timestamp in addition to summary. This specifies the conditions under which the new search criteria are applied:

Create New File List is the default, which starts a new search with the criteria to find a completely new set of files.

Add Matches to List assumes that a search has been made with a previous set of criteria and that the new criteria are to be used to broaden the search, extending list.

Search Only in List limits the search to an existing list of files, narrowing the selection by applying the new criteria.

Advanced Search

| Location | **Summary** | Timestamp |

T̲itle:

A̲uthor: Roy Roach ─

K̲eywords:

S̲ubject:

O̲ptions: Create New List ▼ ─ ☐ **Match Case**

┌**Containing Text**────────────────────

☐ **Use Patte̲rn Matching**   Special ▾

| OK | Cancel | Help |

10   Click the **Timestamp Tab** and complete the dialogue box
      as below.

Last Saved   **Created**

From: Key in the earliest date from which the   This is not applicable to
search is to apply, if you wish to exclude   Excel 5!
earlier files.

To: Key in the latest date up to which the   *Note: The format in which*
search is to apply, if you wish to exclude later   *date is entered is flexible as*
files.   *for Worksheets. Here the*
                                                        earliest date was entered as
By: The author is provided from the   *'11 Apr 94'.*
Summary Tab

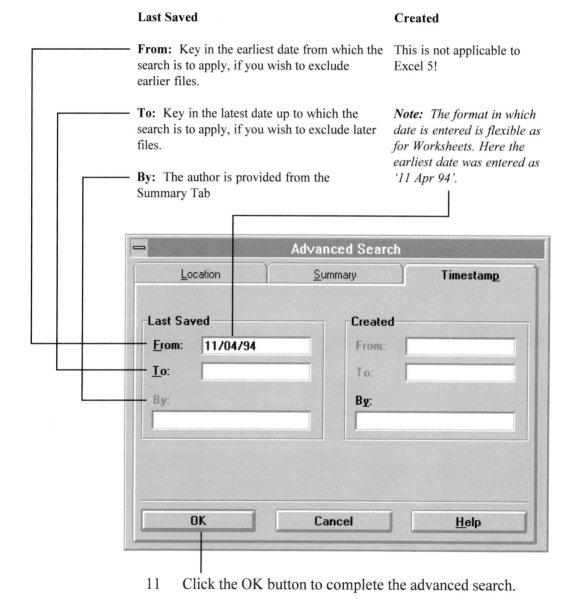

11   Click the OK button to complete the advanced search.

12   The **Search** dialogue box will be re-displayed.

Saved Searches displays the names of previously saved search criteria.

Save Search As... displays the dialogue box, which enables you to enter a name for your search criteria.

Delete Search enables you to delete the highlighted name of a set of search criteria from the list above.

Rebuild File List: If a search has already been made, this enables the list of files to be cleared - this was already covered in the Advanced Search dialogue box.

Include Subdirectories: This was checked in the Advanced Search box to extend the search to the whole of the hard disk drive.

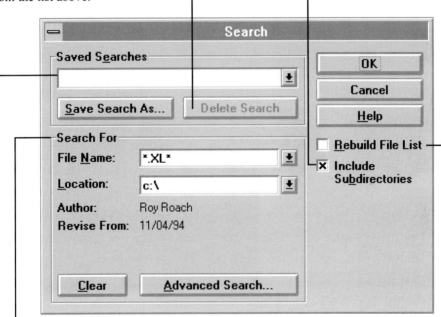

Search For lists the criteria to be applied to the search:

File Name: General wildcard specification for Excel files.

Location: The whole of the hard disk.

Added to this is any additional criteria, in this case... **Author:**
Revise From:

Note: This search has been made very wide deliberately. Normally a search would be restricted to one directory and its sub-directories. Always remember that more restrictive specifications speed up the search process.

13   Click OK to start the search.

14   The **Find File** dialogue box will be redisplayed. (For the record, this wide search of a very full 110 Mbyte hard disk drive took under a minute on a 486DX 25 MHz PC.)

15   As expected the search located the path C:\EXCEL_5\EXAMPLES and listed four files which satisfied the criteria.

16   Clicking any filename will display a preview of the Workbook, i.e. the top left hand corner of the first Worksheet.

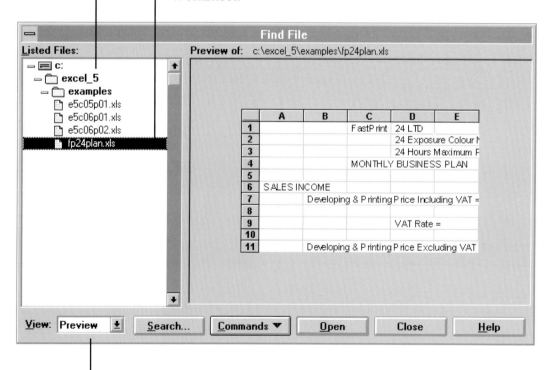

17   Alternatively, the **View** can be changed to the **Summary**, as shown on the opposite page, by selecting it from the View drop down list.

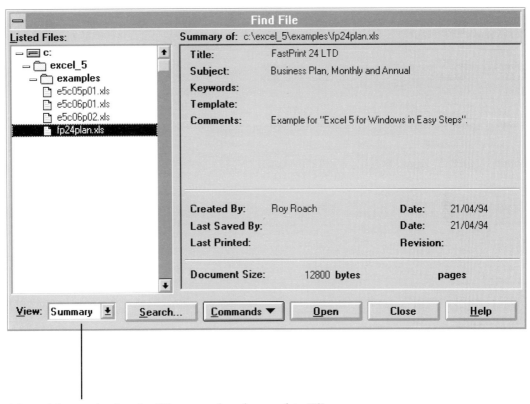

18   Alternatively, the **View** can be changed to **File Information**, as shown on the next page, by selecting it from the View drop down list.

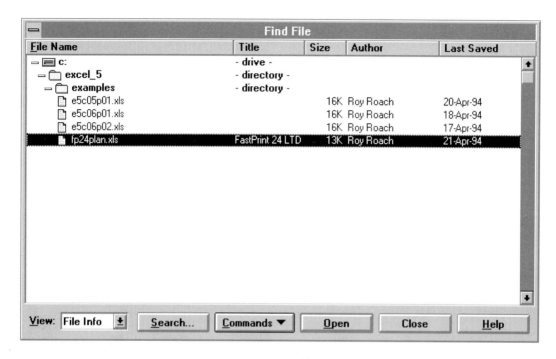

19   Clicking **Open** will open the located file.

20   Alternatively, clicking **Commands** displays the Commands
      sub-menu, which enables file management by further
      dialogue boxes or commands:

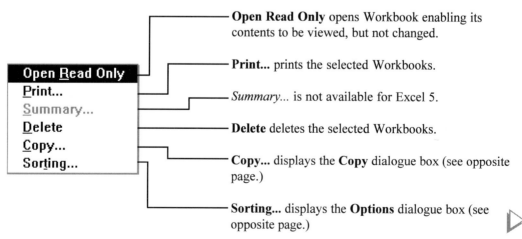

Open Read Only opens Workbook enabling its
contents to be viewed, but not changed.

Print... prints the selected Workbooks.

Summary... is not available for Excel 5.

Delete deletes the selected Workbooks.

Copy... displays the **Copy** dialogue box (see opposite
page.)

Sorting... displays the **Options** dialogue box (see
opposite page.)

In the **Copy** dialogue box:
(from the Commands sub-menu Copy...
option)

    Select the **Drive**

    and the **Directories**

    to display the **Path**

where the copy of the selected Workbook
is to be stored.

Alternatively, click the **New** button to
display the **Create Directory** dialogue
box and key in the name of new directory
which is to be created as a sub-directory
of the current directory.

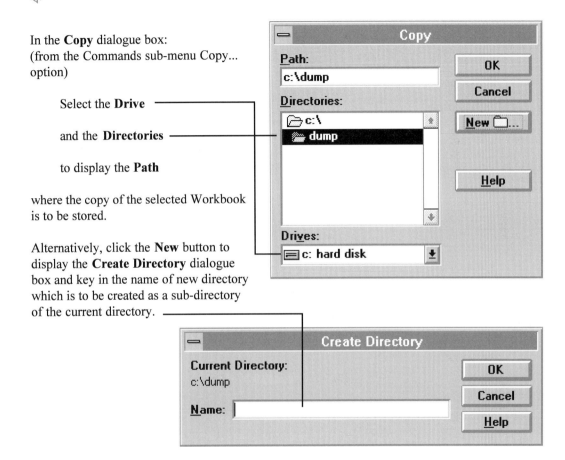

In the **Options** dialogue box:
(from the Commands sub-menu
Sorting... option)

    Select the **Sort Files By** option

    and the **List Files By** option

to determine how the located files are
ordered and listed respectively.

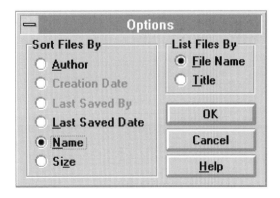

The File New Command

Purpose

The purpose of the File New command is to open a new empty Workbook in order to start a completely new Workbook.

Method of Use

    Either from the **File Menu** select the **New** option
    or on the **Standard Toolbar** click the **New** button.

Illustration of File New and Window Menu

The technique by which File New is normally employed is best illustrated by a typical sequence showing its use. This also introduces the Window menu.

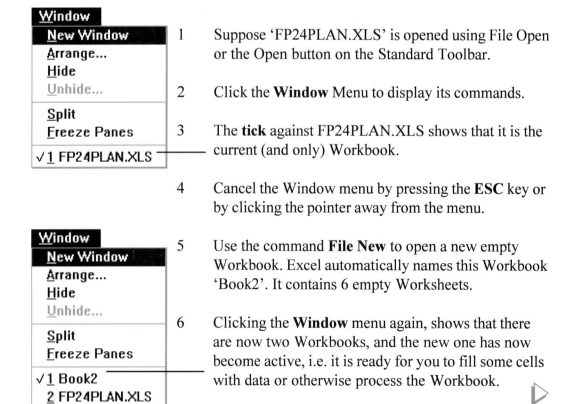

1   Suppose 'FP24PLAN.XLS' is opened using File Open or the Open button on the Standard Toolbar.

2   Click the **Window** Menu to display its commands.

3   The **tick** against FP24PLAN.XLS shows that it is the current (and only) Workbook.

4   Cancel the Window menu by pressing the **ESC** key or by clicking the pointer away from the menu.

5   Use the command **File New** to open a new empty Workbook. Excel automatically names this Workbook 'Book2'. It contains 6 empty Worksheets.

6   Clicking the **Window** menu again, shows that there are now two Workbooks, and the new one has now become active, i.e. it is ready for you to fill some cells with data or otherwise process the Workbook.

◁

7   Suppose some text is keyed into cell A1 of Sheet1 to
    identify the new Workbook. Don't worry about how the
    text has been formatted for now.

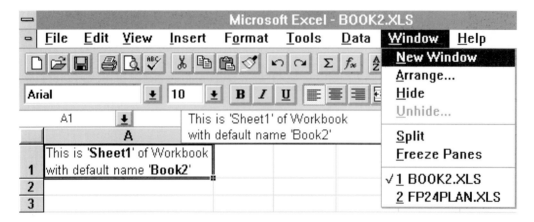

8   Suppose a second new Workbook is opened, called by
    default 'Book3', which contains 6 empty Worksheets.

9   Similar identifying text is keyed into cell A1.

10 Again the Window menu identifies this as the active
    Workbook.

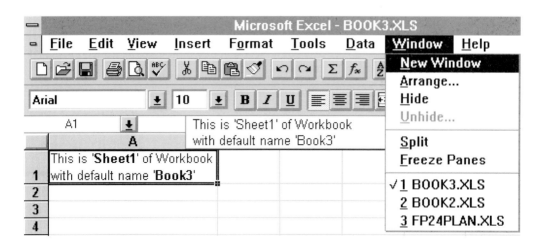

Activating Workbook versus Activating Worksheet

To change the active Workbook, you must click on the Window menu the filename you require so that it is checked, i.e. it has a tick placed against it.

To change the active Worksheet within the active Workbook, you must click the Worksheet tab.

To illustrate this:

1   Suppose that 'Book3' was still the active Workbook.

2   Click the 'Sheet2' Tab to display the second Worksheet.

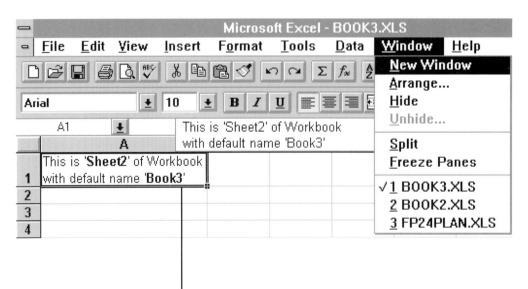

3   Again identifying text is keyed into cell A1:

Opening Extra Windows

To display *either* 'Sheet1' *or* 'Sheet2', you must click the corresponding Sheet tab. To display *both* 'Sheet1' *and* 'Sheet2' *simultaneously*, you must open another Window. The sequence follows:

1 Suppose 'Sheet2' of 'Book3' was made active by clicking its tab.

2 From the **Window** menu, select the **New Window** option.

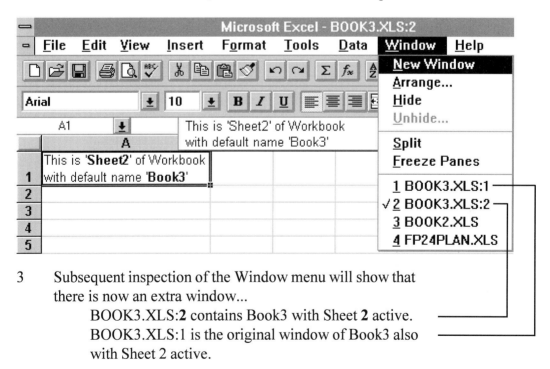

3 Subsequent inspection of the Window menu will show that there is now an extra window...
BOOK3.XLS:**2** contains Book3 with Sheet **2** active.
BOOK3.XLS:1 is the original window of Book3 also with Sheet 2 active.

4 Click BOOK3.XLS:1 to make it the active window.

5 Click 'Sheet1' tab so that
BOOK3.XLS:**1** contains Book3 with Sheet **1** active.

6 To view both worksheets simultaneously, see next section.

The Window Arrange Command

Viewing Several Workbooks and/or Worksheets

It is possible to view several Workbooks and/or Worksheets simultaneously, by using the Window Arrange dialogue box:

1 From the **Window** menu click the **Arrange...** option.

2 The **Arrange Windows** dialogue box will be displayed.

3 Select the options required.

Select the **Arrange** option:

Tiled will display the Windows side by side, arranged by Excel into an appropriate number of rows and columns.

Horizontal will produce a column of tiles, i.e. with *horizontal* subdivisions.

Vertical will produce a row of tiles, i.e. with *vertical* subdivisions.

Cascade will overlay the multiple windows with a slight offset, making each title bar just visible so that it can be clicked with the mouse to make the window active.

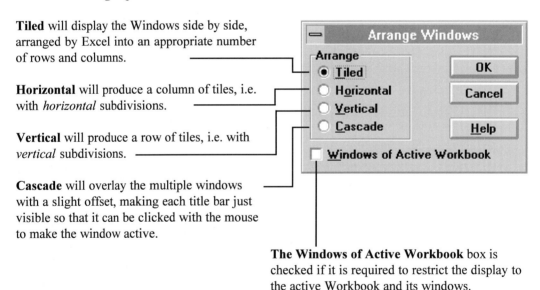

The **Windows of Active Workbook** box is checked if it is required to restrict the display to the active Workbook and its windows.

Remember
You can close an extra window just as you close any window. Simply double click its Control Menu button at the top left-hand corner.

The next two pages give a selection of examples of its use...

Why View Several Windows?

Why is it so useful to be able to view several windows simultaneously? The usual reason is that the Workbooks and Worksheets are **linked** so that they share common data. This will be covered in Chapter 9, 'Linking Worksheets and Workbooks'.

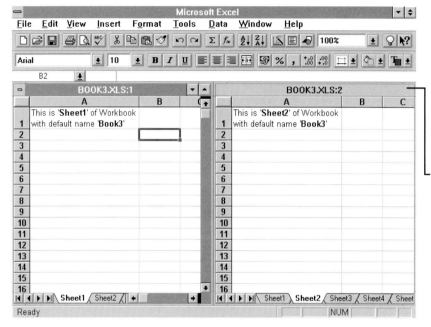

Note
*Arrange Windows Settings: Arrange-**Tiled.** Windows of Active Workbook-***Check.***

Only Sheet1 and Sheet2 of active Workbook are displayed.

Tip
To change the active Worksheet, simply click its window title bar, or click within body of sheet.

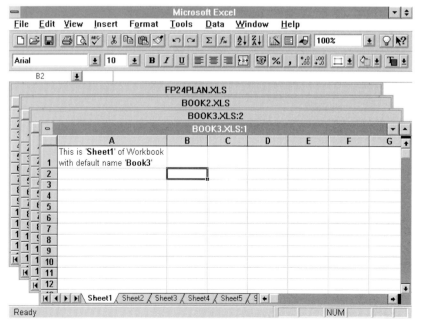

Note
*Arrange Windows Settings: Arrange-**Cascade.** Windows of Active Workbook-**Uncheck.***

Here all sheets of open workbooks are displayed: Sheet1 of Book3, Sheet2 of Book3, Sheet1 of Book2, Monthly Plan of FP24PLAN.XLS

Note
Arrange Windows
Settings: Arrange-
Tiled. *Windows of*
Active Workbook-
Uncheck.

Tip
The quickest way
to revert to
viewing one
window is to make
it active and click
its maximise
button.

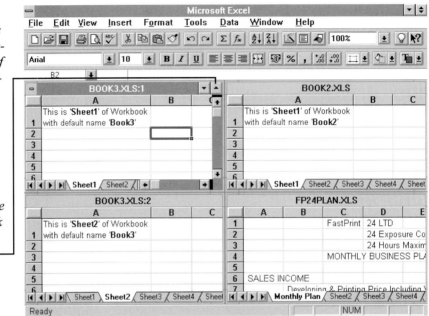

Note
Arrange Windows
Settings: as above.
However, the
tiling has been
rearranged by,

Moving tiles-
point to title bar
and drag.

Sizing tiles- *point*
to border and
drag.

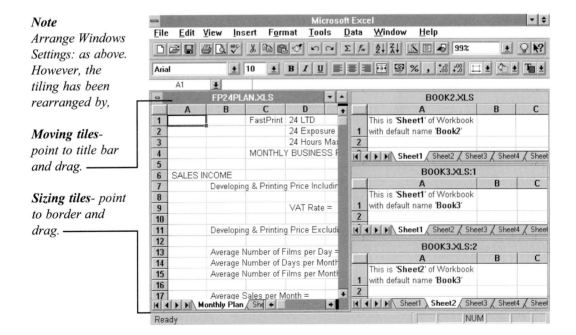

The File Save Workspace Command

Purpose

Some applications require that several Workbooks are open and that various Worksheets are displayed simultaneously. Not only does the opening of such Workbooks require a record of those files required, but the setting up of the tiled or cascaded windows can be very time consuming. To avoid repeating such operations, Excel gives the option of *Saving the Workspace,* i.e. keeping a record of both the files to be opened, the windows to be opened and displayed and their sizes and positions.

Method of Use

The method of use can be illustrated by reference to the previous section. Here three Workbooks were opened, consisting of four Worksheets. In the final tiling arrangement shown on the previous page, a lot of manipulation of the position and size was necessary. To reproduce this in future, follow the sequence:

1   From the **File** menu, select the **Save Workspace...** option.

2   Complete the **Save Workspace** dialogue box.

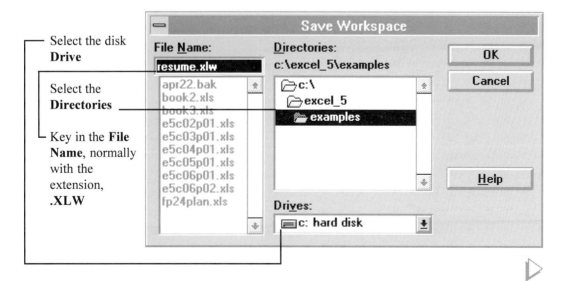

File	
New	**Ctrl+N**
Open...	Ctrl+O
Close	
Save	Ctrl+S
Save As...	
Save Workspace...	
Find File...	
Summary Info...	
Page Setup...	
Print Preview	
Print...	Ctrl+P
Print Report...	
1 TILE_DEM.XLW	
2 BOOK3.XLS	
3 BOOK2.XLS	
4 FP24PLAN.XLS	
Exit	

3   Excel offers the default file name,
     'RESUME.XLW'. You may accept this or key
     in your own name, although you are
     recommended to use the same extension. For
     this example the name 'TILE_DEM.XLW' was
     used.

4   **Close** your files normally.

5   Subsequently on using Excel, the Workspace can
     be restored by opening the file
     TILE_DEM.XLW.

Tip
To open the Work Space automatically when starting Excel,
*copy it to the '**Startup Directory**', '**XLSTART**', or to the*
*'**Alternative Startup Directory**' (See the Tools Options General*
tab dialogue box.)

Don't move your files to the startup directory!

CHAPTER

5

Cell Referencing

Overview

There are four ways of referencing cells:

(1)   Relative References,   e.g.   G9

(2)   Absolute References,   e.g. $G$9

(3)   Mixed References,   e.g. $G9
                                           or   G$9

(4)   Named References,   e.g.   'VAT_Rate'.

So far only the default method, relative referencing, has been used although it has been seen that Excel sometimes uses absolute references for cells. It is important for you to understand the difference between relative and absolute referencing and this chapter will give examples to demonstrate the necessity of using both types of references.

However if the distinguishing between absolute and relative referencing causes any problems, then they can be avoided by using named references. The added advantages of using names are so numerous that much greater emphasis will be placed on this method and on the techniques of naming and using named cells.

It is appropriate at this stage to introduce the most commonly used function for summing rows or columns of numbers, the SUM() function. Chapter 6, 'Formulas and Functions', will concentrate on functions generally and the techniques of incorporating them into formulas.

These new techniques will be introduced by developing further the simplified monthly business plan for 'FastPrint 24 LTD'.

The Advantage of Relative Referencing

Suppose the 'FastPrint 24' monthly business plan was extended to include the 'LABOUR' component of 'SALES COSTS', as shown below. This shows that the business is to employ a working manager, an operator, who also attends to the shop counter, and a half-time counter assistant, who is employed at busy times. The column for the number of employees has been included to allow for part-time or for future expansion.

Tip
To enter a number into a cell such as B24 so that it will be automatically formatted as a fraction, key it in the format '0 1/2'.

The Worksheet has been formatted as follows:

Columns E, F, H and I are selected. From the **Format** menu, the **Column** sub-menu is selected, from which the **Width...** option is chosen. In the **Column Width** dialogue box a consistent value of 10 is entered.

	B24		0.5					
	A	B	C	D	E	F	G	H	I
8									
9				VAT Rate =			17.5%		
10									
11		Developing & Printing Price Excluding VAT =					£3.83		
12									
13		Average Number of Films per Day =					60		
14		Average Number of Days per Month =					30		
15		Average Number of Films per Month =					1800		
16									
17		Average Sales per Month =							£6,893.62
18									
19	SALES COSTS								
20		LABOUR Costs per Annum							
21		Number		Job Title	Salary	Cost			
22		1		Manager	£10,000.00				
23		1		Operator/Counter	£8,000.00				
24		1/2		Counter Assistant	£6,000.00				
25		Total Annual Labour Cost =							
26									

Monthly Plan / Sheet2 / Sheet3 / Sheet4 / Sheet5 /
Ready   NUM

Cell B24 is selected. From the **Format** menu, the **Cells...** option is selected. The **Category Fraction** is selected and the **Format** '# ?/?' is chosen.

Cells B22 and B23 are selected. From the **Format** menu, the **Cells...** option is selected. The **Category Number** is selected and the **Format** '0' is chosen.

The formulas for the Costs of employing the staff are entered as follows:

1   In Cell F22 store the formula "= B22 * E22", which is the number employed times their salary. This can be done by pointing and clicking with the mouse or by keying in directly.

F22	↓		=B22*E22			
	A	**B**	**C**	**D**	**E**	**F**	**G**
19	SALES COSTS						
20		LABOUR Costs per Annum					
21		Number		Job Title	Salary	Cost	
22		1		Manager	£10,000.00	£10,000.00	
23		1	Operator/Counter		£8,000.00		
24		1/2	Counter Assistant		£6,000.00		
25		Total Annual Labour Cost =					
26							

2   The formula in F22 is copied to the adjacent cells below, by using either Edit Fill Down or the Short-Cut menu or by dragging the cell Fill Handle, as shown below.

—Drag the fill handle of F22 down so that the selection extends to F24

F22	↓		=B22*E22			
	A	**B**	**C**	**D**	**E**	**F**	**G**
19	SALES COSTS						
20		LABOUR Costs per Annum					
21		Number		Job Title	Salary	Cost	
22		1		Manager	£10,000.00	£10,000.00	
23		1	Operator/Counter		£8,000.00	£8,000.00	
24		1/2	Counter Assistant		£6,000.00	£3,000.00	
25		Total Annual Labour Cost =					
26							

3   The costs in all three cells will display the expected values, the formulas in F23 and F24 having been adjusted to reflect the new row numbers.

4   In particular, it can be seen on the formula bar below that cell F24 contains the formula "= B24 * E24".

F24	↓		=B24*E24			
A	**B**	**C**	**D**	**E**	**F**	**G**
19 SALES COSTS						
20	LABOUR Costs per Annum					
21	Number		Job Title	Salary	Cost	
22	1		Manager	£10,000.00	£10,000.00	
23	1	Operator/Counter		£8,000.00	£8,000.00	
24	1/2	Counter Assistant		£6,000.00	£3,000.00	
25	Total Annual Labour Cost =					
26						

How does Excel automatically adjust the formulas...
           from   = B22 * E22
           to   = B23 * E23
           and to   = B24 * E24?

The answer is that it is using Relative Referencing. The original formula in cell F22 actually stores a reference of the form "Take the contents of the cell, which lies on the same row but is four columns to the left, and multiply it by the contents of the cell, which also lies on the same row but is in the column immediately to the left". When such a relative reference is applied, the formulas are adjusted to the positions of the cell to which the formula is copied. This method of referencing cells together with the techniques of copying to adjacent cells provide efficient ways of generating tables of numbers.

The Need for Absolute Referencing

Since relative referencing is the default and proves so powerful, it might appear that absolute referencing is not needed. The deliberate mistake in the example which follows will demonstrate that it is sometimes essential and will show how these two forms of referencing are used together.

Consider the typical example of calculating the cost of a number of items as shown below, with the Worksheet set to display formulas instead of values. The values were contrived to make the calculations self checking in that the number multiplied by the unit price gives the same value for each line, which should result in the same VAT and gross cost. The formulas are simple:

C5 contains the product of the number in A5 and the unit price in B5.

	C5	↓	=A5*B5		
	A	**B**	**C**	**D**	**E**
1					
2		VAT Rate =	0.175		
3					
4	Number	Unit Price	Net Cost	VAT	Gross Cost
5	1	18	=A5*B5	=C5*C2	=C5+D5
6	3	6			
7	4	4.5			
8	8	2.25			
9					

D5 contains the product of the net cost in C5 and the and the VAT rate in C2.

1   If these three selected cells were copied down by dragging the fill handle, then the formulas would be adjusted:

E5 contains the sum of the net cost in C5 and the VAT charged in D5.

	C5	↓	=A5*B5		
	A	**B**	**C**	**D**	**E**
1					
2		VAT Rate =	0.175		
3					
4	Number	Unit Price	Net Cost	VAT	Gross Cost
5	1	18	=A5*B5	=C5*C2	=C5+D5
6	3	6	=A6*B6	=C6*C3	=C6+D6
7	4	4.5	=A7*B7	=C7*C4	=C7+D7
8	8	2.25	=A8*B8	=C8*C5	=C8+D8
9					

2   If you display the results of calculating these formulas by holding down the Control key and pressing the single open quote key (at the top left hand corner of the keyboard), then the problems below will be revealed:

D5		=C5*C2		
A	**B**	**C**	**D**	**E**
1				
2	VAT Rate =	17.5%		
3				
4 Number	Unit Price	Net Cost	VAT	Gross Cost
5 1	£18.00	£18.00	£3.15	£21.15
6 3	£6.00	£18.00	£0.00	£18.00
7 4	£4.50	£18.00	#VALUE!	#VALUE!
8 8	£2.25	£18.00	£324.00	£342.00
9				

The first line is correct, since the formula for VAT in D5 is valid.

The remaining lines should give the same values but are wrong:

D6 takes the VAT rate from C3 which is empty and Excel assumes a zero value.

D7 attempts to take the VAT rate from C4 which contains the text 'Net Cost', resulting in the error message shown.

D8 takes the VAT rate from C5 which contains the net cost for the first line and interprets the VAT rate as 1800%!

The reason for these mistakes is the use of a relative reference for cell C2.

3   Change the formula in D5 so that it refers to the VAT rate absolutely, i.e. **$C$2**. This can be done by editing or using F4.

Tip
To switch between relative and absolute cell references in a formula, press the **F4 key** *after selecting the cell reference or after keying in the cell reference or after clicking the cell.*

D5		=C5*$C$2		
A	**B**	**C**	**D**	**E**
1				
2	VAT Rate =	0.175		
3				
4 Number	Unit Price	Net Cost	VAT	Gross Cost
5 1	18	=A5*B5	=C5*$C$2	=C5+D5
6 3	6			
7 4	4.5			
8 8	2.25			
9				

4   Select the cells C5:E5 and drag the fill handle down to the cells below to copy the formulas as shown. Note that the relative references are adjusted as before, but the absolute reference to the VAT rate, $C$2, remains constant ——

C5	↓		=A5*B5		
	A	**B**	**C**	**D**	**E**
1					
2		VAT Rate =	0.175		
3					
4	Number	Unit Price	Net Cost	VAT	Gross Cost
5	1	18	=A5*B5	=C5*$C$2	=C5+D5
6	3	6	=A6*B6	=C6*$C$2	=C6+D6
7	4	4.5	=A7*B7	=C7*$C$2	=C7+D7
8	8	2.25	=A8*B8	=C8*$C$2	=C8+D8
9					

5   Changing the display to results rather than formulas will reveal the correct calculations as below.

C5	↓		=A5*B5		
	A	**B**	**C**	**D**	**E**
1					
2		VAT Rate =	17.5%		
3					
4	Number	Unit Price	Net Cost	VAT	Gross Cost
5	1	£18.00	£18.00	£3.15	£21.15
6	3	£6.00	£18.00	£3.15	£21.15
7	4	£4.50	£18.00	£3.15	£21.15
8	8	£2.25	£18.00	£3.15	£21.15
9					

The Need for Mixed Referencing

Sometimes applications need Mixed References in formulas. Such references specify *either* the column as absolute and the row as relative *or* vice versa.

Compare the following references:

Absolute: $G$9   This refers to the cell which lies at the intersection of column G and row 9 and may not refer to any other cell.

Mixed: $G9   This refers to the cell which must always lie in column G but lies in row 9 only relative to the cell which contains the formula.

Mixed: G$9   This refers to the cell which must always lie in row 9 but lies in column G only relative to the cell which contains the formula.

Relative: G9   This refers to the cell which lies in column G and row 9 both relative to the cell which contains the formula.

To illustrate the need for mixed references, consider the trivial example of generating part of the multiplication table, as shown below. Don't worry for now how the borders have been inserted. This will be covered in a later chapter. The main question to consider is how to reference the formula in cell B3, so that it multiplies the contents of cells A3 and B2, and more importantly, so that it can be copied to the rest of the body of the table.

Warning
The formula in B3 may not simply contain the relative references "=A3 * B2". The formula needs mixed references so that it can be copied to the rest of the table!

A1				
A	**B**	**C**	**D**	**E**
1				
2		10	11	12
3	10	100	110	120
4	11	110	121	132
5	12	120	132	144
6				

Several procedures may be used for generating the required
formulas and the following is one such sequence:

1   Select cell B3, press
the equals key, and
point to cell A3 with
the mouse and click.

A3		f_x =A3		
A	**B**	**C**	**D**	**E**
1				
2		10	11	12
3	10 =A3			
4	11			
5	12			
6				

2   Press the Function
key **F4** (at the top of
the keyboard) **three
times** to change the
reference to A3:
from A3   to $A$3
from $A$3 to A$3
from A$3   to $A3.

A3		f_x =$A3		
A	**B**	**C**	**D**	**E**
1				
2		10	11	12
3	10 =$A3			
4	11			
5	12			
6				

3   Key in an asterisk and
point to cell B2 and
click.
Press the Function
key **F4 twice** to
change the reference
to B2:
from B2   to $B$2
from $B$2 to B$2.

B2		f_x =$A3*B$2		
A	**B**	**C**	**D**	**E**
1				
2		10	11	12
3	10 =$A3*B$2			
4	11			
5	12			
6				

$A fixes the reference
absolutely on column A, which
contains one set of values to be
multiplied.

$2 fixes the reference
absolutely on row 2, which
contains the other set of values
to be multiplied.

4   Drag the fill handle on
    cell B3 so that the
    border expands,
    extending the
    selection to cell D3
    and copying the
    formula across.

B3		↓		=$A3*B$2		
	A	**B**	**C**	**D**	**E**
1					
2		10	11	12	
3	10	100	110	120	
4	11				
5	12				
6					

5   Drag the fill handle on
    the selection B3:D3
    down so that it
    extends the selection
    down to row 5 and
    copies the formulas to
    the adjacent rows.

B3		↓		=$A3*B$2		
	A	**B**	**C**	**D**	**E**
1					
2		10	11	12	
3	10	100	110	120	
4	11	110	121	132	
5	12	120	132	144	
6					

6   Switch the display so
    that formulas are
    shown by holding
    down the Control key
    and pressing the open
    single quote key (top
    left hand corner of
    keyboard).

B3		↓		=$A3*B$2		
	A	**B**	**C**	**D**	**E**
1					
2		10	11	12	
3	10	=$A3*B$2	=$A3*C$2	=$A3*D$2	
4	11	=$A4*B$2	=$A4*C$2	=$A4*D$2	
5	12	=$A5*B$2	=$A5*C$2	=$A5*D$2	
6					

Row relative references

Column relative references

Note
The relative references have changed for the rows and columns,
while the absolute references have remained fixed.

R1C1 Versus A1 Referencing Styles

There is an older alternative style of referencing cells, called the 'R1C1' method, by which both columns and rows are numbered. It has the advantage that the distinction between absolute and relative referencing is easier to understand. Its disadvantage is that it is not as brief as the 'A1' method, which is the default for Excel. This section will show you how to change to this alternative referencing style if you prefer to use it. However, it is worth reading this if you are at all confused about the difference between absolute and relative referencing in 'A1' style.

The procedure for changing the reference style is:

1   From the **Tools** menu, select the **Options...** command.

2   Click the **General** tab.

3   Select the **R1C1** option and click OK.

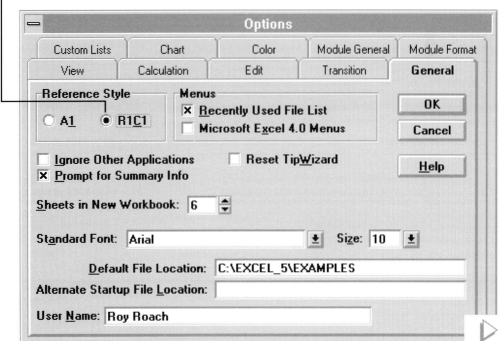

◁

In this style, '**R2C3**' means the absolute reference given by the intersection of **Row 2** and **Column 3,** corresponding to '**C2**' in the default style.

Generally, a relative reference employs square brackets to indicate the offsets relative to the cell containing the formula. For example **R[2]C[-3]** means **2 rows down** and **three columns to the left**. Therefore the reference is longer but unambiguous.

If a single **R** or a single **C** is used in the reference it means the same **Row** or the same **Column** respectively.

The example on VAT from the previous section should illustrate the technique:

R5C3	▾	=RC[-2]*RC[-1]		
	1	**2**	**3**	**4**	**5**

	1	**2**	**3**	**4**	**5**
1					
2		VAT Rate =	0.175		
3					
4	Number	Unit Price	Net Cost	VAT	Gross Cost
5	1	18	=RC[-2]*RC[-1]	=RC[-1]*R2C3	=RC[-2]+RC[-1]
6	3	6	=RC[-2]*RC[-1]	=RC[-1]*R2C3	=RC[-2]+RC[-1]
7	4	4.5	=RC[-2]*RC[-1]	=RC[-1]*R2C3	=RC[-2]+RC[-1]
8	8	2.25	=RC[-2]*RC[-1]	=RC[-1]*R2C3	=RC[-2]+RC[-1]
9					

Tip
*Use which ever referencing style you find easier but if you want to use the easiest technique change to **Naming** cells, which follows.*

This is a relative reference to the cell on the same row, R, but two columns to the left, C[-2],

This is an absolute reference to the cell at the intersection of row 2 and column 3, i.e. the VAT rate.

Introduction to the SUM Function

Suppose the Worksheet for the 'FastPrint 24' monthly business plan is further extended so that the Sales Costs include additionally the cost of Materials and Electricity, as shown below.

It is now necessary to add up a couple of columns of values. This is such a common requirement, that the procedure has been made very simple:

1   Select the cell where the total is required, e.g. F25.

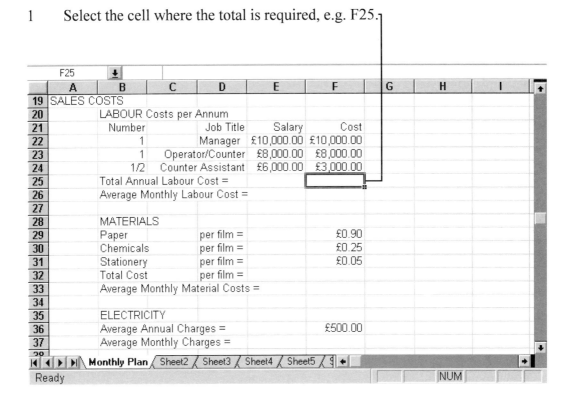

	A	B	C	D	E	F	G	H	I
19	SALES COSTS								
20		LABOUR Costs per Annum							
21		Number		Job Title	Salary	Cost			
22		1		Manager	£10,000.00	£10,000.00			
23		1	Operator/Counter	£8,000.00	£8,000.00				
24		1/2	Counter Assistant	£6,000.00	£3,000.00				
25		Total Annual Labour Cost =							
26		Average Monthly Labour Cost =							
27									
28		MATERIALS							
29		Paper		per film =		£0.90			
30		Chemicals		per film =		£0.25			
31		Stationery		per film =		£0.05			
32		Total Cost		per film =					
33		Average Monthly Material Costs =							
34									
35		ELECTRICITY							
36		Average Annual Charges =				£500.00			
37		Average Monthly Charges =							

Monthly Plan / Sheet2 / Sheet3 / Sheet4 / Sheet5 /

Ready   NUM

2   On the **Standard Toolbar**, click the **AutoSum** button. The icon for this is Greek letter capital sigma, which is the universal mathematical symbol for summation. This is shown on the next page.

◁

3   The AutoSum command makes Excel insert the SUM( )
     function in a formula in cell F25.

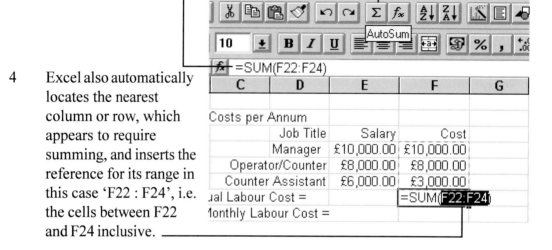

4   Excel also automatically
     locates the nearest
     column or row, which
     appears to require
     summing, and inserts the
     reference for its range in
     this case 'F22 : F24', i.e.
     the cells between F22
     and F24 inclusive.

5   Since the range is
     correct, press the Enter
     key and the correct
     results of the calculation
     will appear in F25.

6   The same technique is
     applied to the sum in cell
     F32. Here the range
     suggested for summing
     is 'F29 : F31', which is
     accepted by pressing
     Enter, leaving the
     expected value in F32.

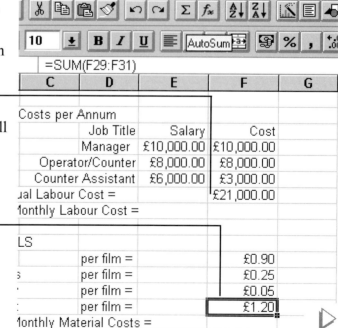

More detail on functions will
be given in Chapter 6,
'Formulas and Functions'.

The remaining three formulas are inserted in the usual way by pointing and clicking the cells for referencing:

H33: Multiply the 'average number of films per month' by the 'total costs per film' : "= G15 * F32".

H26: Divide the 'total annual labour cost' by 12 to give the average monthly cost : "= F25 / 12".

H37: Divide the 'average annual electricity charges' by 12 to give the average monthly cost : "= F36 / 12".

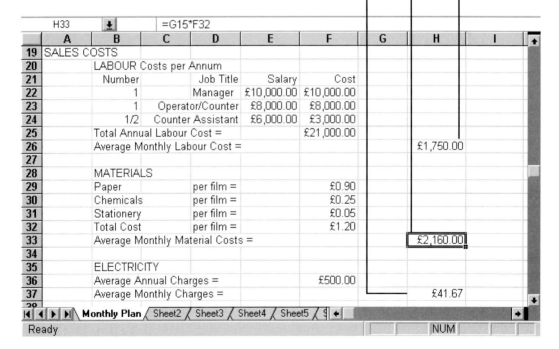

	H33	↓		=G15*F32					
	A	B	C	D	E	F	G	H	I
19	SALES COSTS								
20		LABOUR Costs per Annum							
21		Number		Job Title	Salary	Cost			
22		1		Manager	£10,000.00	£10,000.00			
23		1		Operator/Counter	£8,000.00	£8,000.00			
24		1/2		Counter Assistant	£6,000.00	£3,000.00			
25		Total Annual Labour Cost =				£21,000.00			
26		Average Monthly Labour Cost =						£1,750.00	
27									
28		MATERIALS							
29		Paper		per film =		£0.90			
30		Chemicals		per film =		£0.25			
31		Stationery		per film =		£0.05			
32		Total Cost		per film =		£1.20			
33		Average Monthly Material Costs =						£2,160.00	
34									
35		ELECTRICITY							
36		Average Annual Charges =				£500.00			
37		Average Monthly Charges =						£41.67	

Monthly Plan / Sheet2 / Sheet3 / Sheet4 / Sheet5 /

Ready   NUM

Finally add the following text, ready for the next section.

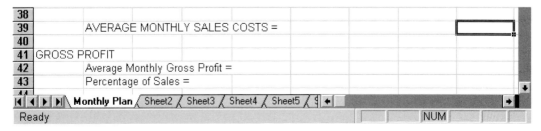

38									
39		AVERAGE MONTHLY SALES COSTS =							
40									
41	GROSS PROFIT								
42		Average Monthly Gross Profit =							
43		Percentage of Sales =							

Monthly Plan / Sheet2 / Sheet3 / Sheet4 / Sheet5 /

Ready   NUM

Naming Cells using the Name Box

An alternative way of referencing cells is to give them a 'Name' or 'Identifier' which describes the cells' contents. The advantages of doing this are too numerous to list here in this introduction. Suffice it to say for now that it is much easier to understand a formula expressed in words rather than in absolute or mixed cell references. This section will concentrate on the quickest ways of using named cells. Later sections will cover the wider issues.

Defining Names Using the Name Box

The easiest way to define names for cells is to use the Name Box on the Formula Bar. This will be illustrated for the 'FastPrint 24' example. The procedure is:

1   Select the cell to be named, e.g. H26. Its reference will appear on the formula bar.

2   Click the Name Box Button on the Formula Bar to display the Name Box, which at this stage will be empty.

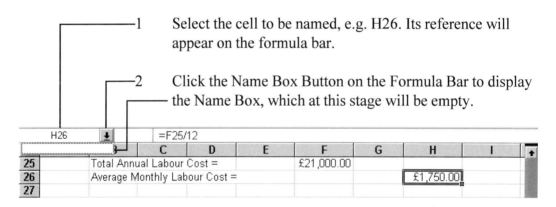

3   In place of the cell reference, 'H26', key in the name, say 'Labour', to represent this cell.

4   If any corrections are necessary whilst keying in the name, use the usual editing keys. Press Enter to complete the name. It will be added to the Workbook list of names.

5   To confirm that it has been added to the list of names, click
    the button again to display the Name Box.

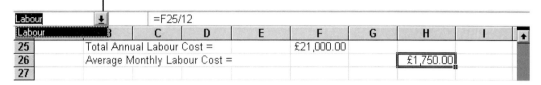

Labour	↓	=F25/12						
Labour		C	D	E	F	G	H	I
25		Total Annual Labour Cost =			£21,000.00			
26		Average Monthly Labour Cost =					£1,750.00	
27								

6   Repeat the procedure to name any other cells, in this case
    'Materials' for H33 and 'Electricity' for H37. Displaying
    the Name Box will reveal all three names in alphabetical
    order.

Electricity	↓	=F36/12						
Electricity		C	D	E	F	G	H	I
Labour		Annual Labour Cost =			£21,000.00			
Materials		Average Monthly Labour Cost =					£1,750.00	
27								

Other Uses for Names in Names List

The main purpose of names is to use them as cell references in
formulas, as will be shown next. However, there are other useful
applications which are worth trying:

(a) If the formula bar is not activated for the receipt of a
     formula, clicking a name in Name Box will select the
     named cell(s). This is like the Edit Goto command.

(b) If you type a name into the reference area and the name is
     already on the Workbook list of names, then the named
     cell(s) will be selected. This provides a warning against
     duplicating names.

(c) If you select a cell or block of cells which have been
     named, the name will appear in the cell reference area on
     the formula bar. If you press the mouse left button, the
     relative reference will replace the name temporarily.

Pasting Names Using the Name Box

The easiest way to paste names into formulas is to use the Name
Box. Again this will be illustrated for 'FastPrint 24'. The
'average monthly sales costs' are calculated by adding the
average monthly 'Labour', 'Materials' and 'Electricity' costs.
The procedure follows:

1   Select the cell in which to store the formula, i.e. I39.

2   You must press the keyboard equals sign, '=', to alert
     Excel to expect a formula and to activate the formula bar.

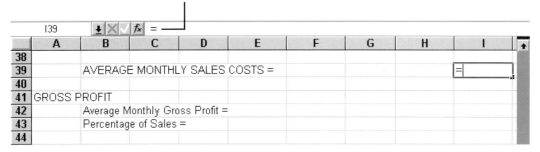

3   On the Formula Bar click the name button to display the
     Name Box.

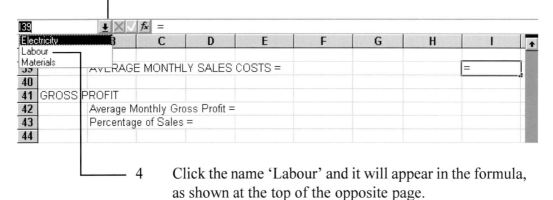

4   Click the name 'Labour' and it will appear in the formula,
     as shown at the top of the opposite page.

Tip
For long lists of names, type in the first letter of the name to speed up its location.

	A	B	C	D	E	F	G	H	I
H26			fx	=Labour					
26		Average Monthly Labour Cost =						£1,750.00	
27									
28		MATERIALS							
29		Paper		per film =		£0.90			
30		Chemicals		per film =		£0.25			
31		Stationery		per film =		£0.05			
32		Total Cost		per film =		£1.20			
33		Average Monthly Material Costs =						£2,160.00	
34									
35		ELECTRICITY							
36		Average Annual Charges =				£500.00			
37		Average Monthly Charges =						£41.67	
38									
39		AVERAGE MONTHLY SALES COSTS =							=Labour
40									

5   Press the keyboard plus key, '+'. (If you omit this step, Excel will provide the addition operator by default, whether or not it is appropriate!).

	A	B	C	D	E	F	G	H	I
I39			fx	=Labour+					
38									
39		AVERAGE MONTHLY SALES COSTS =							=Labour+
40									
41	GROSS PROFIT								
42		Average Monthly Gross Profit =							
43		Percentage of Sales =							
44									

6   Again click the name box button, select the name 'Materials', and press the plus key.

	A	B	C	D	E	F	G	H	I
I39			fx	=Labour+Materials+					
38									
39		AVERAGE MONTHLY SALES COSTS =							=Labour+
40									Materials+
41	GROSS PROFIT								
42		Average Monthly Gross Profit =							
43		Percentage of Sales =							
44									

7   Again click the name box button and select the name
     'Electricity'.

	H37	↓ X ✓ fx	=Labour+Materials+Electricity						
	A	B	C	D	E	F	G	H	I
26		Average Monthly Labour Cost =						£1,750.00	
27									
28		MATERIALS							
29		Paper		per film =		£0.90			
30		Chemicals		per film =		£0.25			
31		Stationery		per film =		£0.05			
32		Total Cost		per film =		£1.20			
33		Average Monthly Material Costs =						£2,160.00	
34									
35		ELECTRICITY							
36		Average Annual Charges =				£500.00			
37		Average Monthly Charges =						£41.67	
38									
39		AVERAGE MONTHLY SALES COSTS =							=Labour+
40									Materials+
41	GROSS PROFIT								Electricity
42		Average Monthly Gross Profit =							
43		Percentage of Sales =							
44									

8   Press the Enter key to complete the formula and display
     the correct addition in cell I39.

	I39	↓		=Labour+Materials+Electricity						
	A	B	C	D	E	F	G	H	I
38									
39		AVERAGE MONTHLY SALES COSTS =							£3,951.67
40									
41	GROSS PROFIT								
42		Average Monthly Gross Profit =							
43		Percentage of Sales =							
44									

Note
*The formula in I39
is much more
meaningful than
"= $H$26 +
$H$33 + $H$37".*

If you are a competent typist, it may be quicker for you to retype
the cell names. If you do this, your spelling must be consistent,
otherwise you may experience errors of the type shown in the
next section.

Typing Unknown or Incorrect Cell Names

Suppose for the 'Average Monthly Gross Profit' the following
deliberate mistake is made:

1   Cell I42 is selected and the formula, "= Sales - Costs", is
keyed in.

	I42			fx	=Sales - Costs					
	A	B	C	D	E	F	G	H	I	
38										
39		AVERAGE MONTHLY SALES COSTS =							£3,951.67	
40										
41	GROSS PROFIT									
42		Average Monthly Gross Profit =							=Sales -	
43		Percentage of Sales =							Costs	
44										

2   On pressing the Enter key to complete the formula, the
error message, "#NAME!", is displayed. Usually this
indicates an undefined or misspelt name. In this case it is
the former.

	I42			=Sales - Costs						
	A	B	C	D	E	F	G	H	I	
38										
39		AVERAGE MONTHLY SALES COSTS =							£3,951.67	
40										
41	GROSS PROFIT									
42		Average Monthly Gross Profit =							#NAME?	
43		Percentage of Sales =								
44										

3   The mistake is corrected by defining the names 'Sales' and
'Costs' for cells I17 and I39 respectively. Finally I42 is
named 'Gross_Profit', the formula shown is stored in I43
and I43 is formatted as a percentage.

Note
Spaces are not
allowed in names.
Use underlines as
here or full stops.

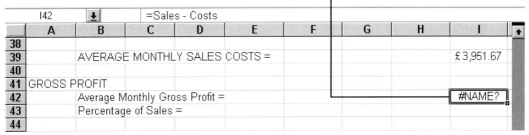

SUM Function versus Addition Operator

New users are sometimes confused as to whether to use the SUM() function or to use the addition sign (+) in a formula. Generally they are interchangeable so that there are no hard and fast rules. However it is probably easier to follow the guidelines:

SUM -   Use the SUM() Function for contiguous (i.e. adjacent) cells in rows, columns or blocks.

+   -   Use the Addition Operator for separated cells.

Both techniques have been used in 'FastPrint 24'. The simple example below of summing columns compares the use of both techniques for adjacent and separated cells.

	A	B	C	D	E	F
1						
2		2	2		2	2
3		3	3			
4		4	4		4	4
5		5	5			
6		6	6		6	6
7						
8		=SUM(B2:B6)	=C2+C3+C4+C5+C6		=SUM(E2:E6)	=F2+F4+F6
9						

SUM is the preferred method for adjacent cells, particularly since it can be applied by the AutoSum button on the Standard Toolbar

The + operator is inefficient because of having to key in each cell reference and plus signs, especially for large numbers of cells.

SUM and AutoSum work for separated cells. However a problem may arise subsequently if extra cells are filled within the specified range, especially where the cells are widely separated.

The + operator is probably safer for separated cells.

Naming Cell Ranges

Ranges of cells, i.e. adjacent cells in rows, columns or blocks, can be named in the same way as single cells. Using the Name Box, this technique will be applied to the simple example on the multiplication table used to illustrate mixed reference in a previous section:

1 Name the cells containing the first values for multiplication, i.e. name the cells A3:A5 'First'.

2 Correspondingly name the cells B2:D2 'Second'.

3 In cell B3 store the formula "=First*Second".

Second		↓		10		
	A	**B**	**C**	**D**	**E**
1					
2		10	11	12	
3	10	=First*Second	=First*Second	=First*Second	
4	11	=First*Second	=First*Second	=First*Second	
5	12	=First*Second	=First*Second	=First*Second	
6					

4 Copy this formula to the rest of the cells in the body of the table, i.e. to the block of cells B3:D5.

5 Holding down the Control key and pressing the single open quote key will display the same table as before.

Implicit Intersection

Clearly, this is far more simple than having to think about mixed, absolute and relative references. In the formula, how does Excel treat the names which each reference three cells? In cases like this, it takes the values from the corresponding row or column. This is caThe Insert Name Sub-menu

First		↓		10	
	A	**B**	**C**	**D**	**E**
1					
2		10	11	12	
3	10	100	110	120	
4	11	110	121	132	
5	12	120	132	144	
6					

Rules for Names

Rules for Defining Names

1   The **First Character** must be a letter (A,a...Z,z) or the underline character (_).

2   The **Other Characters** may be any sequence of letters and digits (0...9), provided it doesn't form a cell reference.

3   **Separators** must be either the underline (_) or the full stop (), since spaces are not allowed, e.g. Valid_Name.

4   The **Length** may be up to 255 characters.

5   Excel is **not Case Sensitive** to cell names - no distinction is made between capitals and lower case letters.

Names Are Normally Absolute References

Note
The early use of the 'A1' method of cell addressing may cause new users confusion. This is the use of the relative reference when specifying cells. If the absolute reference '$A$1' was always used when it should be, the distinction between absolute and relative references would be clearer. Excel is stricter when defining names.

Although Excel can be made to define names as relative references, this is not advisable because it is an unnecessary complication for most users. By default names are treated as absolute references to cells. For this reason it will be seen that Excel defines a name, say 'VAT_Rate', in terms of the cell's absolute reference, say '$C$2'.

Furthermore, Excel often specifies the sheet in which the name is located, giving the full reference as say...

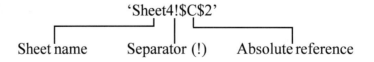

'Sheet4!$C$2'

Sheet name   Separator (!)   Absolute reference

It is apparent from the previous example on naming cell ranges that the effect of 'implicit intersection', whereby the current row or current column is selected from a range of values, effectively provides named cells with a relative referencing facility.

The Insert Name Sub-menu

As usual the Command Menu bar offers more facilities for naming cells and applying cell names than the Name Box on the Formula Bar. Whereas the name box is more efficient for pasting names into formulas, the menu bar provides more powerful techniques for naming cells:

From the **Insert** menu the sub-menu **Name** offers four dialogue boxes.

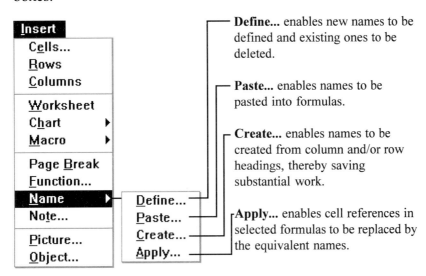

Define... enables new names to be defined and existing ones to be deleted.

Paste... enables names to be pasted into formulas.

Create... enables names to be created from column and/or row headings, thereby saving substantial work.

Apply... enables cell references in selected formulas to be replaced by the equivalent names.

These dialogue boxes will be covered in the next sections, based largely on the previous example on absolute referencing:

	C2	↓	0.175		
	A	B	C	D	E
1					
2		VAT Rate =	0.175		
3					
4	Number	Unit Price	Net Cost	VAT	Gross Cost
5	1	18	=A5*B5	=C5*$C$2	=C5+D5
6	3	6	=A6*B6	=C6*$C$2	=C6+D6
7	4	4.5	=A7*B7	=C7*$C$2	=C7+D7
8	8	2.25	=A8*B8	=C8*$C$2	=C8+D8
9					

The Define Name Dialogue Box

1   Select the single cell or range of cells to be named, e.g. C2.

2   From the **Insert** menu and the **Name** sub-menu, select the **Define...** option.

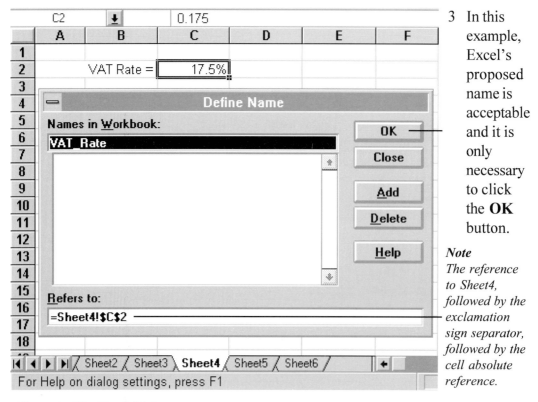

3   In this example, Excel's proposed name is acceptable and it is only necessary to click the **OK** button.

Note
The reference to Sheet4, followed by the exclamation sign separator, followed by the cell absolute reference.

Names in Workbook List:

The list is empty since none have yet been defined for this workbook.

A bonus in this case is that Excel proposes automatically the name 'VAT_Rate' based on the label in the cell adjacent to C2.

Refers to Box: This contains a precise reference to the Sheet name and to the absolute reference of the selected cells.

The **Add Button** is used when you wish to add a series of names to the Workbook list. You would have to key in each cell reference and its name and click the add button for each one.

The **Delete Button** enables existing names in the Workbook list to be deleted by selecting each in turn and clicking the delete button.

The Create Names Dialogue Box

1   In this case, you must select the range of cells to be named
and the appropriate row and/or column headings, e.g. the
whole of the table below, including the column titles.

	A	B	C	D	E	F
1						
2		VAT Rate =	17.5%			
3						
4	Number	Unit Price	Net Cost	VAT	Gross Cost	
5	1	£18.00	£18.00	£3.15	£21.15	
6	3	£6.00	£18.00	£3.15	£21.15	
7	4	£4.50	£18.00	£3.15	£21.15	
8	8	£2.25	£18.00	£3.15	£21.15	
9						

A4   ↕   Number

Note
*This selection
need not be
applied to a
completed
table. The
body of the
table may
contain empty
cells, awaiting
the insertion of
formulas.*

2   From the **Insert** menu and the **Name** sub-menu, select the
Create... option.

3   Complete the dialogue
box, by selecting the
location of the table
labels.

Create Names

Create Names in
- ☒ **Top Row**
- ☐ **Left Column**
- ☐ **Bottom Row**
- ☐ **Right Column**

OK

Cancel

Help

Note
*For some
applications, two
boxes will be
checked, e.g. 'top
row' and 'left
column'.*

4   Click OK or press Enter.

5   Click the Name Box button on the
Formula Bar to display the newly created
names. It will be seen here that Excel has
adapted the column headings by
replacing spaces by underlines. The
efficiency of this process should appeal!

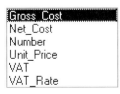

Gross_Cost
Net_Cost
Number
Unit_Price
VAT
VAT_Rate

Note
*'VAT_Rate' was
already defined.
All the other
names have been
created
automatically
from the column
headings.*

The Apply Names Dialogue Box

1   From the **Insert** menu and the **Name** sub-menu, select the
     Apply... option.

2   Complete the
     dialogue box.

Apply Names:

Select the cell names, which
are to be applied in formulas.
Hold down the Control key
while clicking the required
names.

Ignore Relative/Absolute
Keep this checked so that cell
references are replaced by
names, irrespective of their
reference types. Otherwise, it
will mean adding the
complication of defining
names as relative as well as
absolute.

Use Row and Column Names
Generally this should be
checked. This means that if an
exact name for a cell is not
available, Excel will use the
names of cell ranges which
include a row or column
which contains the cell.

Options >>
If this is clicked the dialogue
box will be extended to
include more options for
selecting row and column
names.

3   Click OK and display the formulas to show that the cell references have been
     replaced by names, with a further saving in effort.

	A	B	C	D	E
1					
2		VAT Rate =0.175			
3					
4	Number	Unit Price	Net Cost	VAT	Gross Cost
5	1	18	=Number*Unit_Price	=Net_Cost*VAT_Rate	=Net_Cost+VAT
6	3	6	=Number*Unit_Price	=Net_Cost*VAT_Rate	=Net_Cost+VAT
7	4	4.5	=Number*Unit_Price	=Net_Cost*VAT_Rate	=Net_Cost+VAT
8	8	2.25	=Number*Unit_Price	=Net_Cost*VAT_Rate	=Net_Cost+VAT
9					

The Paste Name Dialogue Box

The Paste Name dialogue box can be used to paste names in formulas, although it is usually easier to use the Name Box. However, an additional use for it is to list on the Worksheet all the names and cell references:

1   Select the single cell to mark the top left hand corner of the table of names, e.g. B10. Care must be taken to allow sufficient space - it is easy to overlay data!

2   From the **Insert** menu and the **Name** sub-menu, select the **Paste...** option.

3   Click the **Paste List** button.

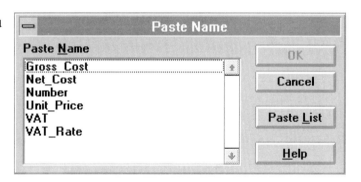

B10	↓		Gross_Cost		
	A	B	C	D	E
1					
2		VAT Rate =	17.5%		
3					
4	Number	Unit Price	Net Cost	VAT	Gross Cost
5	1	£18.00	£18.00	£3.15	£21.15
6	3	£6.00	£18.00	£3.15	£21.15
7	4	£4.50	£18.00	£3.15	£21.15
8	8	£2.25	£18.00	£3.15	£21.15
9					
10		Gross_Cost	=Sheet4!$E$5:$E$8		
11		Net_Cost	=Sheet4!$C$5:$C$8		
12		Number	=Sheet4!$A$5:$A$8		
13		Unit_Price	=Sheet4!$B$5:$B$8		
14		VAT	=Sheet4!$D$5:$D$8		
15		VAT_Rate	=Sheet4!$C$2		
16					

Note
The cells forming this table contain text, not formulas.

Using Cell Reference Operators

Cell Reference Operators are used to link cell references:

The **Range Operator** (the colon ':') means the rectangular block of cells formed between the two cell references which it separates.

The Union Operator (the comma ',') means the set of cells formed by the list of cell references which it separates.

The Intersection Operator (the space ' ') means the cells defined at the intersection of the cell ranges which it separates. These ranges must overlap, otherwise an error message will appear.

	A	B	C	D	E
1					
2		Qtr 1	Qtr 2	Qtr 3	Qtr 4
3	1991:	£8,000	£10,000	£15,000	£12,000
4					
5	1992:	£9,000	£11,000	£17,000	£13,000
6					
7	1993:	£10,000	£12,000	£19,000	£14,000
8					
9	Total Sales for 1992 =				£50,000
10	Quarter 3 Sales for 1991 to 1993 =				£51,000
11	Quarter 3 Sales for 1992 =				£17,000

This first example illustrates the use of the three operators in three summations as shown. E9 contains a reference to a range of cells, E10 contains a reference to a list of cells and E11 contains a reference to the intersection of two ranges.

	E	*Note...*
9	=SUM(B5:E5)	—— *Colon*
10	=SUM(D3,D5,D7)	—— *Comma*
11	=SUM(B5:E5 D3:D7)	— *Space*

Intersection operators make better sense when applied to named ranges of cells as in this second example. Here the careful choice of names makes the meanings more clear, even though the grammar is not strictly correct. In the formula in F23, the 'Number Operators' refers to cell B23 and the 'Operators Salary' refers to cell E23.

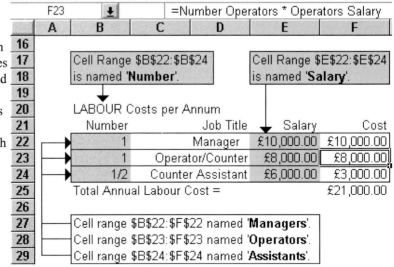

6

Formulas and Functions

In easy steps

Overview

Functions are used in Formulas. Typically they are used for special mathematical calculations but some functions are used to manipulate text. Some carry out very simple arithmetic, whereas others involve much more complex operations. Often these operations are common to many applications. Functions are easy to recognise in formulas because their names are always in capital letters and they are always followed by open and close brackets, for example...

SUM(*argument*), which adds up the total for the cells specified in the argument. We have already seen that this is used by the AutoSum function on the Standard Toolbar.

MAX(*argument*), which finds the maximum value in a list of cells specified by the argument.

MEDIAN(*argument*), which calculates the median value for the cells specified by the argument.

Because *functions* are in capitals, it is recommended that *cell names* use lower case and caps (mixed case) in order to distinguish them. (See tip below.)

The selection of functions built into Excel is extensive with wide ranging applications. The applications are so wide that they will satisfy most disciplines, e.g. accountancy, business, engineering, mathematics and science. The range is so great that it is only possible in a book of this length to sample a small fraction of functions. However the techniques of using them can be applied to many specialist applications, which gives Excel its flexibility.

This chapter will further develop the use of the AutoSum function. It will introduce the Function Wizard, demonstrating commonly used functions. Finally it will survey formula error messages and trouble shooting using the Auditing Toolbar.

Tip: Microsoft suggest that if you wish to type cell names and functions in your formulas, they can be made self checking as follows. Always use caps and lower case to define your names. Subsequently, always use lower case to key in cell and function names. If Excel recognises them, it will convert them to caps and lower case or all caps respectively. Otherwise, they are undefined or misspelt.

More Features of AutoSum

The following example shows features which AutoSum is able to offer additionally to simply adding rows or columns. These are summing *ranges* of cells and adding *grand totals*. Don't worry for now about the formatting of the cells, which will be covered later in Chapter 10.

1   To sum a range of cells, you can *either* select the cells in which the totals are to appear *or* you can select the block of cells to be added, as shown below.

Tip
Remember that 'Quarter 1' is part of a series which Excel will continue by dragging the fill handle of the first cell.

	B5	↓		34000		
	A	**B**	**C**	**D**	**E**	**F**
1						
2		Quarter 1	Quarter 2	Quarter 3	Quarter 4	Annual
3						
4	**1993 Sales**					
5	Factory A:	£34,000	£36,500	£30,750	£31,800	
6	Factory B:	£20,550	£24,640	£17,950	£22,340	
7	Totals:					
8						
9	**1994 Sales**					
10	Factory A:	£35,120	£38,120	£31,500	£34,080	
11	Factory B:	£20,990	£26,220	£18,050	£25,990	
12	Totals:					
13						
14	**93/94 Sales**					

2   Click the **AutoSum** button on the **Standard Toolbar**.

Tip
The keyboard code for AutoSum is to hold down the Alt key and press equals:
ALT =

3   By either method, Excel will enter the formulas in the range B7 : E7, using the SUM() function, for example...

in cell B7 :   "=SUM(B5:B6)",

in cell E7 :   "=SUM(E5:E6)".

▷

B10	↓	35120			
	A	**B**	**C**	**D**	**E**	**F**

	A	B	C	D	E	F
1						
2		Quarter 1	Quarter 2	Quarter 3	Quarter 4	Annual
3						
4	**1993 Sales**					
5	Factory A:	£34,000	£36,500	£30,750	£31,800	
6	Factory B:	£20,550	£24,640	£17,950	£22,340	
7	Totals:	£54,550	£61,140	£48,700	£54,140	
8						
9	**1994 Sales**					
10	Factory A:	£35,120	£38,120	£31,500	£34,080	
11	Factory B:	£20,990	£26,220	£18,050	£25,990	
12	Totals:					
13						
14	**93/94 Sales**					

Note
The range of totals in row 7 are produced automatically by AutoSum.

4   As a more positive alternative for summing ranges, you can
    select the block of cells to be added together with the
    range of empty cells to contain the totals, as above.

B5	↓	34000			
	A	**B**	**C**	**D**	**E**	**F**

	A	B	C	D	E	F
1						
2		Quarter 1	Quarter 2	Quarter 3	Quarter 4	Annual
3						
4	**1993 Sales**					
5	Factory A:	£34,000	£36,500	£30,750	£31,800	
6	Factory B:	£20,550	£24,640	£17,950	£22,340	
7	Totals:	£54,550	£61,140	£48,700	£54,140	
8						
9	**1994 Sales**					
10	Factory A:	£35,120	£38,120	£31,500	£34,080	
11	Factory B:	£20,990	£26,220	£18,050	£25,990	
12	Totals:	£56,110	£64,340	£49,550	£60,070	
13						
14	**93/94 Sales**					

Tip
AutoSum is not as flexible for grand totals as it might appear. Avoid filling any cells within the grand total ranges with say extra text. Otherwise Excel will change the location of the grand totals to a range of empty cells!

5   To add grand totals automatically, you must first select the range of cells which includes the data, the sub-totals and the empty ranges to accommodate the grand totals, as shown on the previous page.

6   Click the AutoSum button to give the grand totals for both the vertical and horizontal totals, as shown below.

B14	↓	=SUM(B12,B7)			
A	**B**	**C**	**D**	**E**	**F**
1					
2		Quarter 1	Quarter 2	Quarter 3	Quarter 4	Annual
3					
4 **1993 Sales**					
5 Factory A:	£34,000	£36,500	£30,750	£31,800	£133,050
6 Factory B:	£20,550	£24,640	£17,950	£22,340	£85,480
7 Totals:	£54,550	£61,140	£48,700	£54,140	£218,530
8					
9 **1994 Sales**					
10 Factory A:	£35,120	£38,120	£31,500	£34,080	£138,820
11 Factory B:	£20,990	£26,220	£18,050	£25,990	£91,250
12 Totals:	£56,110	£64,340	£49,550	£60,070	£230,070
13					
14 **93/94 Sales**	£110,660	£125,480	£98,250	£114,210	£448,600

Note the difference in the form of the *arguments* for the grand totals between the horizontal and vertical summations:

Horizontal -   e.g. F14 = SUM(E14 : B14)
            The colon represents the *range* of cells
            i.e. block between and including E14 and B14.

Vertical -   e.g. B14 = SUM(B12 , B7)
            The comma represents the *union* of cells
            i.e. cell B12 and cell B7.

The Function Wizard

Usually the Function Wizard can be recognised throughout Excel by its icon, f_x, which is an abbreviation for the mathematical term for any function, $f(x)$. The Function Wizard dialogue box can be activated in several ways:

1   *Either* from the **Insert** menu, select the **Function...** option.

2   *Or* on the **Standard Toolbar** click the **Function Wizard** button.

3   *Or* if the **Formula Bar** is activated, i.e. it is ready to receive or in the process of receiving a formula, then click the **Function Wizard** button.

4   *Or* from within the **Function Wizard dialogue box** itself.

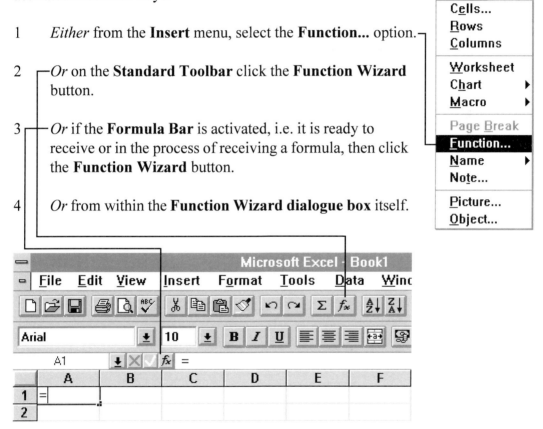

The Function Wizard dialogue boxes are presented in two stages, the first to guide you to choose the function name, the second to guide you to fill in the appropriate arguments.

e.g.   LOOKUP(Lookup_Value , Array)

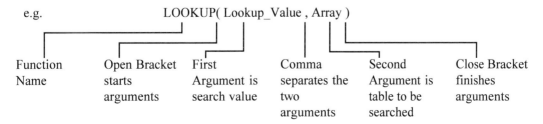

| Function Name | Open Bracket starts arguments | First Argument is search value | Comma separates the two arguments | Second Argument is table to be searched | Close Bracket finishes arguments |

Completion of Monthly Business Plan

The monthly plan for 'FastPrint 24' will now be completed, by adding the 'EXPENSES', which are constants independent of the sales. The text and numeric values are keyed in and the formulas entered as shown below:

1   Cell H47 is selected and the formula "=F46/12" entered. This is a relative reference to the cell on the previous line and two columns to the left. The same formula can be applied to the other annual rates by any technique of copying separated cells.

2   To copy this formula, H47 is selected and the **Copy** button is clicked on the Standard Toolbar. H49 is selected and holding down the Control key, the selection is extended to cells H51, H53, H55 and H57. Pressing the **Enter** key then **Paste**s the formula into all five cells.

H57	↓		=F56/12						
	A	B	C	D	E	F	G	H	I
39		AVERAGE MONTHLY SALES COSTS =							£3,951.67
40									
41	GROSS PROFIT								
42		Average Monthly Gross Profit =							£2,941.95
43		Percentage of Sales =							42.7%
44									
45	EXPENSES								
46		ACCOUNTANCY		Annual Average =		£400.00			
47				Monthly Average =				£33.33	
48		ADVERTISING		Annual Average =		£1,000.00			
49				Monthly Average =				£83.33	
50		INSURANCE		Annual Average =		£400.00			
51				Monthly Average =				£33.33	
52		MAINTENANCE		Annual Average =		£500.00			
53				Monthly Average =				£41.67	
54		TELEPHONE		Annual Average =		£300.00			
55				Monthly Average =				£25.00	
56		RENT/RATES		Annual Average =		£6,000.00			
57				Monthly Average =				£500.00	

3   The following cells will need to be named for future reference.

$G$7:	'Retail_Price'
$G$11:	'Net_Price'
$F$29:	'Paper'
$F$30:	'Chemicals'
$F$31:	'Stationery'

4   The cells containing the monthly rates are named as follows.

$H$47 :	'Accountancy'
$H$49 :	'Advertising'
$H$51 :	'Insurance'
$H$53 :	'Maintenance'
$H$55 :	'Telephone'
$H$57 :	'Rent_Rates'

◁

The rest of the text and numbers are added to complete this Worksheet. The final expenses are the capital costs of purchasing the processing equipment, some of which will be second hand, and the cost of counters and signs, etc., for the shop. It is assumed that the capital will be raised from a lease company. The formulas await completion as shown below.

5   Cell F61 is selected and **ALT + = is** pressed to call up AutoSum, which offers to SUM the range 'F59:F60', and this is accepted by pressing **Enter**.

6   The range of cells, $B$65 : $C$69, i.e. the columns containing the lease periods and the lease rates are selected and named 'Lease_Table'.

| F59 | ↓ × ✓ _fx_ | =SUM(F59:F60) |

	A	B	C	D	E	F	G	H	I
58		CAPITAL COSTS							
59			Processing Equipment =			£35,000.00			
60			Fitting out Shop =			£5,000.00			
61			Total Capital Costs =			=SUM(F59:F60)			
62									
63		Monthly Lease Rates per £1000 borrowed							
64		Years	Rates						
65		1	£89.08						
66		2	£47.31						
67		3	£33.45						
68		4	£26.58		Lease Term in Years =		5		
69		5	£22.50		Monthly Lease Costs =				
70									
71		AVERAGE MONTHLY EXPENSES =							
72									
73	NET PROFIT								
74		Average Monthly Net Profit =							
75		Percentage of Sales =							
76									

7   The following single cells are also named:
    $F$61 :   'Capital'
    $G$68 :   'Lease_Term'
    $H$69 :   'Lease_Costs'
    $I$71 :   'Expenses'
    $I$74 :   'Net_Profit'

8   The formula for the lease costs in $H$69 will be inserted in the next section.

9   The rest of the formulas are inserted.

    $I$71 : "=Accountancy + Advertising + Insurance + Maintenance + Telephone + Rent_Rates + Lease_Costs"

    $I$74 : "=Sales - Costs - Expenses"

    $I$75 : "=Net_Profit/Sales"

Using the LOOKUP Function

As an example of using the Function Wizard, we return to the 'FastPrint 24' example from the last section. The formula for the 'Lease_Costs' in cell $H$69 will be completed. The first part of this formula requires reference to the table of lease rates. Now it is clear to us that if the owner of the business chooses the maximum 'Lease_Term' of 5 years, by entering 5 in cell G68, the monthly rate for each £1000 of capital borrowed will be £22.50. To make Excel look up this value requires the LOOKUP function. The procedure to insert this into a formula follows:

1   Select the cell to receive the formula, e.g. H69. Note that the name 'Lease_Costs' of this cell will appear in place of the cell reference on the formula bar.

2   Press the '=' key to activate the formula bar, ready to receive a formula.

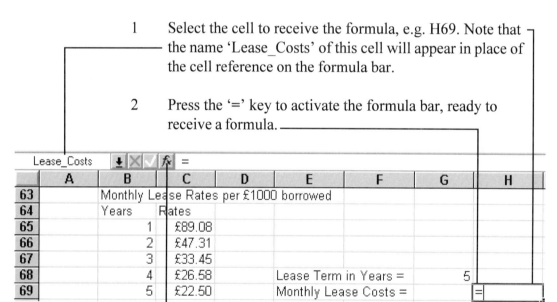

3   Click the **Function Wizard** button on the formula bar to display the first Function Wizard dialogue box shown on the next page.

Note
*The **Function Category** gives a choice of groups of functions to speed up the selection process, except for the 'All' group which enables you to view the whole large list. Some of these categories and most of the functions may never be required by you, depending on your type of work.*

4   Complete the dialogue box by following its instructions.

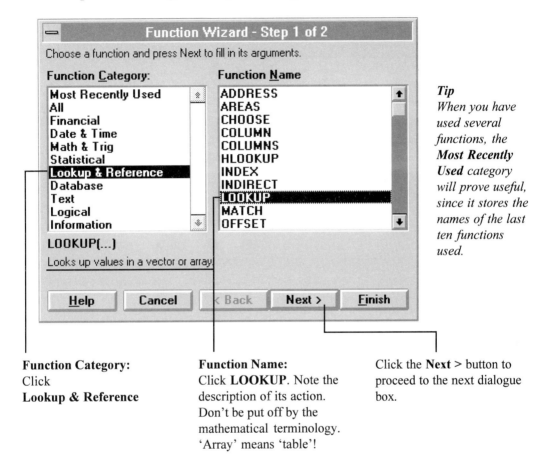

Function Category:
Click
Lookup & Reference

Function Name:
Click **LOOKUP**. Note the description of its action. Don't be put off by the mathematical terminology. 'Array' means 'table'!

Click the **Next >** button to proceed to the next dialogue box.

Tip
*When you have used several functions, the **Most Recently Used** category will prove useful, since it stores the names of the last ten functions used.*

Note
There are two functions which are very similar to LOOKUP. VLOOKUP must be used on a **V**ertical table and HLOOKUP on a **H**orizontal table. The LOOKUP function has been chosen for its compatibility with other spreadsheet programs. It does in fact decide whether a table is vertical (tall) or horizontal (wide). In the former case it searches the first column for the nearest match and returns the value in the last column of the corresponding row. In the latter case it operates on the top and bottom rows of the table.

5   Complete the intermediate dialogue box which is needed
     for this function since there are two versions. Click the
     simpler alternative, which has two arguments.

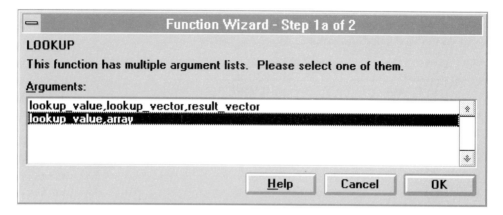

6   Click OK to move to the next stage.

7   The dialogue box for the two argument LOOKUP function
     will be displayed. This is the second stage of the Function
     Wizard process of guidance. It now proceeds to help you
     insert the required arguments, by defining each in turn.
     Here it tells you that the first argument is the value to be
     matched in the first column of the table.

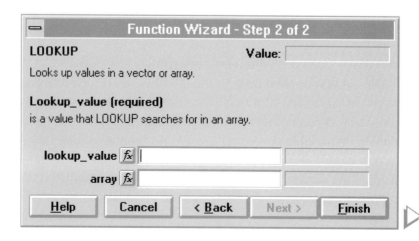

8   In this case the Lookup Value is the number contained in the cell named 'Lease_Term'. To insert this name in the function, click the Name Box button on the Formula Bar and click Lease_Term in the Name Box. (Alternatively, if you are using cell references, you can click the required cell.)

Tip
To view the Name Box and cells, you may have to move the Function Wizard dialogue box by dragging its title bar.

9   The selected name will appear within the function brackets, simultaneously on the formula bar, in cell H69 and in the dialogue box.

Note
The cell named Lease_Term will be highlighted with a dotted line border.

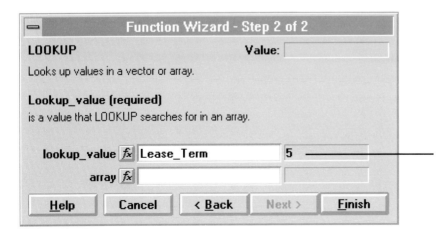

Note
The value stored in the cell named Lease_Term is also displayed.

10   To move on to the next argument, press the Tab key or click the empty box for 'array'.

11   The second argument is the Array or Table to be searched.
     This was named 'Lease_Table' and it can also be located in
     the Name Box.

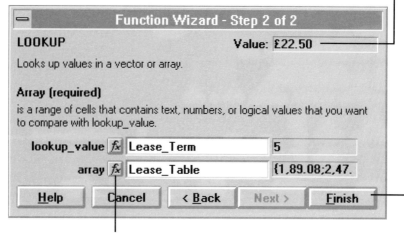

Note
*The cell range
named
Lease_Table will
be highlighted
with a dotted line
border.*

12   Lease_Table will appear on the formula bar, in cell H69,
     and in the dialogue box.

13   As a check on the function, the value returned by the
     function is also displayed.

14   Since this is correct, click the Finish button to complete
     the function.

Function Wizard - Step 2 of 2

LOOKUP   Value: £22.50

Looks up values in a vector or array.

Note
*The values stored
in the lease table
also appear in the
dialogue box.*

Array (required)

is a range of cells that contains text, numbers, or logical values that you want
to compare with lookup_value.

lookup_value *fx* Lease_Term   5

array *fx* Lease_Table   {1,89.08;2,47.

Help	Cancel	< Back	Next >	Finish

*Note the Function Wizard button, which appears against each argument.
This is provided for those cases where the argument is itself a function,
allowing for functions within functions. (See later section.)*

15   To complete the formula, the selected monthly lease rate per £1000 must be multiplied by the number of units of £1000 of borrowed capital, i.e. multiplied by 'Capital' and divided by 1000.

16   The asterisk is keyed in to signify multiplication and the Name Box is used to add the name 'Capital'.

Capital		fx	=LOOKUP(Lease_Term,Lease_Table)*Capital				
Capital	3	C	D	E	F	G	H
Costs		Total Capital Costs =			£40,000.00		
Electricity							
Expenses							
Gross_Profit		hly Lease Rates per £1000 borrowed					
Insurance	s	Rates					
Labour	1	£89.08					
Lease_Costs	2	£47.31					
Lease_Table	3	£33.45					
b/							

17   Finally the oblique stroke is added followed by 1000.

18   Pressing Enter completes the monthly business plan.

Lease_Costs			=LOOKUP(Lease_Term,Lease_Table)*Capital/1000						
	A	B	C	D	E	F	G	H	I
58		CAPITAL COSTS							
59			Processing Equipment =			£35,000.00			
60			Fitting out Shop =			£5,000.00			
61			Total Capital Costs =			£40,000.00			
62									
63		Monthly Lease Rates per £1000 borrowed							
64		Years	Rates						
65		1	£89.08						
66		2	£47.31						
67		3	£33.45						
68		4	£26.58			Lease Term in Years =	5		
69		5	£22.50			Monthly Lease Costs =		£900.00	
70									
71		AVERAGE MONTHLY EXPENSES =							£1,616.67
72									
73	NET PROFIT								
74			Average Monthly Net Profit =						£1,325.28
75			Percentage of Sales =						19.2%

Using the IF Function

The IF( ) function is possibly one of the most versatile functions and, of all the functions, it deserves at least a mention. It can be found in the **Logical** category of the **Function Wizard**. It is defined as follows:

IF(logical_test , value_if_true , value_if_false)

A logical test which yields the logical value TRUE or FALSE.

If the result of logical_test is TRUE, then this argument defines the value to be displayed.

If the result of logical_test is FALSE, then this argument defines the value to be displayed.

The logical test normally uses the **Comparison Operators**:

=	equal to	<>	not equal to
>	greater than	>=	greater than or equal to
<	less than	<=	less than or equal to

Consider IF($C$7>=0 , "Positive or Zero" , "Negative"). If cell $C$7 contained 25, the cell containing the formula would display the text, "Positive or Zero". If cell $C$7 contained -10, the cell containing the formula would display the text, "Negative".

The logical tests may be based on numbers or on text. The values displayed for true or false may be text, numbers or formulas, or indeed logical values.

More complex tests can be expressed by combining logical tests with the logical functions AND(), OR() and NOT(). Also available are functions TRUE() and FALSE().

Consider the example on VAT used in a previous chapter. This has been extended to include a column which indicates whether any items are exempt from VAT (e.g. food, children's clothing, books).

▷

E5			=IF(VAT_Exempt, 0, Net_Cost*VAT_Rate)		
A	**B**	**C**	**D**	**E**	**F**
1					
2	VAT Rate =	17.5%			
3					
4	Number	Unit Price	Net Cost	VAT Exempt	VAT	Gross Cost
5	1	£18.00	£18.00	TRUE	£0.00	£18.00
6	2	£9.00	£18.00	-1	£0.00	£18.00
7	3	£6.00	£18.00	3600	£0.00	£18.00
8	4	£4.50	£18.00	FALSE	£3.15	£21.15
9	6	£3.00	£18.00	0	£3.15	£21.15
10	8	£2.25	£18.00		£3.15	£21.15

The cell range $D$5:$D$10 has been named 'VAT_Exempt'.

All the cells in the range $E$5:$E$10 contain the formula
IF(VAT_Exempt , 0 , Net_Cost * VAT_Rate)

Consider the result of applying the IF function. The first three lines have been zero rated whereas the remaining three lines carry the usual tax. The reason for this is that the first three lines of the VAT Exempt column contains values which Excel treats as TRUE and the last three lines as FALSE.

In fact, Excel recognises as FALSE...
- (1)   The logical value FALSE (numeric value zero).
- (2)   The numeric value zero.
- (3)   An empty cell, which it treats as zero.

Excel recognises as TRUE...
- (1)   The logical value TRUE (numeric value plus one).
- (2)   All numeric values, other than zero.

Although Excel allows the use of the logical values TRUE and FALSE in cells, they are not everyday English and may be inconveniently long. Also the vast number of numeric values which yield TRUE make the technique less than reliable. The next section develops an alternative approach.

Nesting Functions within Functions

Just as functions are used within formulas, formulas can be used within functions as the function argument. This means that functions can be used within functions, the technique being referred to as 'Nesting'. It is for this purpose that the Function Wizard button appears against each argument box in the second stage of the Function Wizard. As an example of this application let us modify the exemption of VAT calculation in the previous section so that it allows the exemption to be indicated in ordinary English, i.e. 'Yes' or 'y'. The Function Wizard can be used to edit an existing formula. The procedure follows:

1   Select the cell which contains the formula to be edited.

2   On the formula bar, select the argument to be replaced.

3   Click the Function Wizard button.

4   From the Function Wizard **Step 1 of 2** dialogue box, select the **Text** category and the **LOWER** function, and click the **Next** button.

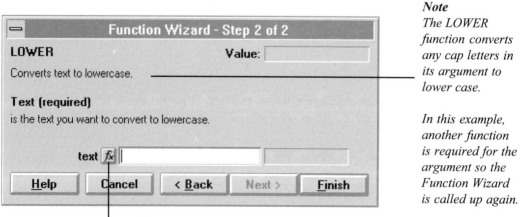

Note
The LOWER function converts any cap letters in its argument to lower case.

In this example, another function is required for the argument so the Function Wizard is called up again.

5   Click the Function Wizard button to insert nested function.

6   From the Function Wizard **Step 1 of 2 (Nested)** dialogue
     box, select the **Text** category and the **LEFT** function, and
     click the Next button.

7   Complete the **Step 2 of 2 (Nested)** dialogue box.

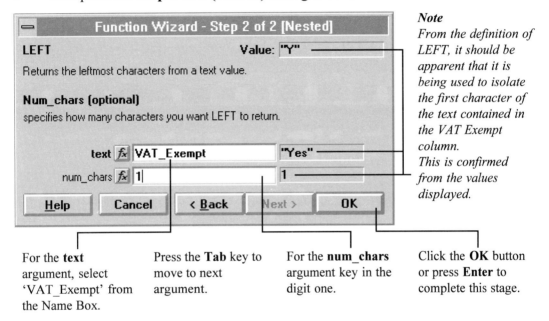

Note
From the definition of
LEFT, it should be
apparent that it is
being used to isolate
the first character of
the text contained in
the VAT Exempt
column.
This is confirmed
from the values
displayed.

For the **text**   Press the **Tab** key to   For the **num_chars**   Click the **OK** button
argument, select   move to next   argument key in the   or press **Enter** to
'VAT_Exempt' from   argument.   digit one.   complete this stage.
the Name Box.

8   The previous **Step 2 of 2** dialogue box will be re-displayed.
     Click the **Finish** button to terminate the Function Wizard.

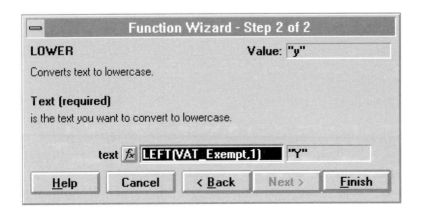

Note
The values show
how cap 'Y' has
been changed to
lower case 'y'.

9   The insertion point will appear on the formula bar, awaiting further editing, if required.

E5	± X ✓ fx	=IF(LOWER(LEFT(VAT_Exempt,1)), 0, Net_Cost*VAT_Rate)					
A	B	C	D	E	F	G	H

10   Key in the rest of the logical test which forms the first argument of the existing IF function.

E5	± X ✓ fx	=IF(LOWER(LEFT(VAT_Exempt,1)) = "y", 0, Net_Cost*VAT_Rate)					
A	B	C	D	E	F	G	H

11   Press the **Enter** key to complete the editing of formula on the formula bar.

12   In this case the edited cell would need to be copied to the cells below, giving the following results which show that any word beginning with 'y' or 'Y' will give exemption.

	E5	±		=IF(LOWER(LEFT(VAT_Exempt,1)) = "y", 0, Net_Cost*VAT_Rate)				
	A	B	C	D	E	F	G	H
1								
2		VAT Rate =	17.5%					
3								
4	Number	Unit Price	Net Cost	VAT Exempt	VAT	Gross Cost		
5	1	£18.00	£18.00	Yes	£0.00	£18.00		
6	2	£9.00	£18.00	yes	£0.00	£18.00		
7	3	£6.00	£18.00	y	£0.00	£18.00		
8	4	£4.50	£18.00		£3.15	£21.15		
9	6	£3.00	£18.00	No	£3.15	£21.15		
10	8	£2.25	£18.00	Rubbish!	£3.15	£21.15		

Note
If you are a new user, the aid to using functions provided by the Function Wizard is wonderful, especially as it covers the full and extensive range of in-built functions. If you have experience of computer programming such as BASIC, you will recognise many functions.

Cell Error Values

If Excel fails to evaluate the formula in a cell, then it displays an Error Value in the cell. All such errors commence with the '#' symbol. So far three such errors have been encountered in the previous chapters. In this chapter it seems appropriate to review all these errors, so that when they occur, you will have a better idea of what is causing them. In the examples, all the errors have been generated deliberately. On the left is the data, with the resulting error values. On the right the formulas are displayed:

(1) **#DIV/0!** This error is caused by an attempt to **divide** 2.5 by **zero**. Theoretically this should generate infinity. In practice any such value is too big, even for a computer, and the calculation is suppressed.

(2) **#N/A** This means that **N**o value is **A**vailable, since the first argument of the LOOKUP function is cell B8 which contains text, instead of D8 which contains a number.

	A	B	C	D		D
	A1	↓		'(1)		
1	(1)					
2		2.5	0	#DIV/0!		=B2/C2
3						
4	(2)					
5	Amount:	£0	£500	£1,000		1000
6	Discount:	0.0%	5.0%	10.0%		0.1
7						
8		Price =		£750		750
9		Discount Rate =		#N/A		=LOOKUP(B8, B5:D6)
10						
11	(3)					
12		-0.25		#NAME?		=IS(B12=0, "Zero", "Non-zero")
13						
14	(4)					
15		5	10	15		15
16	2					
17	4					
18	6			#NULL!		=B15:D15 A16:A18

(3) **#NAME?** Here (on the previous page) Excel fails to recognise the **Name** of the function 'IS', which has been incorrectly typed for 'IF'.

(4) **#NULL!** This formula (on the previous page) uses the **Intersection Operator** (a space) to locate the cell at the intersection of ranges B15:D15 and A16:A18. Since they do not intersect, Excel displays the error message.

(5) **#NUM!** This error value indicates problems with **Numbers**. The first example of this error (see below) attempts to generate the value 100^{1000}, i.e. 100 multiplied by itself 1000 times, which is too large for the computer to store and the calculation is suppressed. In the second example the attempt to calculate the square root (SQRT function) of a negative value is suppressed.

(6) **#VALUE!** This error occurs when the data in a cell isn't appropriate for the operation, or the operation doesn't apply to the type of data. Here an attempt has been made to divide 'Text' by 50.

	A20	↓	'(5)		
	A	**B**	**C**	**D**	
20	(5)				
21		100	1000	#NUM!	=B21^C21
22		16		#NUM!	=SQRT(-B22)
23					
24	(6)				
25		Text		50 #VALUE!	=B25/C25
26					
27	(7)				
28				########	100000000
29					
30	(8)				
31		100			
32			50	2	=B31/C32

(7) ###### This error (on the previous page) is not necessarily
generated by a formula. In this case the number stored is
simply too long for the cell width.

(8) **#REF!** To generate this error requires another stage.
It was seen (on the previous page) that the original
formula divided the content of cell B31 by the content of
cell C32, initially producing the correct answer.

Row 31 is selected by clicking its heading.

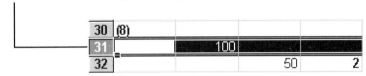

From the **Edit** menu the command **Delete** is selected to
delete the whole row.

D31	↓		=#REF!/C31	
	A	**B**	**C**	**D**
30	(8)			
31			50	#REF!

Since the cell previously referred to as B31 has been
deleted, the error message is displayed because the
Reference to the cell is no longer valid.

Note on the formula bar that the formula has been changed
so   that the B31 reference is replaced by #REF!
and   that the C32 reference is updated to C31.

These examples have been contrived deliberately to give simple
practical examples of what causes the error values. In practice it
is not usually as obvious because a single error may cause a
proliferation of error values.

Troubleshooting using Auditing Tools

The Auditing features are available...
> from the **Tools** menu by selecting the **Auditing** sub-menu
> or from the **Auditing Toolbar**.

In this case the Auditing Toolbar provides more features than the
Menu bar, as is indicated by the comparison below. To display
the Auditing Toolbar, the corresponding command must be
checked in the Auditing sub-menu.

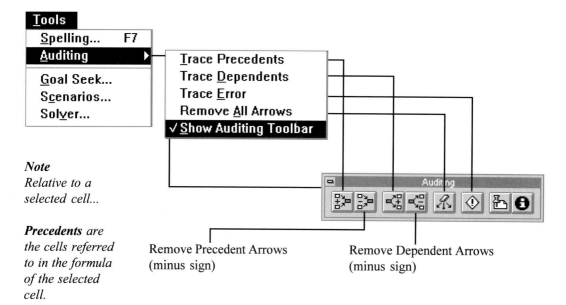

*Remove Precedent Arrows
(minus sign)*

*Remove Dependent Arrows
(minus sign)*

Note
*Relative to a
selected cell...*

Precedents *are
the cells referred
to in the formula
of the selected
cell.*

Dependents *are
the cells which
contain formulas
which refer to the
selected cell.*

Preparing Worksheets for Auditing

Auditing displays tracer arrows between selected cells and their
precedents and dependents. In order to make these arrows
clearer, it is better to remove the grid lines.

To move between precedent and dependent cells requires you to
double click the tracer arrows. To avoid inadvertently going into
editing mode by double clicking an underlying cell, it is better to
temporarily suspend this direct editing feature.

They can be removed/suspended at the same time:

1   From the **Tools** menu, select the **Options...** command.

2   Click the **View** tab and under the **Window Options** *uncheck* the **Gridlines** option.

3   Click the **Edit** tab and under **Settings** *uncheck* the **Edit Directly in Cell** option.

Inserting Precedent Tracers

The 'FastPrint 24' example will be used to illustrate the insertion of tracer arrows:

1   Select the cell which contains a formula with references to other cells or cell ranges, i.e. **Precedents.**

Note
Arrows from precedent cells and box around table.

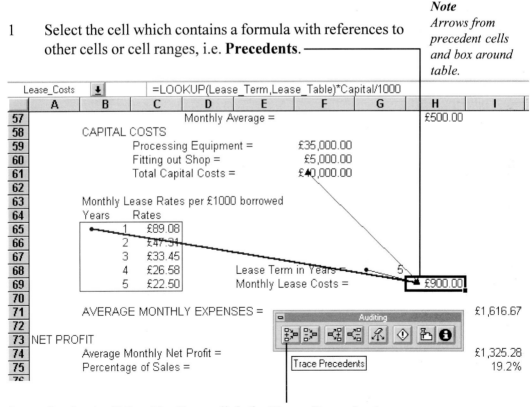

2   On the **Auditing Toolbar**, click the **Trace Precedents** button to display the blue arrows (colour monitor) or continuous black arrows (monochrome).

3   Click the **Trace Precedents** button to extend the arrows to display the next level of cell precedents. In this case only one more level exists, and the computer will 'beep' at you if you try to go beyond this!

4   Correspondingly, you can remove one level of precedent tracer arrows each time you click the **Remove Precedent Arrows** button.

Inserting Dependent Tracers

Note
Relative to cell
H69 there are two
precedent levels.

From the selected cell, click the **Trace Dependents** button once for each level. In the example below, with cell H69 selected, three such levels may be detected.

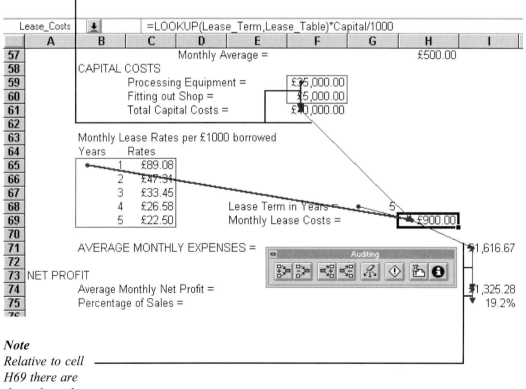

Note
Relative to cell
H69 there are
three dependent
levels.

Navigating Tracer Arrows

To change the selected cell by moving within the inter-connecting network of tracer arrows:

1   Point to the tracer arrow so that the *pointer* cross itself changes to an *arrow*, when the tracer is located. This is particularly critical for small tracer arrows. ——————

2   *Double click* the mouse left button. ——————

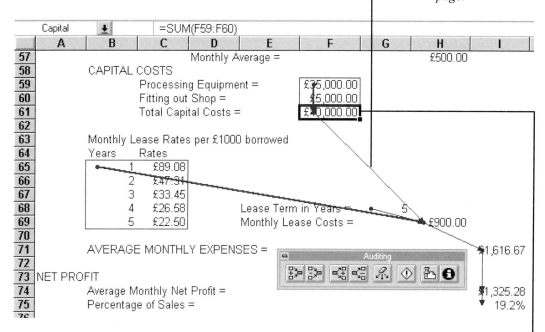

This technique of navigating the tracer arrows is particularly advantageous when moving about a worksheet which extends off the screen, since it adjusts the window view automatically.

Note
Cell F61 is now selected and its name and formula are displayed on the formula bar.

Removing All Tracer Arrows

To remove the whole set of tracer arrows on the worksheet, e.g. to finish the audit or perhaps to recommence from a different cell, simply click the **Remove All Arrows** button.

Alternative Method of Tracing Precedent Cells

This technique is mentioned not only for its speed and usefulness but because it may be activated accidentally! Assuming that 'Direct Editing in Cells' is suspended:

1   Select the cell which contains the formula, e.g. H69.

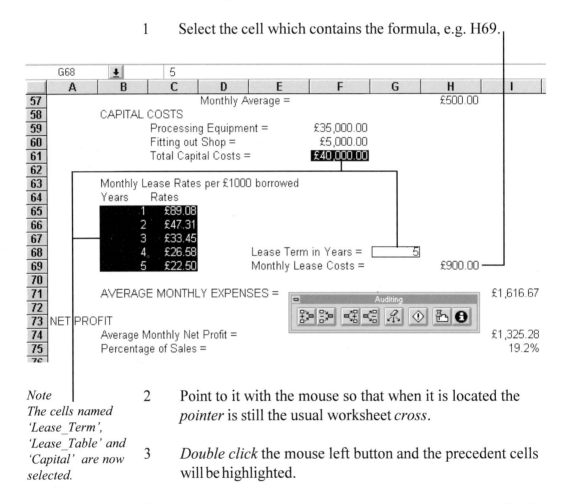

Note
The cells named 'Lease_Term', 'Lease_Table' and 'Capital' are now selected.

2   Point to it with the mouse so that when it is located the *pointer* is still the usual worksheet *cross*.

3   *Double click* the mouse left button and the precedent cells will be highlighted.

Remember that this feature is independent of the Auditing Tools.

Using the Error Tracer

To illustrate the application of the Error Tracer, three simple typical errors have been introduced into the 'FastPrint 24' worksheet, which results in error values being displayed:

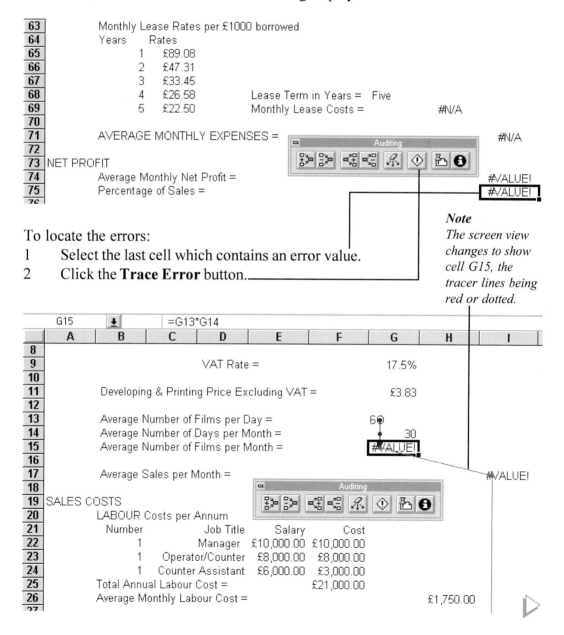

To locate the errors:

1   Select the last cell which contains an error value.
2   Click the **Trace Error** button.

Note

The screen view changes to show cell G15, the tracer lines being red or dotted.

Note
Trace Error
locates all the
cells affected by
the original error
but it makes active
the cell which
contains the first
occurrence.

3   Cell G15 is selected. It contains the error value '#VALUE', which means that one of the cells referenced in the formula has the wrong type of value for the operation required. In this case G13 and G14 are to be multiplied and inspection shows that G13 contains '6O', i.e. digit 6 followed by capital O, instead of '60'.

4   Select G13 and key in '60'. The error value in G15 will be replaced by the correct result, '1800'.

Tip
*Always **clear**
existing tracer
arrows before re-
using Trace Error.

5   Move to the end of the worksheet again (Control + End), making I75 the active cell.

Note
The screen view
changes to show
cell I39, the tracer
lines being red or
dotted.

6   Click the **Delete All Arrows** button to clear existing tracers.

7   Click the **Trace Error** button. This will trace the errors back to cell I39, adjusting the screen display automatically to show it.

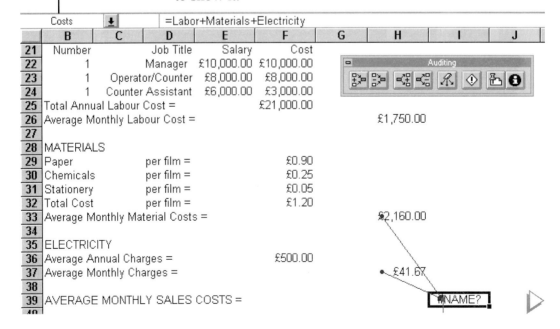

8   Cell I39 displays the '#NAME?' error. According to the formula bar it contains the formula "=Labor + Materials + Electricity". Precedent tracers arrows come from Materials and Electricity but none from Labor. The problem is the American spelling, since it was defined as 'Labour'. Edit I39 and the error message is replaced by the correct total.

9   Again move to the end of the worksheet, making I75 the active cell.

10   Click the **Delete All Arrows** button to clear the existing tracers.

11   Click the **Trace Error** button. This will trace the errors back to cell H69, via cells I75, I74 and I71, all containing the '#N/A' error value, which means that a value is not available.

Note

The screen view remains the same, the tracer lines being red or dotted showing the earliest occurrence of error in cell G15.

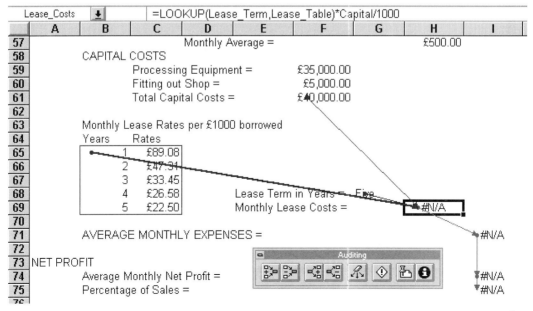

12   As shown on the formula bar, H69 contains the formula which makes reference to three names which are located by precedent arrows. The problem in this case lies in cell G68, named 'Lease_Term', which contains the text 'Five' instead of the number '5'. This means that one argument for the function 'LOOKUP' is of the incorrect type, which makes 'not available' the value returned by this function. Select G68 and key in 5 to remove this final error.

It should be appreciated that originally cell I75 was subject to the three errors caused by earlier cells. As the three error values, #VALUE!, #NAME? and #N/A were removed, the error value displayed in cell I75 changed accordingly.

Locating Precedents on Other Sheets

It will be shown in Chapter 9, 'Linking Worksheets and Workbooks', that links can be formed between Worksheets within a particular Workbook and between Worksheets contained in different Workbooks. Don't worry for now about the technique or the form of the reference required.

The example below applies to the Workbook containing the 'FastPrint 24' **Monthly Plan** Worksheet. A single formula has been entered into cell C17 of **Sheet2**. The technique of locating a precedent on another sheet is simple:

1   Select the cell containing the reference to other sheet. Its formula is shown on the formula bar. In this case it makes reference to three named cells on the Monthly Plan.

2   Click the **Trace Precedents** button to create the tracer arrow which is drawn from an icon which represents the other Worksheet.

3 Point to the tracer arrow and when the pointer itself changes to an arrow, double click the mouse button.

4 The **Go To** dialogue box will appear.

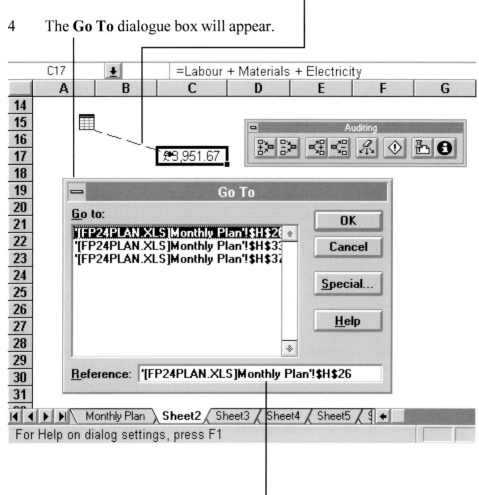

5 Select the reference required and click the OK button. It is a pity that the names are not used in the references! (The reference specification will be explained later.)

6 The screen display will switch to the new sheet and the active cell will be that selected, in this case the cell named 'Labour' on the 'Monthly Plan'.

Using Cell Notes

You may attach notes to cells for various reasons, but one use is where complex formulas have been used and may need some explanation for future reference. This is why the Auditing Toolbar contains the buttons 'Attach Note' and 'Show Information Window'. Alternatively, the Command Menu bar can be used but is much slower.

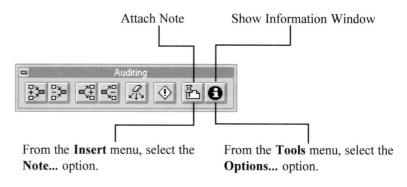

Attach Note   Show Information Window

From the **Insert** menu, select the **Note...** option.

From the **Tools** menu, select the **Options...** option.

In the Options dialogue box, click the **View** tab and check the **Information Window** box.

Adding a Note to a Cell

1   Select the cell.

2   Click the **Attach Note** button on the Auditing Toolbar.

3   Complete the **Cell Note** dialogue box shown on the next page.

4   Enter the note in the **Text Note** box.

5   **Don't forget** to click the **Add** button, otherwise your note will be lost!

6   Finally click the **OK** button.

Note
Although you can use simple editing, as for editing data at a cell or on the formula bar, Cut, Copy and Paste are not available. So get the order right!

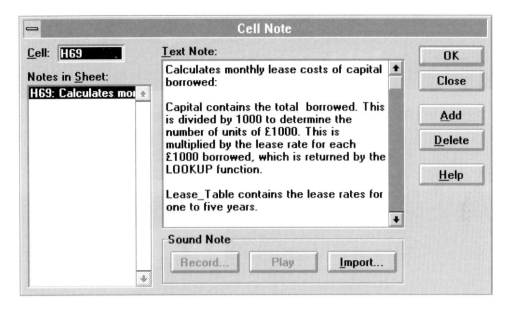

To Delete a Note from a Cell

1   Click the **Attach Note** button on the Auditing Toolbar to
     display the **Cell Note** dialogue box.

2   From the **Notes in Sheet** list, select the cell and note to be
     deleted.

3   Click the **Delete** button and confirm this in response to the
     subsequent dialogue box.

To Read a Cell Note

1   Select the cell. It may have a **Note Indicator** (a small red
     box in the top right hand corner of the cell).

2   Display the Information Window by clicking the **Display
     Info** button on the **Auditing Toolbar**.

3   The Information Window can be viewed alongside the
     sheet window by using the **Arrange...** command from the
     Window menu. Its position can be adjusted if required.

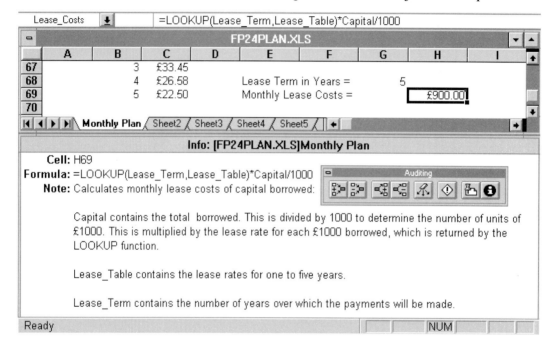

4   The Information Window can be closed just like any other
     window by double clicking the control menu button.

To Display Note Indicators on Cells

1   From the **Tools** menu, select the **Options...** command.

2   In the Options dialogue box, click the **View** tab and *check*
     the **Note Indicator** box.

Note
*Note Indicator is small
red box in top right hand
corner of cell.*

CHAPTER

7

Workbook and Worksheet Security

THIS CHAPTER COVERS

In easy Steps

Overview

Excel provides a comprehensive framework of security at various levels. This chapter subdivides the techniques into three levels:

- Workbook file level

- Workbook structure and windows level

- Workbook sheet level.

Why is such protection necessary?

At the highest file level, some data may be confidential and should be made available only to certain levels of management within a company. At the next level down, considerable time and effort may have been devoted to setting up the structure of the Worksheets within a Workbook and the optimum windows arrangement for viewing these sheets. Certainly at the lowest level of detail on a Worksheet, the work involved in keying in headings and labels, data and formulas, in locating and correcting errors in formulas and in formatting the appearance of the Worksheet, will be even greater. Without any form of protection, any text, data or formulas can be simply overtyped, formatting can be changed and the structure altered. You can do this very easily by yourself accidentally, and spreadsheets are particularly vulnerable to changes by less experienced users.

How is such protection implemented?

Largely protection is afforded by assigning a set of passwords, which are issued only to the users who are required to make changes, at the levels at which the passwords apply.

What kind of protection is available?

At the highest level, files can be made available only to password holders and may be made 'Read Only'. At the intermediate level, the Worksheet structure and/or windows can be fixed. At the lowest level of detail, individual cells can be locked, preventing any unwanted changes. Formulas can be hidden, if required.

Protecting Workbook Files

Rules for
Passwords
The maximum
length *allowed for*
a password is 15
characters.

They can be ***any***
combination *of*
letters, digits and
other symbols.

They are ***case***
sensitive.

Protecting Files

The access to Workbook files can be restricted to users who have been provided with the necessary password(s). The following sequence will illustrate this.

1   Supposing 'FP24PLAN.XLS' was saved under a new file name 'FP24PROT.XLS', which is to be password protected, by using the **File** menu **Save As...** option.

2   In the **Save As** dialogue box, click the **Options...** button.

3   Three levels of protection for the new file are available:

Note
As for most
passwords, entry
is 'blind', the only
indication being
the number of
characters keyed
in.

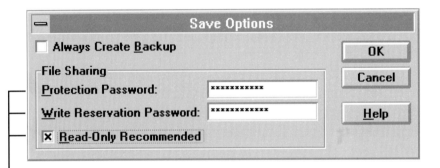

Note
Although not
particularly
relevant for
general use, the
two passwords
keyed for this
example were
'Read_Enable'
and
'Write_Enable'.

The **Protection Password** will be supplied to users to allow them to open the file and to access its data. However, although they will be allowed to alter the contents of the Workbook, they will not be allowed to save such changes under the existing file name. To save the changes, they will be obliged to use the File menu Save As... option to create a new file name.

The **Write Reservation Password** will be supplied additionally to those users who are trusted to make changes under the existing file name.

The **Read Only Recommended** box is *checked* so that a warning is issued to users, especially those with the Write Reservation Password, in an attempt to dissuade them from changing the existing file, unless it is absolutely necessary!

▷

4   Confirmation will be requested of the password(s).

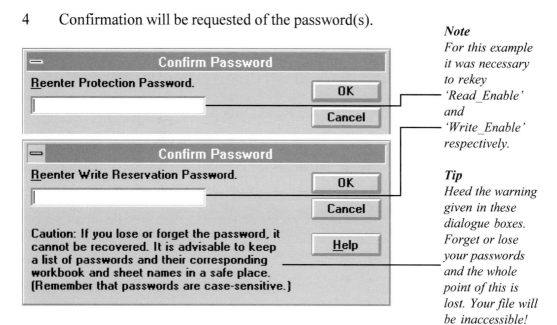

Note
For this example it was necessary to rekey 'Read_Enable' and 'Write_Enable' respectively.

Tip
Heed the warning given in these dialogue boxes. Forget or lose your passwords and the whole point of this is lost. Your file will be inaccessible!

Subsequent Opening of Protected File

1   Use the **File** menu **Open...** option.

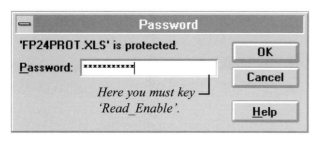

2   On supplying the file name, you will be asked for the **Protection Password**. (The Write Reservation Password is unacceptable!).

3   On supplying the correct Protection Password, another Password dialogue box will be displayed.

This gives two further options:

3a   *Either* to key in the **Write Reservation Password**.
        This is only for users who are trusted to change the file.

3b   *Or* to click the **Read Only** button. This applies to all users.

4   On attempting to save the file under its existing name, a
        warning will be issued if the Read Only Recommended box
        has been checked.

5   If subsequently a user attempts to use the File menu Save
        option on a file which is read-only, the relevant warning
        will be issued.

Removal of Password Protection

1   Select the **File** menu **Open** option.

2   Key in both the **Protection** and the **Write Reservation**
        passwords.

3   Select the **File** menu **Save As** option.

4   Click the **Options...** button and delete both passwords.

5   *Uncheck* the **Read Only Recommended** box, if this
        warning is no longer relevant.

6   Complete the **Save As** dialogue box for the existing file
        name.

Protecting Workbook Structure and Windows

Applying Protection

It is possible to protect the Structure of a Workbook, i.e. the number, the order and the names of the sheets within the Workbook. The same dialogue box can be used to protect the Windows that have been set up for the Workbook to make sure that they are always the same size and in the same position:

1   From the **Tools** menu, select the sub-menu **Protection**.

2   From the **Protection** sub-menu, select the **Protect Workbook...** option.

3   Complete the **Protect Workbook** dialogue box.

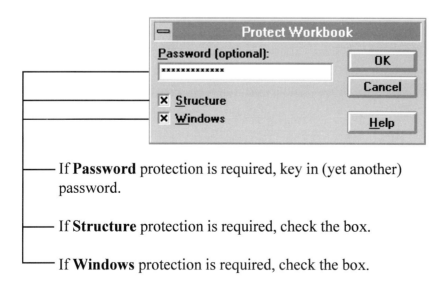

— If **Password** protection is required, key in (yet another) password.

— If **Structure** protection is required, check the box.

— If **Windows** protection is required, check the box.

4   If a password is given, you will be requested to confirm it by re-keying it.

Effect on Structure

When protection is applied, certain commands are 'greyed out':

In **Edit** menu	*Delete Sheet*
	Move or Copy Sheet...
In **Format** menu	all the **Sheet** sub-menu commands
	Rename...
	Hide
	Unhide...

If from the **Insert** menu the command **Worksheet** is attempted, then a warning is displayed.

Note
This doesn't prevent the Information Window being displayed, moved and sized, subject to the limitations on the Workbook sheet windows.

Effect on Windows

When protection is applied, the following are *hidden*:

On the Command Menu bar
the *Minimise and Maximise Icons*
the *Control-Menu Box*
Around the edges
the *Window Sizing Borders*.

Removing Protection

The procedure is effectively reversed:

1   From the **Options** menu, select the sub-menu **Protection**.

2   From the **Protection** sub-menu, select the **Unprotect Workbook...** option.

3   If a password was used, rekey it in the **Unprotect Workbook** dialogue box.

Protecting Workbook Sheets

Decide Which Cells Need Protection

It is possible to apply protection at an individual cell level for the active Worksheet in a Workbook. Before doing this you need to be clear about which cells require protection. Consider again the 'FastPrint 24' example:

1   Decide which cells require protecting against deliberate or accidental changes. Normally this will include...

Cells which contain text which form labels or headings, e.g. 'SALES INCOME', 'VAT Rate ='.

Cells which contain formulas, e.g. "= Sales - Costs".

Cells which contain numbers which are constant, e.g. the average number of days per month, '30'.

Cells which have been left empty deliberately to provide spacing between items or sections of the Worksheet.

2   Usually, it is easier to decide which cells a potential user or yourself might require to change, such as...

the developing and printing price including VAT,

and the average number of films processed per day.

3   Normally by default all the cells in a Worksheet will be set to 'Locked'. This has absolutely no effect until the sheet protection is activated. Once the sheet is protected, this would mean that no cells could be changed. Assuming that the majority of the cells on the sheet are to remain locked, it is easier to select and set the cells which are to be unlocked.

Tip
Even if you are working as a single user, this level of protection is invaluable, if only to save you from accidental changes to your Worksheets. In such cases it is unnecessary to use passwords.

Warning
If you are new to worksheet protection, you may be confused by the two stage process for protecting cells:

First, unlock the cells which need to remain variable.

Second, activate the Sheet protection.

Applying Protection

1   Select the Worksheet to be protected so that it is activated, e.g. 'Monthly Plan' of 'FP24PROT.XLS'.

2   *Either* assume that all the cells are set to **Locked** by default *or* click the **Select All** button and re-initialise all cells to **Locked** as shown in steps 4, 5 and 6 which follow.

3   Select the cells to be **Unlocked**. This can be done individually but it is quicker to do it collectively, e.g. select all the following by clicking the cells or dragging across cell ranges while holding down the Control key:

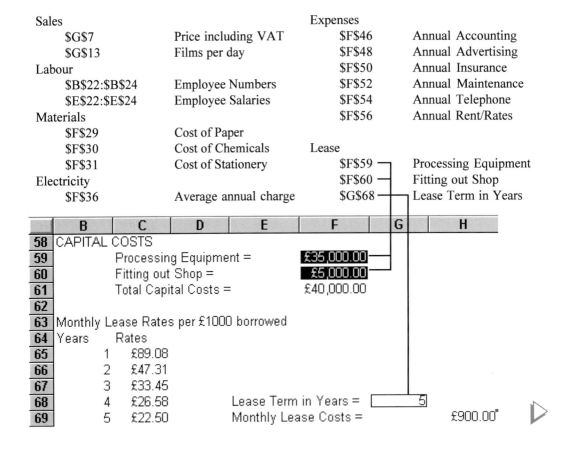

Sales		Expenses	
$G$7	Price including VAT	$F$46	Annual Accounting
$G$13	Films per day	$F$48	Annual Advertising
Labour		$F$50	Annual Insurance
$B$22:$B$24	Employee Numbers	$F$52	Annual Maintenance
$E$22:$E$24	Employee Salaries	$F$54	Annual Telephone
Materials		$F$56	Annual Rent/Rates
$F$29	Cost of Paper		
$F$30	Cost of Chemicals	Lease	
$F$31	Cost of Stationery	$F$59	Processing Equipment
Electricity		$F$60	Fitting out Shop
$F$36	Average annual charge	$G$68	Lease Term in Years

	B	C	D	E	F	G	H
58	CAPITAL COSTS						
59		Processing Equipment =			£35,000.00		
60		Fitting out Shop =			£5,000.00		
61		Total Capital Costs =			£40,000.00		
62							
63	Monthly Lease Rates per £1000 borrowed						
64	Years	Rates					
65		1	£89.08				
66		2	£47.31				
67		3	£33.45				
68		4	£26.58		Lease Term in Years =		5
69		5	£22.50		Monthly Lease Costs =		£900.00

◁

4   From the **Format** menu, select the **Cells...** option.

5   In the **Format Cells** dialogue box, click the **Protection** tab.

6   *Uncheck* **Locked** and click OK.

*Note
The Hidden option applies only to cells containing formulas - see next page.*

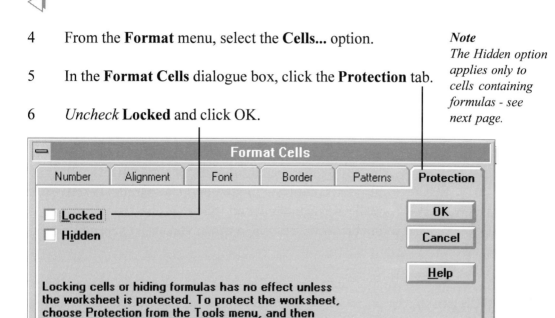

7   From the **Tools** menu, select the **Protection** sub-menu and then select the **Protect Sheet...** option.

8   Complete the **Protect Sheet** dialogue box.

Password: A fourth(!) password is optional.

Contents: This must be checked.

Objects and **Scenarios**: These would normally be checked - see Chapters 12 and 8 respectively.

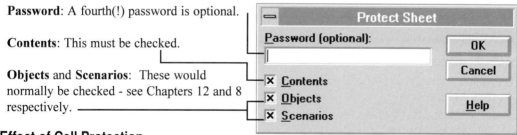

Effect of Cell Protection

1   If you attempt to edit or overtype a cell which is **Locked**, then this error message will be displayed, irrespective of the sort of data the cell contains or whether it is empty.

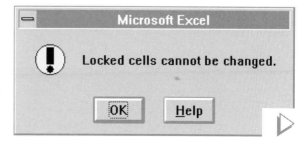

2   If you select a **Locked** cell, certain commands on the Command Menu bar
     will be 'greyed out'.

3   Any changes can be made as normal to **Unlocked** cells. If this changes the
     value of a cell, which has dependent formulas, then any changes will ripple
     through the Worksheet.

4   If you press the **Tab** key, then the selected cell will change to the next
     Unlocked cell, following the order from top to bottom and from left to right.
     Pressing **Shift** + **Tab** will reverse the order of selection. This is a very
     efficient way of locating the unlocked cell(s) which you need to change.

Changing a Cell's Protection

If you need to change a cell from Lock to Unlock or vice versa, then the previous
procedure is reversed:

1   Select the cell(s).
2   From the **Tools** menu, choose the **Protection** sub-menu and then select the
     Unprotect Sheet option.
3   If a Password was used to protect the sheet, then this will be requested.
4   From the **Format** menu, select the **Cells...** option and click the **Protection** tab.
5   *Uncheck* or *Check* **Locked** as required and click OK.

Hiding Cell Formulas

In some applications, it may be thought advisable to hide strategic formula(s) in
particular cell(s). The procedure is the same as that for Locking cells, except that
the **Hidden** option is *checked* in the **Protection** tab of the **Format Cells** dialogue
box. The effect of this is to prevent the formula being displayed:

1   On the formula bar.
2   If the Window display is changed to Formulas instead of Results, using the
     Control plus open quote keyboard short-cut (**CTRL** + `).
3   At the cell as a result of double clicking the cell, assuming that the 'Edit
     Directly in Cell' option is enabled.

CHAPTER

8

What-If
Tests

in easy steps

Overview

The illustrations in this book have been taken from screen shots of the Excel screen. Those which show spreadsheet examples could have been keyed in using a word processor or a desktop publishing package. The printed results from such packages can appear very similar to the printout from spreadsheets such as Excel. However on the screen with the computer in front of you, the difference is fundamental! Alter the content of a cell which is a precedent for a formula cell and the dependent cell will change almost instantaneously. If that cell is a precedent for further levels of formula cells, then this change will ripple through the subsequent levels. The screen view of a spreadsheet is live and interactive, the printed snapshot of it fixed and lifeless. Initially, if you have no practical experience of spreadsheets, you may have difficulty with this important concept.

This is, of course, the basis of **What_If** testing. Change the value of numeric data in cells and investigate the effect on dependent formulas. To reflect its importance, this technique has already been introduced in Chapter 2, 'Creating and Editing a Simple Spreadsheet'. Here the technique will be developed further, illustrating how facilities such as **Split Screens** and **Locked Cells** can be used to aid What-If Tests.

In addition to basic What-If tests, Excel provides more sophisticated tecniques of **What_If Analysis**. Practical examples will again be used to illustrate the use of:

Goal Seek - Finding the value of one precedent cell to produce a specified result in a dependent formula.

Data Tables - Summarising the results of varying one or two precedent cell values on a specified dependent cell.

Scenarios - Setting up several named sets of dependent cells with initial values to be used to produce reports of their effects on a set of dependent cells.

Solver - Finding the initial values of a set of precedent cells to optimise a target cell, subject to specified constraints.

Aids to What-If Tests

Use of Locked Cells

Although the 'FastPrint 24' example is oversimplified, it can be used to illustrate the power of What-If testing. Suppose the 'Monthly Plan' sheet has most of its cells locked and this protection is activated as described in the previous chapter. Not only does this safeguard you from accidentally overwriting cells which should remain fixed, but it aids you to locate the precedent cells by pressing the **Tab** and **Shift + Tab** keys.

Use of Split Screen

A problem that arises even with comparatively small spreadsheets, such as the 'FastPrint 24' Monthly Plan, is that the final result may be off the screen while changes are being made to earlier cells. This can be overcome by splitting the screen into two panes as shown on the opposite page:

1   Adjust the view of the sheet so that in this case Row 75, which contains the 'percentage net profit' is just visible at the bottom of the screen.

Either Use the Command Menu...   *Or* Use the Mouse...

2   Select Row 73, which contains the 2   Point with the mouse to the **Screen**
     text, 'NET PROFIT', by clicking   **Horizontal Split Box**, so that
     the row heading.   when located the pointer changes
                                              to a double headed arrow.

3   From the **Window** menu, select the 3   Click and drag the pointer and split
     Split option.   screen border, so that it coincides
                                              with the intersection between rows
                                              72 and 73.

4   The screen will be split into two Panes. The lower one will
     be left as it is to display the final profit. The upper one will
     be scrolled to locate the precedent cells.   ▷

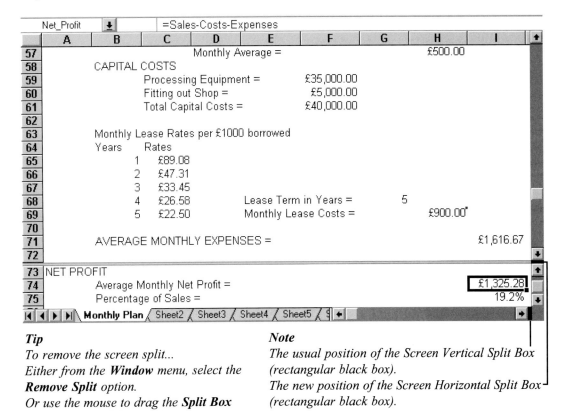

	A	B	C	D	E	F	G	H	I	
57				Monthly Average =				£500.00		
58		CAPITAL COSTS								
59			Processing Equipment =			£35,000.00				
60			Fitting out Shop =			£5,000.00				
61			Total Capital Costs =			£40,000.00				
62										
63		Monthly Lease Rates per £1000 borrowed								
64		Years	Rates							
65			1	£89.08						
66			2	£47.31						
67			3	£33.45						
68			4	£26.58		Lease Term in Years =	5			
69			5	£22.50		Monthly Lease Costs =		£900.00		
70										
71		AVERAGE MONTHLY EXPENSES =							£1,616.67	
72										
73	NET PROFIT									
74			Average Monthly Net Profit =						£1,325.28	
75			Percentage of Sales =						19.2%	

The formula bar reads: Net_Profit `=Sales-Costs-Expenses`

The sheet tabs at the bottom read: **Monthly Plan** / Sheet2 / Sheet3 / Sheet4 / Sheet5 / 9

Tip
To remove the screen split...
Either from the **Window** *menu, select the*
Remove Split *option.*
Or use the mouse to drag the **Split Box**
back to its usual (un-split) position.
Or double click the **Split Box** *or* **Bar**.

Note
The usual position of the Screen Vertical Split Box
(rectangular black box).
The new position of the Screen Horizontal Split Box
(rectangular black box).

Simple What-If Tests

Suppose the owner of 'FastPrint 24' wishes to investigate the possibility of expanding the average monthly sales. How could the number of films processed be doubled? Possibly by reducing the price to attract more customers:

1   Make the upper pane active by selecting any cell.

2   Locate the 'Developing and Printing Price including VAT' (Retail_Price) by repeatedly pressing the **Tab** key (to move down/right) or **Shift** + **Tab** keys (to move up/left).

3   Key in the new price £3.95.

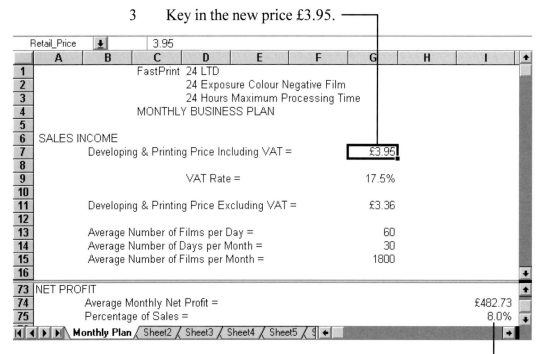

4   Immediately observe the reduction in profit to 8.0%.

Advertising expenditure might be quadrupled to make customers
aware of the lower price. If the throughput of work doubles, the
manager might negotiate a 20% rise. Also another Operator
might need to be taken on. The knock on effect of all these
changes can be easily and quickly investigated:

Change...		Resulting Profit
1	Reduce retail price from £4.50 to £3.95.	8.0%
2	Increase annual advertising from £1000 to £4000.	3.8%
3	Assume sales double! - number of films from 60 to 120.	34.1%
4	Compensate manager with 20% rise.	32.7%
5	Take on an extra operator.	27.2%

Automatic versus Manual Calculation

By default, Excel automatically recalculates the values of
formulas in dependent cells when you change the values of
precedent cells. Usually this occurs so fast that there is no
noticable delay. However if the network of dependent formulas is
large and complex, this may not always be the case. It can prove
particularly frustrating if you wish to change several values and
you are made to wait after each one while Excel has finished
recalculating the rest of the worksheet. In such cases it is better
to switch to manual calculation:

1   From the **Tools** menu, select the **Options...** command.

Note
The alternative
options of
recalculating
2   Click the **Calculation** tab and check the **Manual** option.   *Workbook (F9) or*
     The option of suspending **Recalculate before Save** is now   *Worksheet*
     available.

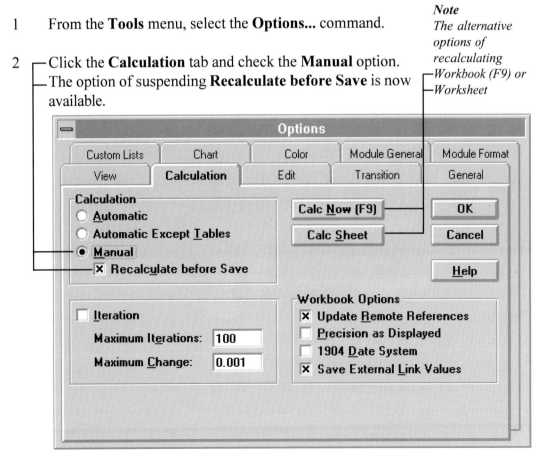

3   You must now remember to return to this dialogue box or
     to press the **F9** key every time you require a recalculation.

Using the Goal Seek Command

Suppose the owner of 'FastPrint 24' wanted to know the average number of films per day necessary to break even, i.e. to cover all the sales costs and expenses (before the changes of the previous section), so that the net profit was 0.0%. This is still a What_If test, but the order has to be reversed. In some cases, it may be possible to work out the reverse sequence of formulas to enable this to be calculated, but Excel allows this to be evaluated automatically using Goal Seek. Assume that the split screen is set up as it was prior to the changes of the last section:

1   In the lower pane, select cell I75, which contains the formula for the net percentage profit.

2   From the **Tools** menu, select the **Goal Seek...** option.

3   Complete the **Goal Seek** dialogue box. Key in cell references and the target value. Click OK.

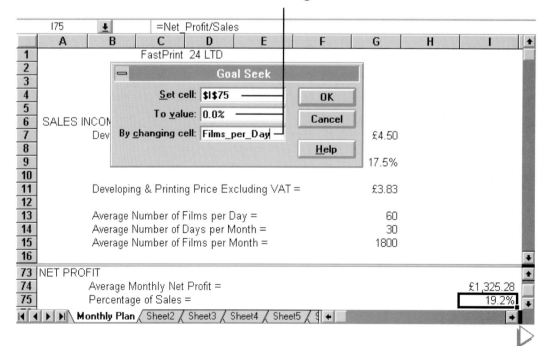

4   The solution, as shown below, is returned almost
     instantaneously.

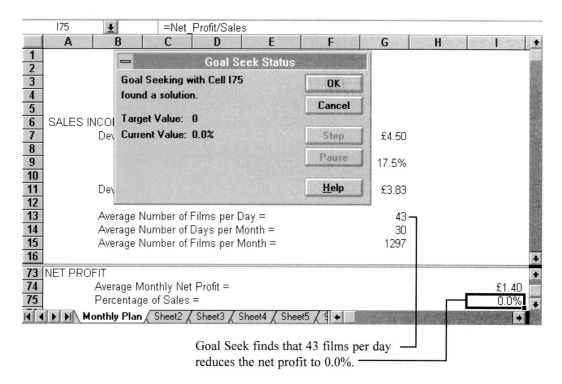

Goal Seek finds that 43 films per day
reduces the net profit to 0.0%.

5   The break-even level is an average of 43 films per day, as
     shown on the Worksheet.

6   *Either* click the **OK** button to confirm these changes to the
     Worksheet,

     Or click the **Cancel** button to restore the previous values.

Using One-Input Data Tables

Supposing the owner of 'FastPrint 24' wanted to know how the net profit would vary relative to the 'Developing and Printing Price Including VAT', named 'Retail_Price'. He could use the simple What_If technique of varying the Retail_Price and recording the corresponding change in the Percentage Net Profit. However, this is more easily done using a Data Table, as shown below. Don't worry about the formatting for now. This will be covered in Chapter 10, 'Formatting Worksheets'.

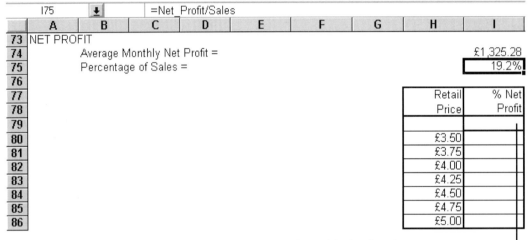

The procedure to complete the table is simple:

1   Select cell I79. Note that this position above the second column is critical!

2   In cell I79, key in the formula which calculates the percentage net profit. In this example, this calculation is based on a network of dependent formulas, the last being located in cell I75. Here it is easier to refer simply to the value of this cell, i.e. "= I75".

3   Select the table as shown on the next page. This selection is critical and must include cell I79 and both columns, i.e. H79 : I86.

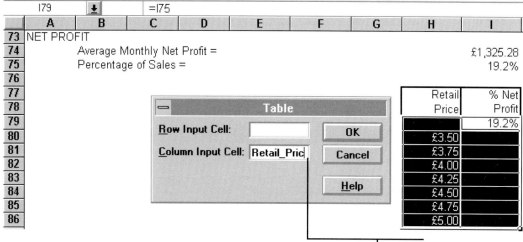

	I79		↓	=I75					
	A	B	C	D	E	F	G	H	I
73	NET PROFIT								
74		Average Monthly Net Profit =							£1,325.28
75		Percentage of Sales =							19.2%
76									

4 From the **Data** menu, select the **Table...** option.

5 Complete the **Table** dialogue box as above. Since a **one-input vertical table** is required, it is only necessary to complete the **Column Input Cell**. This is the name or cell reference into which the value in the left hand column of the table is to be substituted. Here 'Retail_Price' is keyed in.

6 Clicking **OK** will give the completed table below.

Note
*For a **one-input horizontal table**, it is necessary to enter only the **Row Input Cell**.*

You can key in names, cell references, or point to the cell and click mouse.

	I75		↓	=Net_Profit/Sales					
	A	B	C	D	E	F	G	H	I
73	NET PROFIT								
74		Average Monthly Net Profit =							£1,325.28
75		Percentage of Sales =							19.2%
76									
77								Retail	% Net
78								Price	Profit
79									19.2%
80								£3.50	-3.9%
81								£3.75	3.1%
82								£4.00	9.1%
83								£4.25	14.5%
84								£4.50	19.2%
85								£4.75	23.5%
86								£5.00	27.3%

Using Two-Input Data Tables

Supposing the owner of 'FastPrint 24' wanted to know how the net profit would vary relative to the 'Retail_Price' and also relative to the average number of films processed per day, 'Films_per_Day'. Simple What-If techniques of varying the Retail_Price and the Films_per_Day to obtain the corresponding change in the Percentage Net Profit would require a substantial amount of work. However, the Data Table technique can be extended to two input values, as shown below.

The procedure to complete the table is simple:

1   Select cell D79. Again this position is critical! It is located at the intersection of the row containing the first input value (Films_per_Day) and the column containing the second input value (Retail_Price).

2   In cell D79, key in the formula which calculates the percentage net profit. As for the previous section, this calculation is based on a network of dependent formulas, the last being located in cell I75. Again it is easier to refer simply to the value of this cell, i.e. "= I75".

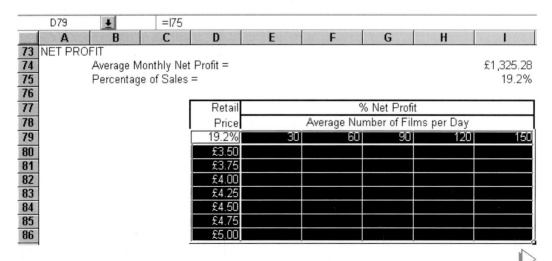

3   Select the table as shown on the previous page. This
     selection is critical and is the rectangular area which must
     include cell D79, the column and row of input data and the
     empty body of the table, i.e. D79 : I86.

4   From the **Data** menu, select the **Table...** option.

5   Complete the **Table** dialogue box.

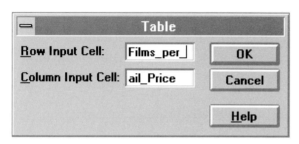

For the **Row Input Cell**, key in
'Films_per_Day'.

For the **Column Input Cell**, key in
'Retail_Price'.

*The corresponding pair of row and column values will be used to replace these cell names or cell
references in the recalculations of the 'net profits'.*

6   Clicking **OK** will produce the extended table below.

The table is calculated rapidly and shows at a glance the inter-
relationship between the retail price and the throughput of films.

	D79		⬇		=I75				
	A	B	C	D	E	F	G	H	I
73	NET PROFIT								
74		Average Monthly Net Profit =							£1,325.28
75		Percentage of Sales =							19.2%
76									
77				Retail		% Net Profit			
78				Price		Average Number of Films per Day			
79				19.2%	30	60	90	120	150
80				£3.50	-67.4%	-3.9%	17.3%	27.9%	34.3%
81				£3.75	-56.3%	3.1%	22.8%	32.7%	38.7%
82				£4.00	-46.5%	9.1%	27.7%	36.9%	42.5%
83				£4.25	-37.9%	14.5%	31.9%	40.6%	45.9%
84				£4.50	-30.2%	19.2%	35.7%	43.9%	48.9%
85				£4.75	-23.4%	23.5%	39.1%	46.9%	51.6%
86				£5.00	-17.2%	27.3%	42.1%	49.6%	54.0%

Using What-If Scenarios

What is a Scenario?

A Scenario is a set of What-If precedent cell references and their input values, which you name for subsequent recall. This enables sets of input values to be changed very quickly in What_If tests and saves having to record them and rekey them each time they are required. Facilities are provided for editing Scenarios and for automatically producing reports of their effects in What-If tests.

These techniques are available by using the **Tools** menu **Scenarios...** option or by using the **Scenarios Box** on the **Workgroup Toolbar**. In practice it is found that although the latter has less facilities, it is more efficient to use it to build new Scenarios.

As usual the best use of each will be illustrated by a practical sequence based on 'FastPrint 24'.

Displaying the Workgroup Toolbar.

1   From the **View** menu, select the **Toolbars...** option.

Tip
It is more convenient to drag the Workgroup Toolbar to the position shown on the next page.

2   In the **Toolbars** dialogue box, *check* the **Workgroup** box.

3   The Workgroup Toolbar may well be '**docked**', i.e. placed with the other toolbars, usually immediately above the Formula Bar. It can be '**floated**' onto the Worksheet by pointing to its background and dragging it into position.

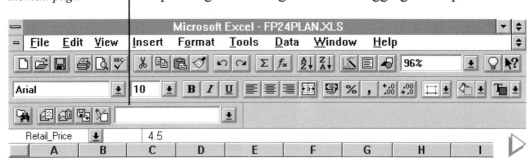

Adding Scenarios using the Scenario Box

Suppose the owner of 'FastPrint 24' wished to set up three sets
of input values, representing the average, worst and best cases.
Excel allows up to 32 input values in each scenario but, in these
examples, the number will be restricted deliberately to 5, simply
so that all the values can be viewed together on the screen. The
input values chosen are those with the most influence on the
finances of the business, namely the 'Retail_Price', the
'Films_per_Day' and the numbers of the three categories of staff
employed. For the final report, it is preferable that all cells are
named, and so these cells would be named 'Number_Managers',
'Number_Operators', 'Number_Assistants'. The procedure for
adding the scenarios follows:

Warning
Although Excel
will accept
intersection
references for the
input of cells, e.g.
'Number Managers'
it converts them to
an absolute cell
reference, e.g.
$B$22. To avoid
such references in
the final report, it
is advisable to
name each cell
individually, e.g.
'Number_Managers'.

1   Key in the values required in the chosen set of input values.
     In this case the existing values would apply for the average
     scenario, i.e. £4.50, 60, 1, 1, 1/2.

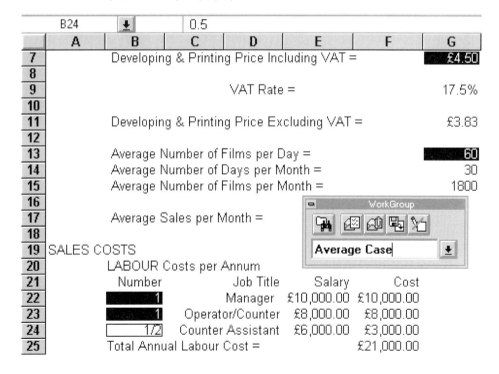

2   Select all these input values, by clicking the first and then
     holding down the Control key while you click the
     remainder. (See previous page.)

3   Since no scenarios have yet been defined, the Scenario Box
     on the Workgroup toolbar will be empty. Key in the name
     of the first scenario, 'Average Case', and press Enter. (See
     previous page.)

4   Suppose the owner of 'FastPrint 24' decides that the
     'Worst Case' scenario would be a throughput of only 10
     films per day, which would mean he couldn't afford to
     employ any staff but would have to cope single handed.
     Again the input values would be entered, the cells selected
     and the previous scenario name would be overtyped with
     the new name as shown below.

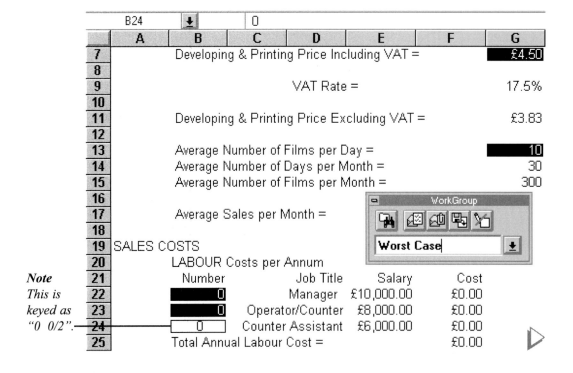

Note
This is
keyed as
"0 0/2".

5   The final scenario, 'Best Case', would be set up with the
corresponding values £3.95, 180, 1, 2, 1 1/2, the increased
throughput reflecting the reduced price and allowing the
staff numbers to be increased accordingly.

Displaying Scenario Values using the Scenario Box
The Scenario box is particularly efficient for the display of
scenarios:

1   Click the arrow to the right of the Scenario box.

2   From the list of Scenario names, select the one required.

3   The input cells for this Scenario will be altered to the
specified values, and the changes will ripple through the
Worksheet.

Note
Select any
Scenario name to
change the input
values.

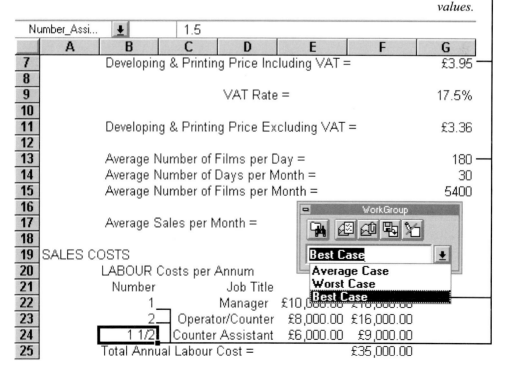

Editing Scenario Values using the Scenario Box

The Scenario Box can be used to change the input values:

1   Select the Scenario Name to be edited. The values of input
        cells on the Worksheet will change accordingly.

2   Key in the new input values.

3   Reselect the Scenario Name again.

4   The following dialogue box will appear.

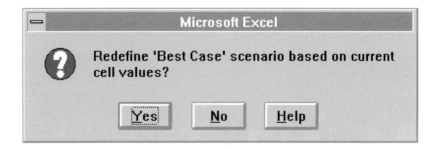

5   Click 'Yes' button to confirm changes.

Using the Scenario Manager Dialogue Box

The Scenario Manager dialogue box has many more features and
is probably better for editing:

1   From the **Tools** menu, select the **Scenario...** option.

2   Complete the **Scenario** dialogue box shown on the
        opposite page.

Select the **Name** of the required **Scenario**.

Click the **Show** button to display the Scenario values in the input cells.

Note the list of its **Changing** input cells.

Click the **Delete** button if you wish to remove the selected Scenario.

Note under **Comment** that the user name and date is recorded automatically each time a change is made.

Click the **Close** button when you have finished.

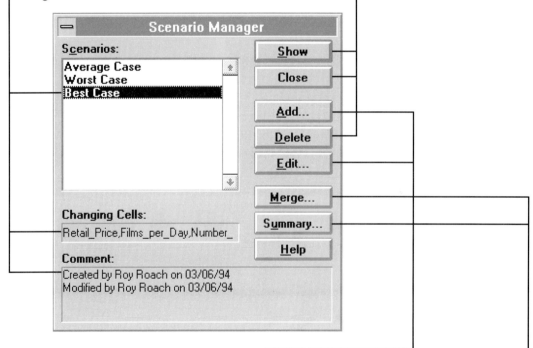

Click the **Add...** button to add another scenario. See the dialogue box on the next page.

Click the **Merge...** button to merge a scenario from another Worksheet or Workbook. See dialogue box on a subsequent page.

First select the name of a Scenario to be edited and then click the **Edit...** button. See the description on the next page.

Click the **Summary...** button to produce a report on the scenarios. See dialogue box on a subsequent page.

Adding a Scenario

1 Key in the **Name** for new scenario.

2 Key in the cell references or names for the **Changing** input **Cells**, or select these cells directly on the Worksheet.

3 Add further **Comments** if you wish.

4 Set protection if required by checking **Prevent Changes** button.

5 Click **OK** to display the **Scenario Values** dialogue box.

6 Key in the **new values**, using the tab key to move between the boxes.

7 *Either* click the **Add** button to return to the previous dialogue box, *or* click the **OK** button to return to the Scenario Manager dialogue box.

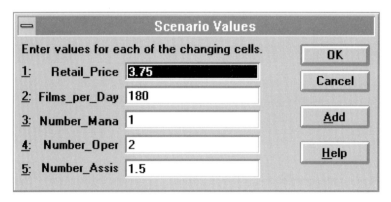

Editing a Scenario

The procedure is very similar to that of adding a scenario and the dialogue boxes are identical, apart from one name. With the Edit Scenario dialogue box, you may change the selected 'Changing Cells' and then call up the Scenario Values dialogue box to alter their values.

Merging Other Scenarios

Before attempting this procedure, open the Workbooks which contain the Scenarios which you require to merge. Alternatively, you can merge from Worksheets in the current Workbook.

Tip
Keep things simple! Only merge scenarios from worksheets which contain identical What_If models.

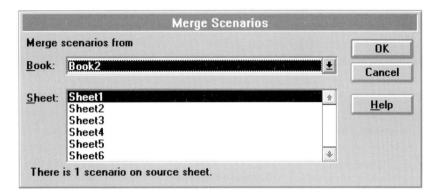

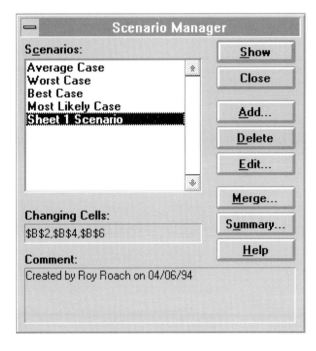

1 Select the **Workbook**.

2 Select the **Worksheet**.

3 The Merge Scenarios dialogue box will indicate whether there are any scenarios and if so how many.

4 Click **OK** button and you will be returned to the Scenario Manager dialogue box. All the Scenarios from the selected Worksheet in the selected Workbook will be copied into the current Worksheet.

◁

Summaries via the Scenario Dialogue Box

1   Select Scenario Summary. ——

2   Key in the names or references for
    the dependent cells of What-If
    tests, in this case Sales, Costs,
    Gross_Profit, Expenses, and
    Net_Profit.

3   Click OK to produce report below
    automatically.

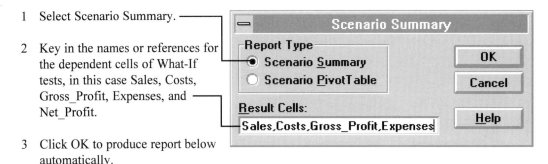

*Note: the automatic
formatting and
outlining, e.g. click the
plus button to reveal
hidden detail about
scenario updates.
Click a minus button to
suppress detail.*

*Warning: If cells are
not named, then cell
references would be
given in this report,
e.g. '$G$7' instead of
'Retail_Price'!*

*Note: This report is
inserted in a new sheet,
called by default the
'Scenario Summary'.
It is made up of text
and numbers, as shown
for cell F16.*

*Note: This report
shows at a glance the
effect of scenarios on
the dependent cells, in
this case the Sales,
Costs, Expenses,
Profits and Losses.*

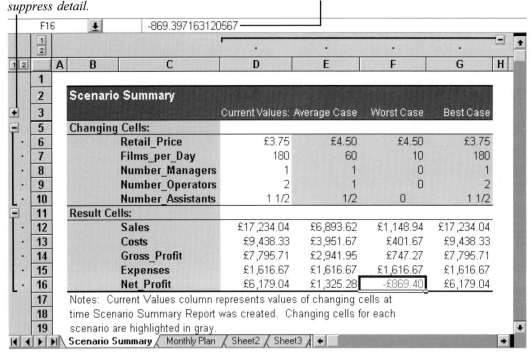

Using Solver

What is Solver?

Solver is a powerful sophisticated add-in feature which facilitates the solving of complex problems on Worksheets. At its simplest, it might be described as an extension of the Goal Seek command. But whereas Goal Seek adjusts only one precedent cell in order to change a dependent cell to a particular value, Solver will adjust several precedent cells to reach an optimal solution for the dependent cell. However, it also has the option of applying the type of constraints which apply in real life situations.

Although Solver is easy to use, its actions may be less easy to understand unless you have the necessary mathematical background. This book has been written for the majority of users who have a basic knowledge of arithmetic and simple algebra. It is easier to apply solver if you understand mathematical terms such as iteration, starting values, convergence, linear and non-linear functions. If you are familiar with these terms, this brief introduction will be sufficient to get you started with Solver. If these terms are new to you, then you may need more help than it is possible to give in one short section of this chapter.

Preparing Worksheet for Use with Solver

In many cases it is necessary to modify a Worksheet so that Solver can be properly and fully utilised. As usual, the 'FastPrint 24' example will be used to show this practically. We have seen that 'Films_per_Day' is likely to be influenced by 'Advertising' and by 'Retail_Price'. If we knew the precise relationship, Solver could find the optimum values...

Note
This formula is pure speculation by the author to illustrate the use of Solver!

1   Suppose cell $G$13, 'Films_per_Day', is replaced by the formula:

$$= 480 * (1\text{-EXP(-Advertising/360))} * \text{EXP(-((Retail\_Price/3)}^2)/2)$$

Maximum number of films per day that can be reached by advertising.

Advertising factor, which increases with monthly expenditure on advertising.

Price factor, which decreases as the price is raised.

It is assumed that 480 films per day is the absolute maximum that would be possible by saturation advertising together with competitive prices.

As the monthly advertising expenditure is raised from zero, the advertising factor increases rapidly at first but the rate of increase tails off as more is spent. The (£)360 constant is the monthly amount that would give approximately 63% of the maximum achievable by the advertising factor in isolation.

As the retail price is increased from zero, the price factor decreases from 1 slowly at first, but then drops more rapidly as the price goes beyond the (£)3 constant.

2   If Solver is to seek an optimum solution automatically, the staff numbers need to change correspondingly to adjust to the throughput. Suppose we say that an extra operator is required for every 80 films per day or part, and that an extra half-time assistant is required for every 60 films per day, rounded to the nearest operator or half assistant:

Replace cell $B$23 by the formula "= ROUNDUP(Films_per_Day / 80 , 0)" and cell $B$24 by the formula "= ROUNDUP(Films_per_Day / 60 , 0) / 2".

3   In the case of the manager, his salary could be increased by a bonus based conveniently on the percentage net profit in cell I75.

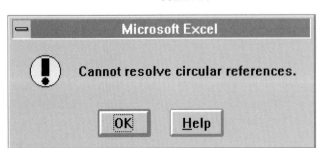

Unfortunately if cell $E$22 is replaced by the formula "= 10000 * (1 + I75)", this error message appears.

The 'Circular Reference' means simply that cell I75 contains a formula which is dependent on a network of formulas, whose precedents include cell E22. Therefore, E22 cannot itself be dependent on I75, unless *Iteration* is to be used which is the case for Solver. For now this change will be abandoned and the manager's salary left fixed at £10,000.

4   Since it will be more convenient to adjust the annual amount spent on advertising, cell F48 will be named 'Annual_Advertising'.

Setting Up Suitable Starting Values

Before using Solver, it is necessary to set up the starting values for the Worksheet. It will be shown that these are critical in this example. This arises from the mathematical formula used to predict the 'Films_per_Day', the dependence on this of the numbers of staff employed, and the inter-reaction of the rest of the Worksheet. Subsequently this will be referred to as the 'FastPrint 24 Model'. Since this theoretical model demands much higher spending on advertising, the starting value for the annual costs will be raised to £18,000. If the Retail_Price is kept at £4.50, then the Films_per_Day will be calculated to be 153. This would require 2 operators and 3 half-time counter assistants (1.5 full-time equivalents). Initially the manager's salary will remain fixed at £10,000. This would produce an average monthly net profit of £6,111.97, which is 34.7% of sales.

In the rest of this section these results will be summarised in the following table:

Retail_Price £4.50	Net_Profit £6068.91	% Net Profit 34.7%
Annual_Advertising £18,000	Number_Operators 3	Managers Salary
Films_Per_Day 210	Number_Assistants 1 1/2	£10,000.00

Starting Solver

Assuming that Solver is installed, start solver:

1   From the **Tools** menu, select the **Solver...** option.

2   Complete the **Solver Parameters** dialogue box.

Set Target Cell:
Key in cell name or
cell reference or
click the cell on the
Worksheet.

Equal to: Select the
appropriate button,
Max in this case.

By Changing Cells:
Key in cell names or
references, separated
by commas or click
the cells on the
Worksheet.

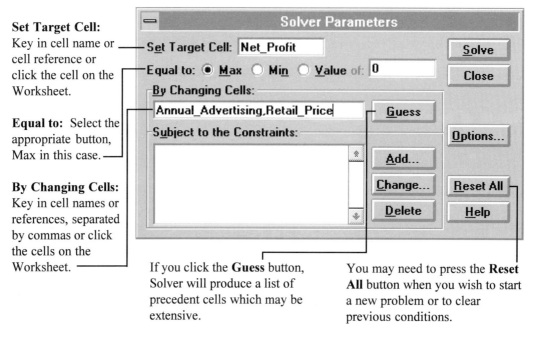

If you click the **Guess** button,
Solver will produce a list of
precedent cells which may be
extensive.

You may need to press the **Reset
All** button when you wish to start
a new problem or to clear
previous conditions.

Subject to Constraints will be
used later.

3   Click the **Options...** button.

4   Complete the **Solver Options** dialogue box shown
     opposite. Here the defaults have been accepted. A major
     consideration is whether the model is linear or non-linear.
     Here the latter *must* be selected. Good definitions of the
     features can be read by pressing the Help button.

Tip
*If the **Solver...** command does
not appear in the **Tools** menu:*

*From the **Tools** menu, select the
Add-In... option.*
*Check the **Solver Add-In** box.*

*If this is not listed, you will have
to install it by running the **Excel**
Setup program.*

Max Time: Limits the number of iterations to this time.

Iterations: Limits the number of iterations to this value.

Precision: Must be a fraction between 0 and 1. It is used to
test how close a constraint value must be to its target.

Tolerance: Only applies to changing cells which are
constrained to *integer* values. It allows an error in optimal
solution.

Assume Linear Model: Check *only* if
linear. If so it speeds up iteration
process.

Show Iteration Results: Check this if
you wish to step through iterations
under your control.

Use Automatic Scaling: Check this if
changing cells and target cells and
constraint values have large differences
in magnitude.

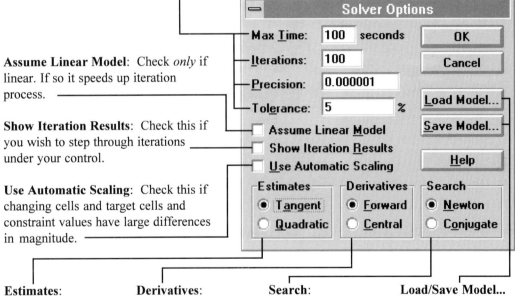

Estimates:
Select Tangent
normally.
Select Quadratic for
highly non-linear
models.

Derivatives:
Forward is the
default.
Central is
recommended for
models which are not
smooth and
continuous.

Search:
Newton uses more
memory.
Conjugate needs less
memory but may
require more
iterations.

Load/Save Model...
Displays the Load/
Save Model dialogue
box, which enables
pre-defined settings
for Solver to be
loaded/ stored.

5   Click the **OK** button in **Solver Options** dialogue box.

Note
On a 486DX
25MHz PC, this
took about 14
iterations in
approximately 7
seconds.

6   Click the **Solve** button in **Solver Parameters** dialogue box. Solver will go through a series of iterations which will be monitored on the status bar.

7   When a solution is found it will display the **Solver Results** dialogue box.

Either accept the default, **Keep Solver Solution**, which keeps the modified worksheet values.

Or click the **Restore Original Values** option to return worksheet to its starting values.

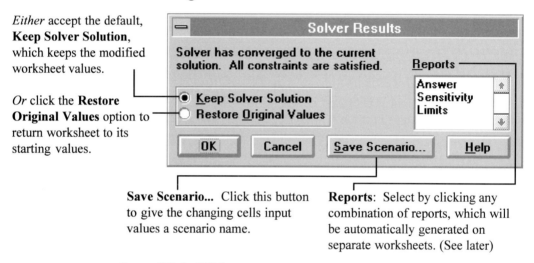

Save Scenario... Click this button to give the changing cells input values a scenario name.

Reports: Select by clicking any combination of reports, which will be automatically generated on separate worksheets. (See later)

8   Click **OK** button.

9   Inspection of the modified Worksheet values will show the following results.

Retail_Price	£4.41	Net_Profit	£6,292.81	% Net Profit	34.9%
Annual_Advertising	£17847	Number_Operators	2	Managers Salary	
Films_Per_Day	160	Number_Assistants	1 1/2		£10,000.00

Note
This is the best
solution that
Solver can find
from the starting
values provided.

It can be seen that Solver has found that a small reduction in annual advertising costs, coupled with a small reduction in retail price, will give a small increase in net profit.

Applying Constraints

An annual advertising budget of nearly £18,000 is a large burden for a small business. Suppose that the owner decides that it would be safer to restrict the budget for advertising to £12,000...

1   Restart Solver by selecting the **Solver...** option from the **Tools** menu. In the **Solver Parameters** dialogue box, the target and changing cells values will be retained from the previous session. Click the **Add...** button to display the **Add Constraints** dialogue box.

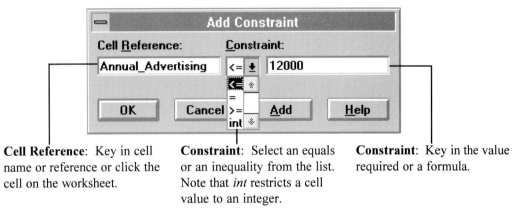

Cell Reference: Key in cell name or reference or click the cell on the worksheet.

Constraint: Select an equals or an inequality from the list. Note that *int* restricts a cell value to an integer.

Constraint: Key in the value required or a formula.

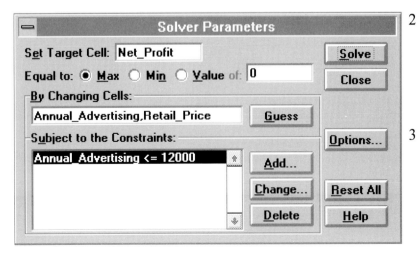

2   Click **OK** to redisplay the **Solver Parameters** dialogue box.

3   Click **Solve** to re-run solver with the starting values given by the previous run.

4   The new solution is shown in the table.

Retail_Price £4.32	Net_Profit £6,375.72	% Net Profit 36.2%
Annual_Advertising £12000	Number_Operators 2	Managers Salary
Films_Per_Day 160	Number_Assistants 1 1/2	£10,000.00

Tip
With a problem like this, you must be prepared to experiment with the starting values to try to locate the optimum solution. Although Solver converges to a solution it does not guarantee it is the best!

In this second attempt, limiting the annual advertising to £12,000 has led to Solver finding an even better solution. The substantial reduction in the advertising commitment, coupled with a small reduction in retail price, has increased the net profit. More suitable starting values may have led Solver to this solution at the first attempt.

5   Suppose a third solution is attempted by further limiting the advertising budget to £10,000. With the second solution providing the starting values, the new solution is...

Retail_Price £4.23	Net_Profit £6,199.79	% Net Profit 35.9%
Annual_Advertising £10000	Number_Operators 2	Managers Salary
Films_Per_Day 160	Number_Assistants 1 1/2	£10,000.00

Tip
In an example such as this, it is very useful to use the Excel's Chart facilities to further explore the model for the optimum solution. See Chapter 12, 'Charts and Graphics'.

Here a further reduction in advertising budget and a further small decrease in retail price has resulted in a small reduction in net profit. However, the reduction is so small that the owner may prefer the lesser risk of a smaller advertising commitment.

Adding Another Constraint

The bonus payment to the manager, which previously caused a 'Circular Reference' error, can now be added in as a second constraint:

1   In the Add Constraint dialogue box, key in the constraint "Managers Salary = 10000 * (1 + $I$75)".

2   Don't forget to add Managers Salary to Changing Cells!

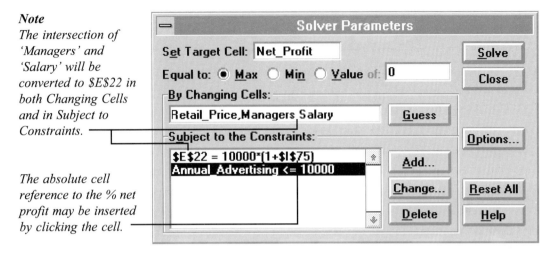

◁

Note
*The intersection of
'Managers' and
'Salary' will be
converted to $E$22 in
both Changing Cells
and in Subject to
Constraints.*

*The absolute cell
reference to the % net
profit may be inserted
by clicking the cell.*

Solver Parameters

Se̲t Target Cell: Net_Profit

Equal to: ● M̲ax   ○ Mi̲n   ○ V̲alue of: 0

B̲y Changing Cells:

Retail_Price,Managers Salary

Subject to the Constraints:

$E$22 = 10000*(1+$I$75)
Annual_Advertising <= 10000

[Buttons: Solve, Close, Guess, Options..., Add..., Change..., Reset All, Delete, Help]

3   Solver uses this second constraint to find the following
     solution.

Retail_Price £3.97	Net_Profit £5,533.51	% Net Profit 30.3%	
Annual_Advertising £10000	Number_Operators 3	Managers Salary	
Films_Per_Day 180	Number_Assistants 1 1/2	£13,030.78	

In this case the Retail_Price has been reduced, which has
increased the Films_per_Day to 180. This has required an
extra operator. Together with the manager's bonus this
reduces the net profit.

Warning
*Do remember that
although this
model provides a
useful example, it
is pure fiction!...*

4   Increasing the starting value of the Retail_Price to £4.50
     will locate a better solution.

Retail_Price £4.23	Net_Profit £5,914.64	% Net Profit 34.2%	
Annual_Advertising £10000	Number_Operators 2	Managers Salary	
Films_Per_Day 160	Number_Assistants 1 1/2	£13,421.87	

Here a higher Retail_Price reduces the Films_per_Day
back to 160. This avoids the need for the extra operator,
giving a slightly larger bonus to the manager, and
increasing the Net_Profit.

*...In practice it is
not as easy to
quantify the effect
of advertising.*

Generating Reports

The **Solver Results** dialogue box carries the options of generating on new separate sheets reports on Answers, Limits and Sensitivity. As an example the 'Answer' report for the final results is reproduced here.

It compares the starting and final values of the target and changing cells. It also lists the constraints.

A1	⬇	Microsoft Excel 5.0 Answer Report

Target Cell (Max)

Cell	Name	Original Value	Final Value
$I$74	Net_Profit	£5,502.20	£5,914.64

Adjustable Cells

Cell	Name	Original Value	Final Value
$F$48	Annual_Advertising	£10,000.00	£10,000.00
$G$7	Retail_Price	£4.50	£4.23
$E$22	Manager Salary	£13,030.78	£13,421.87

Constraints

Cell	Name	Cell Value	Formula	Status	Slack
$E$22	Manager Salary	£13,421.87	$E$22=10000*(1+$I$75)	Not Binding	£0.00
$F$48	Annual_Advertising	£10,000.00	$F$48<=10000	Binding	£0.00

| ⏮ ◀ ▶ ⏭ | Answer Report 1 | Sensitivity Report 1 | Limits Report 1 | N ◀ |

Status:
Not Binding means that the constraint is satisfied.

Binding means that the constraint is satisfied and furthermore that the value assigned is that specified by the inequality.

Slack:
This value gives the difference between the cells final value and the value of the original constraint for that cell.

Linking Worksheets and Workbooks

in easy steps

Overview

A formula in a cell of a Worksheet of a Workbook may refer to data in the cell(s) of another Worksheet of the same or of another Workbook. The dependent formula is then linked to this data, such that if the source of the data changes, then the formula will change dynamically.

The advantages of being able to do this are so extensive that, to be brief, it is possible only to state the obvious advantage; that of avoiding large, cumbersome and complex Worksheets by forming a network of inter-linked Worksheets and Workbooks, which subdivide the work or the data into smaller logical units.

Linking formulas between Worksheets has always been very important so that in this latest Version 5 of Excel it has been made very much easier by making its files Workbooks, which are sets of Worksheets. Within a Workbook, the linking between Worksheets can be as easy as referencing cells from formulas within a Worksheet. Linking between Workbooks requires very similar techniques to those which existed in earlier versions. For this reason, this chapter will distinguish between linking between Worksheets and linking between Workbooks.

When linking between two Workbooks, both Workbooks may be open under Excel. Alternatively, the Workbook which contains the reference data may be closed, in which case it can be accessed from disk, preferably the hard disk for faster access. The latter facility requires less memory (RAM).

Although this chapter concentrates mainly on linking within and between Workbooks, it seems appropriate to introduce the technique of linking to data from other Window's applications.

Also the topic of 3-D references for cells and the definition of 3-D names fits in well with this chapter.

Terminology

Before giving detailed examples of links between Worksheets and Workbooks, it is necessary to define some terms.

Source versus Dependent Workbook

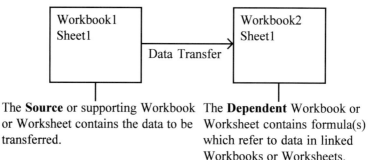

The **Source** or supporting Workbook or Worksheet contains the data to be transferred.

The **Dependent** Workbook or Worksheet contains formula(s) which refer to data in linked Workbooks or Worksheets.

External versus Internal Links

Internal Links are limited to sheets within one Workbook.

External Links apply to sheets which lie in different Workbooks. The Source Workbooks may be open under Excel or may be referenced on disk.

Specification of Links

Note
The more tenuous the link, the longer its specification becomes - see the next page.

The same general specification may be used in formulas to define links in Dependent Workbooks or Worksheets. The next page gives an example of the general specification to the cell named 'Net_Price', i.e. cell $G$11 of the 'Monthly Plan' sheet of 'FP24PLAN.XLS' workbook. It can be seen that the specification of links within the Workbook are much simpler than those external to it.

Use of Names versus Cell References

It will be shown subsequently that it is much easier to use cell names rather than cell references when forming links within and between Workbooks. A cell reference always requires the containing sheet name, whereas this is not usually required for a named cell.

The Full Specification for an (External) Reference

Delimiters: **Single Quotes** are necessary only if sheet name contains spaces.   **Square Brackets** are only necessary to separate file and sheet names.   **Exclamation Mark** must be used to separate cell name or cell reference from the rest.

= 'C:\EXCEL_5\EXAMPLES\[FP24PLAN.XLS]Monthly Plan'!Net_Price

External Reference to Workbook file on disk.

Path is only necessary for file on disk to enable Excel to locate the file.

= '[FP24PLAN.XLS]Monthly Plan'!Net_Price

External Reference to another Workbook currently open under Excel.

Workbook Name is only necessary if linked cell lies in another Workbook.

= 'Monthly Plan'!Net_Price

Reference within Workbook to another Worksheet. (Sheet-level)

Sheet Name is only necessary if the cell name applies only to its containing Worksheet.

= Net_Price

Reference within Workbook to another Worksheet. (Book-level)

Cell Name is all that is necessary if the cell name applies to Workbook.

'FastPrint 24' Annual Business Plan

Tip
Remember that the months of the year are part of an in-built series. Here, it is only necessary to key in 'January' and then drag the cell fill handle across.

Suppose the 'FastPrint 24' business plan is extended by adding a new sheet named 'Annual Plan', which estimates the business performance over a twelve month cycle, allowing for typical seasonal variations. These monthly fluctuations in the number of films processed each month are estimated and are keyed in as numbers. The rest of the numeric data required will be taken by forming a link with the existing 'Monthly Plan' sheet.

	D8	↓		1632					
	A	**B**	**C**	**D**	**E**	**F**	**G**	**H**	**I**
1			FastPrint	24 LTD					
2				24 Exposure Colour Negative Film					
3				24 Hours Maximum Processing Time					
4			ANNUAL BUSINESS PLAN						
5									
6				January	February	March	April	May	June
7									
8	FILMS PER MONTH =			1632	576	768	1152	1344	1920
9									

	O8	↓		960				
	J	**K**	**L**	**M**	**N**	**O**	**P**
6	July	August	September	October	November	December	Totals
7							
8	2304	2880	2496	1824	1344	960	
9							

Note
Cells $D$8:$O$8 are named 'Films_per_Month'

It would be expected that the number of films processed each month will peak in the summer, with a smaller shorter peak in January following Christmas and the New Year. The Worksheet occupies two screen widths to accommodate the columns for the twelve months and the totals.

Below this will be placed the calculations of the 'Sales Income', the 'Sales Costs', the 'Expenses', and the 'Gross' and 'Net Profits'. Here will be formed the link referring back to cells in the 'Monthly Plan' sheet. This will further extend the Worksheet to a depth of two screens.

Forming Links within Workbooks

There are two ways of forming links between Worksheets which belong to the same Workbook:

The *harder way* is to use the cell(s)' reference.

The *easier way* is to use the cell(s)' name.

Using Cell References

Consider the example of the sales income for January:

1   Select the cell, e.g. $D$10 on the sheet 'Annual Plan'.

2   Complete the first part of the formula, using the name box to insert 'Films_per_Month', i.e. "=Films_per_Month*"

3   Click the sheet tab for sheet which contains the required cell, in this case 'Monthly Plan'. Excel will automatically insert the sheet name in the formula, enclosed in single quotes because of its space.

4   In the source sheet, locate the required cell and click it. Here it is $G$11, which contains the price excluding VAT. Excel will insert an exclamation mark and the cell's relative reference in the formula.

5   Press function key F4 to convert the cell reference from its relative form to its more correct absolute form.

6   Press Enter to complete the formula and return you to the dependent sheet, as shown below.

D10	↓		=Films_per_Month*'Monthly Plan'!$G$11		
	A	B	C	D	E	F
6				January	February	March
7						
8	FILMS PER MONTH =			1632	576	768
9						
10	SALES INCOME =			£6,250.21		
11						

Using Cell Names

Alternatively, the formula for the sales income for January can be more efficiently completed by using the name, 'Net_Price', of $G$11 on the 'Monthly Plan' sheet:

1   Select the cell, e.g. $D$10 on the sheet 'Annual Plan'.

2   Complete the first part of the formula, using the name box to insert 'Films_per_Month', i.e. "=Films_per_Month*"

3   Use the name box to locate the name required 'Net_Price'. Excel will automatically switch to the containing sheet, 'Monthly Plan', and it will locate and display the cell.

4   Press Enter to complete the formula and return you to the dependent sheet, as shown below.

Remember
If the 'Net_Price' changes in the 'Monthly Summary' sheet, then the Sales Income in 'Annual Summary' sheet will change correspondingly.

D10	⬇		=Films_per_Month*Net_Price		
	A	B	C	D	E	F
6				January	February	March
7						
8	FILMS PER MONTH =			1632	576	768
9						
10	SALES INCOME =			£6,250.21		
11						

Names are Normally Global to Containing Workbook

The reason that it is so much easier to use a cell's name in links is that the name is available in all sheets within a Workbook, no matter in which sheet the cell is located. This means that the Name Box contains a list of all the names which have been defined for the whole Workbook. The normal computing term for this is 'Global', which means the name is universally available.

Note
Microsoft refer to these names as
*'**Book Level**'.*
They are the default type of names.

More Links for 'FastPrint 24'

The rest of the links are completed for the 'Annual Plan' sheet by inserting the formulas for the Sales, Costs and Expenses, as shown below.

Note that in this partial list of the Name Box, the most recently named range of cells 'Films_per_Month' on the Annual Plan appears amid the names which apply to cells on the Monthly Plan.

| Chemicals |
| Costs |
| Electricity |
| Expenses |
| Films_per_Day |
| Films_per_Month |
| Gross_Profit |
| Insurance |
| Labour |

Note
The extra text headings and labels

Note
The use of the AutoSum button on cells $D$18 and $D$31.

	A12	↓		SALES COSTS		
	A		**B**	**C**		**D**
12	SALES COSTS					
13			Labour =			=Labour
14			Paper =			=Films_per_Month*Paper
15			Chemicals =			=Films_per_Month*Chemicals
16			Stationery =			=Films_per_Month*Stationery
17			Electricity =			=Electricity
18			TOTAL =			=SUM(D13:D17)
19						
20	GROSS PROFIT =					
21	% GROSS PROFIT =					
22						
23	EXPENSES					
24			Accounting =			=Accountancy
25			Advertising =			=Advertising
26			Insurance =			=Insurance
27			Maintenance =			=Maintenance
28			Telephone =			=Telephone
29			Rent/Rates =			=Rent_Rates
30			Lease Costs =			=Lease_Costs
31			TOTAL =			=SUM(D24:D30)
32						

Scenario Summary / Monthly Plan \ **Annual Plan** / She

In order to calculate the gross and net profits for the twelve monthly cycle, it is better to name the ranges of twelve cells containing the monthly values for Sales, Costs and Expenses. Unfortunately, these names have already been used.

The Use of Sheet Level Names

In cases where popular names have already been defined on other sheets, it is probably easier to modify the name slightly, making it a 'Book Level' name. However, if you *insist* on using the same name, you can make the new name 'Sheet Level', which means simply that you must use its containing sheet name when defining it and when referencing it from other sheets. This makes the reference longer and less convenient. To illustrate this, the technique will be applied to Sales, Costs, Expenses, Gross_Profit and Net_Profit for 'FastPrint 24'. Another slight drawback is that you cannot use the Name Box to define the name but you must use the Define Name dialogue box:

Note
A similar term used for 'Sheet Level' is 'Local', which strictly means that the name is only available in its containing sheet.

1   Select the cell or cell range to be named, e.g. $D$10:$O$10.

2   From the **Insert** menu, select the **Name** sub-menu and choose the **Define...** option.

3   Complete the **Define Name** dialogue box.

Names in Workbook:
You must key in the *Sheet Name*, in single quotes if necessary, followed by an *Exclamation Mark*, followed by the *Cell(s)' Name*.

Refers to:
Provided cells were selected, this will be displayed.

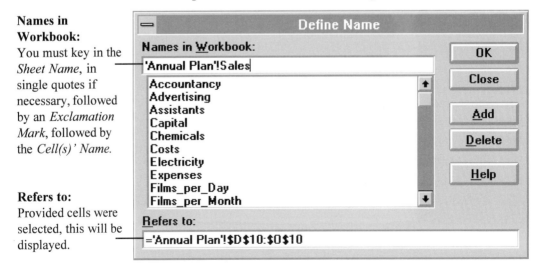

This means that with the 'Annual Plan' sheet active, the name 'Sales' will now apply to the above range of 12 cells.

Specifying Sheet and Book Level Names

The two identical names, 'Sales', can be referenced from *any* sheet in the Workbook, 'FP24PLAN.XLS':

Containing Sheet	Cell(s) Reference	Specification	Reference Sheet
Monthly Plan	$I$17	Sales	Any sheet in Workbook other than 'Annual Plan'
		FP24PLAN.XLS!Sales	'Annual Plan'
Annual Plan	$D$10:$O$10	'Annual Plan'!Sales	Any sheet in Workbook other than 'Annual Plan'
		Sales	'Annual Plan'

Note the difference in the specifications:

Book Level Name
Sheet Level Name

Tip
Generally it seems an unnecessary complication to define sheet level names. In this example, it would have been much simpler to modify the names, e.g. to 'Mthly_Sales' and 'Mthly_Net_Profit', etc.

Completion of Annual Plan Sheet Level Names

Correspondingly the following sheet level names would be defined for the 'Annual Plan' sheet:

$D$18:$O$18:	Costs
$D$31:$O$31:	Expenses
$D$20:$O$20:	Gross_Profit
$D$33:$O$33:	Net_Profit (See next page)

In each case it is necessary to use the Define Name dialogue box and, unfortunately, you would have to key in the sheet name in single quotes in addition to the cell range names.

	A	B	C	D
15		Chemicals =		=Films_per_Month*Chemicals
16		Stationery =		=Films_per_Month*Stationery
17		Electricity =		=Electricity
18		TOTAL =		=SUM(D13:D17)
19				
20	GROSS PROFIT =			=Sales-Costs
21	% GROSS PROFIT =			=Gross_Profit/Sales
22				
23	EXPENSES			
24		Accounting =		=Accountancy
25		Advertising =		=Advertising
26		Insurance =		=Insurance
27		Maintenance =		=Maintenance
28		Telephone =		=Telephone
29		Rent/Rates =		=Rent_Rates
30		Lease Costs =		=Lease_Costs
31		TOTAL =		=SUM(D24:D30)
32				
33	NET PROFIT =			=Sales-Costs-Expenses
34	% NET PROFIT =			=Net_Profit/Sales

The Name Box shows: A15

The formulas for gross and % gross profit can now be entered using the Name Box.

Correspondingly the formulas for net and % net profit can be entered.

Completion of Annual Plan Sheet

The rest of this extensive spreadsheet is easily completed mainly by copying formulas and using AutoSum:

1 Copy Formulas Across 12 Months.

Select the cell range in column D from Sales Income to % Net Profit.
Drag its fill handle so that these formulas are copied across to February...December.

2 Complete the Summations in Column P.

Select the following cells and cell ranges, either collectively or separately and click the AutoSum button:
$P$8, $P$10, $P$13:$P$18, $P$20, $P$24:$P$31, $P$33.

3 Complete the Percentage Totals.

It is critical that the totals for % Gross and % Net Profits are completed using the following formulas:

| $P$21: | =P20/P10 |
| $P$34: | =P33/P10 |

4 Format Cells.

Finally some minor formatting is required using the Currency and Percentage Styles and the Increase Decimal buttons on the Formatting Toolbar.

Hiding Rows or Columns using the Hide Command

The 'Annual Plan' contains a mass of information. To get a clearer overview on the screen it is possible to temporarily *hide* some of the data, in this case the rows containing the detailed sales costs and the expenses:

1   Select the rows or columns to be hidden, e.g. in this case the two ranges, rows 13:17 and rows 24:30.

2   From the **Format** menu and the **Row** (or Column) sub-menu, select the **Hide** option.

3   The screen will give the following display, which shows the main features of the data.

	A	B	C	D	E	F	G	H	I
6				January	February	March	April	May	June
7									
8	FILMS PER MONTH =			1632	576	768	1152	1344	1920
9									
10	SALES INCOME =			£6,250.21	£2,205.96	£2,941.28	£4,411.91	£5,147.23	£7,353.19
11									
12	SALES COSTS								
18		TOTAL =		£3,750.07	£2,482.87	£2,713.27	£3,174.07	£3,404.47	£4,095.67
19									
20	GROSS PROFIT =			£2,500.15	-£276.91	£228.01	£1,237.85	£1,742.77	£3,257.52
21	% GROSS PROFIT =			40.0%	-12.6%	7.8%	28.1%	33.9%	44.3%
22									
23	EXPENSES								
31		TOTAL =		£1,616.67	£1,616.67	£1,616.67	£1,616.67	£1,616.67	£1,616.67
32									
33	NET PROFIT =			£883.48	-£1,893.58	-£1,388.66	-£378.82	£126.10	£1,640.86
34	% NET PROFIT =			14.1%	-85.8%	-47.2%	-8.6%	2.4%	22.3%
35									

Scenario Summary / Monthly Plan \ **Annual Plan** / Sh

To unhide selected rows or columns:

1   Make a selection containing the hidden rows or columns, e.g. rows 12 to 18.

2   From the **Format** menu and the **Row** (or Column) sub-menu, select the **Unhide** option.

Tip
To Unhide all rows and/or columns, click the **Select All** *button first.*

Hiding Rows or Columns using Outlining

You may prefer to use *Outlining* to hide rows or columns:

1   Make *separate* selections of the rows or columns to be hidden, e.g. in this case first the range of rows 13:17 and later the range of rows 24:30.

2   From the **Data** menu and the **Group and Outline** sub-menu, select the **Group...** option.

3   The screen will give the following display, which now includes the **Outline Row Level Bar**. Click the **Hide Detail Symbol** (-) or the **Show Detail Symbol** (+) to control the data on display.

		A	B	C	D	E	F	G	H	I
	10	SALES INCOME =			£6,250.21	£2,205.96	£2,941.28	£4,411.91	£5,147.23	£7,35
	11									
	12	SALES COSTS								
·	13		Labour =		£1,750.00	£1,750.00	£1,750.00	£1,750.00	£1,750.00	£1,75
·	14		Paper =		£1,468.80	£518.40	£691.20	£1,036.80	£1,209.60	£1,72
·	15		Chemicals =		£408.00	£144.00	£192.00	£288.00	£336.00	£48
·	16		Stationery =		£81.60	£28.80	£38.40	£57.60	£67.20	£9
·	17		Electricity =		£41.67	£41.67	£41.67	£41.67	£41.67	£4
−	18		TOTAL =		£3,750.07	£2,482.87	£2,713.27	£3,174.07	£3,404.47	£4,09
	19									
	20	GROSS PROFIT =			£2,500.15	-£276.91	£228.01	£1,237.85	£1,742.77	£3,25
	21	% GROSS PROFIT =			40.0%	-12.6%	7.8%	28.1%	33.9%	44
	22									
	23	EXPENSES								
+	31		TOTAL =		£1,616.67	£1,616.67	£1,616.67	£1,616.67	£1,616.67	£1,61
	32									
	33	NET PROFIT =			£883.48	-£1,893.58	-£1,388.66	-£378.82	£126.10	£1,64
	34	% NET PROFIT =			14.1%	-85.8%	-47.2%	-8.6%	2.4%	22

Scenario Summary / Monthly Plan \ **Annual Plan** / Sh

Tip
*To clear just the Outlining Bar: From **Tools**, select **Options...** Click **View** tab and uncheck **Outline Symbols** box.*

To remove an outline:

1   Make a selection containing the outlined rows or columns, e.g. rows 12 to 18.

2   From the **Data** menu and the **Group and Outline** sub-menu, select the **Clear Outline...** option.

Using Window Split and Freeze Panes

Because the 'Annual Plan' is such a wide spreadsheet, it helps if the screen is split vertically, so that the row labels are separated from the numeric data. Furthermore the left hand pane can be frozen so that it isn't accidentally scrolled:

Note
Here the extra detail is hidden by Outlining, but the Outlining Symbols and the Outlining Bar have been temporarily removed from the display.

1   Split the screen vertically by dragging the Vertical Split box to the boundary between columns C and D, (or use the Split command from the Window menu).

2   From the **Window** menu, select the **Freeze Panes** command.

	A	B	C	K	L	M	N	O	P	
6				August	September	October	November	December	Totals	
7										
8	FILMS PER MONTH =			2880	2496	1824	1344	960	19200	
9										
10	SALES INCOME =			£11,029.79	£9,559.15	£6,985.53	£5,147.23	£3,676.60	£73,531.91	
11										
12	SALES COSTS									
18		TOTAL =		£5,247.67	£4,786.87	£3,980.47	£3,404.47	£2,943.67	£44,540.00	
19										
20	GROSS PROFIT =			£5,782.12	£4,772.28	£3,005.07	£1,742.77	£732.93	£28,991.91	
21	% GROSS PROFIT =			52.4%	49.9%	43.0%	33.9%	19.9%	39.4%	
22										
23	EXPENSES									
31		TOTAL =		£1,616.67	£1,616.67	£1,616.67	£1,616.67	£1,616.67	£19,400.00	
32										
33	NET PROFIT =			£4,165.45	£3,155.62	£1,388.40	£126.10	-£883.74	£9,591.91	
34	% NET PROFIT =			37.8%	33.0%	19.9%	2.4%	-24.0%	13.0%	
35										

Scenario Summary / Monthly Plan \ **Annual Plan** / She ←

Left Pane is frozen - it has no scroll bars - it just follows right pane for vertical scroll.

Right Pane can be scrolled horizontally to pan across the full width of monthly data.

To unfreeze frozen pane and remove window split:

1   From the **Window** menu, select the **Unfreeze Panes** option.

2   From the **Window** menu, select the **Remove Split** option.

Tip
*To remove window split, double click the **split bar** or the **split box**.*

Forming Links between Workbooks

To illustrate how links can be formed between Workbooks, a new example of quarterly sales over three years will be used:

1   Suppose the data shown below was keyed into a Worksheet named 'Annual Summary' in a Workbook file named '91_SALES.XLS'. It can be seen that the four selected cells containing the quarterly sales figures were named 'Qtrly_Sales'.

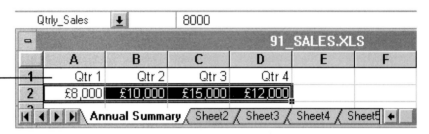

Tip
Remember that Qtr 1... is part of a cyclical series which can be generated by keying in the first term, and then dragging the cell fill handle across.

2   Correspondingly, the sales figures were keyed into exactly the same locations named 'Qtrly_Sales' in Worksheets named 'Annual Summary' in new Workbook files named '92_SALES.XLS' and '93_SALES.XLS' respectively.

3   The first Workbook, '91_SALES.XLS', was then closed, the file being saved on the hard disk in the directory specified by the path 'C:\EXCEL_5\EXAMPLES\'.

4   In Workbook, '93_SALES.XLS', a second Worksheet was named 'Three Year Summary' and was used to record the total sales figures for the three years, as shown on the next page.

5   In '93_SALES.XLS', a second window was opened to display its second Worksheet. The Window menu showed the three windows available. The next page shows the tiled display of these three windows and a display of the formulas used, giving the links specifications.

New Window
Arrange...
Hide
Unhide...
Split
Freeze Panes
1 93_SALES.XLS:1
√2 93_SALES.XLS:2
3 92_SALES.XLS

92_SALES.XLS

	A	B	C	D	E	F
1	Qtr 1	Qtr 2	Qtr 3	Qtr 4		
2	£9,000	£11,000	£17,000	£13,000		

⏮ ◀ ▶ ⏭ \ **Annual Summary** / Sheet2 / Sheet3 / Sheet4 / Sheet5 / She

93_SALES.XLS:1

	A	B	C	D	E	F
1	Qtr 1	Qtr 2	Qtr 3	Qtr 4		
2	£10,000	£12,000	£19,000	£14,000		

⏮ ◀ ▶ ⏭ \ **Annual Summary** / Three Year Summary / Sheet3 / Sheet4 /

93_SALES.XLS:2

	A	B	C	D	E
1		Annual Totals			
2	1991:	£45,000			
3	1992:	£50,000			
4	1993:	£55,000			
5					
6	Three Year Total:	£150,000			

⏮ ◀ ▶ ⏭ \ Annual Summary \ **Three Year Summary** / Sheet3 / S ◀

Tip
To insert in a formula the specification for a link to another Workbook:

Assuming that the Workbook is open, use the Window menu to display the Workbook, click Worksheet tab and either select the cell(s) or use the Name Box to select the name.

If the Workbook is closed, you will have to key in the full specification, including path.

Consider the three different specifications used for the links:

B2: Since the Workbook is closed, the full path for its file must be specified to enable Excel to locate it.

B3: Since the file is open, only the Workbook file name and the cell's name is required.

B4: Since the link is to a Worksheet in the same Workbook, only the name of the cells is required.

93_SALES.XLS:2

	A	B
1		Annual Totals
2	1991:	=SUM('C:\EXCEL_5\EXAMPLES\91_SALES.XLS'!Qtrly_Sales)
3	1992:	=SUM('92_SALES.XLS'!Qtrly_Sales)
4	1993:	=SUM(Qtrly_Sales)
5		
6	Three Year Total:	=SUM(B2:B4)

⏮ ◀ ▶ ⏭ \ Annual Summary \ **Three Year Summary** / Sheet3 / S ◀

Using the Edit Links Command

The Links dialogue box enables links to be opened, changed or updated:

1   Make the **Dependent** Workbook **active**.

2   From the **Edit** menu, select the **Links...** option.

3   Complete the **Links** dialogue box.

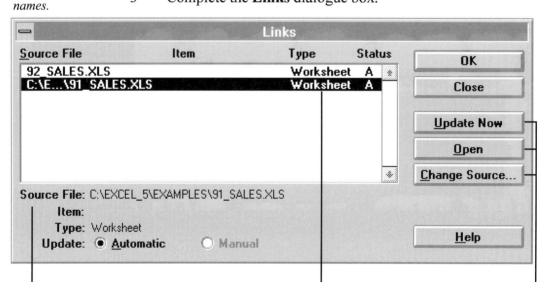

Source File: All the source files will be listed which form both **External Links** to other Excel Workbooks and **Remote Links** to other Windows Applications, which support Dynamic Data Exchange (DDE):

Source File:	specifies path and file.
Item:	lists the source of the link, e.g. 'DDE_LINK'.
Type:	describes the linked item, e.g. application.
Status:	A for Automatic, M for Manual.

You may select a single file or a set of files.

Update Now: Clicking this button will update the links in dependent Workbook to the selected source file(s). It is intended for files which have been set to Manual.

Open: This will Open any files (External or Remote) which are specified to be on disk.

Change Source... This opens the Change Links dialogue box, which is almost identical to the (File) Save As dialogue box and enables you to locate alternative paths and files.

Order of Saving and Opening Linked Workbooks

Closing Linked Workbooks

You should save and close the *Source* Workbooks before the *Dependent* Workbooks. Partly this is to ensure that the Dependent files have the latest data. More importantly, it means that the Dependent files will have a record of the paths of the directories in which the Source files are stored, should this be needed on subsequently opening. In the example of previous sections, the logical order of closing the workbooks would be:

91_SALES.XLS, 92_SALES.XLS, 93_SALES.XLS.

Opening Linked Workbooks

Correspondingly it is easier to open the Source Workbooks before the Dependent Workbooks. This ensures that the links are available as they were during the previous session.

Suppose for the previous example on Quarterly Sales the Dependent Workbook, '93_SALES.XLS', was opened first. The following dialogue box would be displayed:

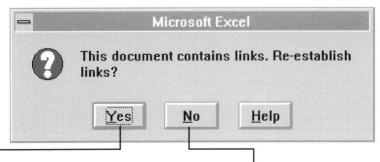

Yes: If you click the Yes button, Excel will take the data from the current version of the Workbook on disk. In the case of the formula which previously referenced the open Workbook, '92_SALES.XLS', it will now insert the path name which it recorded when it was last saved.

No: If you click the No button, Excel will retain the data which it recorded from the Source Workbooks when it was last saved.

If you have forgotten the source files, then you can re-establish the links by using the Links dialogue box from the Edit menu. For **Embedding**, select **Paste** button,

Linking versus Embedding from Remote Applications

Note
Whereas links
between Excel
Workbooks are
referred to as
***External**, links*
between Excel and
other applications
are referred to as
***Remote**.*

Linking versus Embedding

Embedding means to copy static data or objects, such as text or graphics, between applications operating under Windows, provided the packages supports *Object Linking and Embedding* (**OLE**). *Linking* means to dynamically exchange data or objects, such as text or graphics, with another application operating under Windows, provided the packages support OLE or *Dynamic Data Exchange* (**DDE**).

Embedding is used where the information is fixed, linking where it will be updated. The subject is too extensive to be covered fully, but a simple example will show you how easy it is to use.

Linking and Embedding from Word to Excel

To link or embed text from Word for Windows to Excel follow the procedure:

1   Suppose Word is open and two simple lines of text are keyed into a document named 'WIN_WORD.DOC'...
             "A sample of text...
             from Word for Windows."

2   The two lines are selected and stored in the ClipBoard using the **Edit** menu **Copy** command.

3   Excel is opened and cell, which is to receive the text, is made active, e.g. A3.

4   From the **Edit** menu, the **Paste Special...** option is selected.

5   The **Paste Special** dialogue box (next page) is completed.

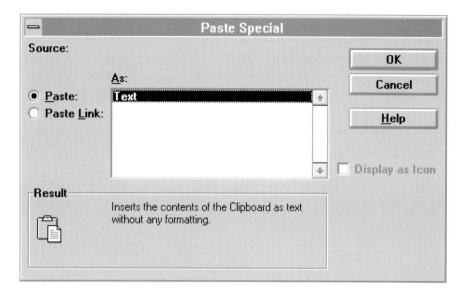

For **Embedding**, select **Paste** button, and click OK button.

6   The two lines of text will be placed in cells A3:A4 (next page).

7   Select Cell A8 and repeat the **Edit** menu **Paste Special...** option on the unchanged contents of the ClipBoard. Complete the **Paste Special** box.

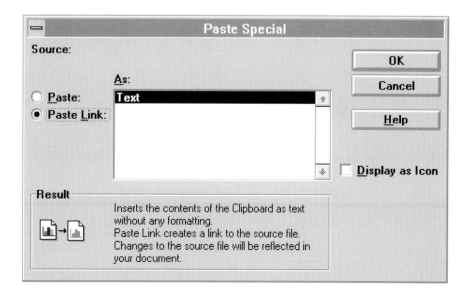

For **Linking**, select **Paste Link** button, and click OK button.

	A	B	C
1	Embedded Text from Word:-		
2			
3	A sample of text...		
4	from Word for Windows.		
5			
6	Linked Text from Word:-		
7			
8	A sample of text...		
9	from Word for Windows.		
10			

8   The text will appear in cells A8:A9, as shown here.

9   The embedded text and the linked text appear identical, but if the formula contents are displayed, it can be seen that text is stored for the embedded case, whereas a link specification is created in the two formulas for the linked case.

Remember
If the selected text is changed in the Source file, it will have no effect on the Embedded text, but the Linked text will change dynamically.

	A
1	Embedded Text from Word:-
2	
3	A sample of text...
4	from Word for Windows.
5	
6	Linked Text from Word:-
7	
8	=WinWord|'C:\EXCEL_5\EXAMPLES\WIN_WORD.DOC'!DDE_LINK8
9	=WinWord|'C:\EXCEL_5\EXAMPLES\WIN_WORD.DOC'!DDE_LINK8
10	

10   From the **Edit** menu, select the **Links...** option to display the Links dialogue box, showing the details of the source file.

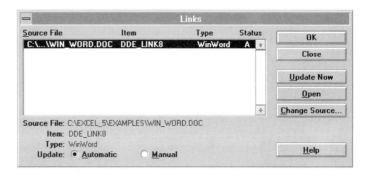

Using 3-D References and Names

3-D Cell References

As an example to illustrate the use of 3-D references the sales data for the four quarters of the three years 1991, 92 and 93 will be used. Here the years will be placed on Worksheets within the same Workbook. The three windows are shown with Horizontal Tiling.

3-D_NAME.XLS:3

	A	B	C	D	E	F
1	Qtr 1	Qtr 2	Qtr 3	Qtr 4		
2	£10,000	£12,000	£19,000	£14,000		
3						

1991 Sales / 1992 Sales / **1993 Sales** / 91-93 Summa

3-D_NAME.XLS:2

	A	B	C	D	E	F
1	Qtr 1	Qtr 2	Qtr 3	Qtr 4		
2	£9,000	£11,000	£17,000	£13,000		
3						

1991 Sales / **1992 Sales** / 1993 Sales / 91-93 Summary / S

3-D_NAME.XLS:1

	A	B	C	D	E	F
1	Qtr 1	Qtr 2	Qtr 3	Qtr 4		
2	£8,000	£10,000	£15,000	£12,000		
3						
4						

1991 Sales / 1992 Sales / 1993 Sales / 91-93 Summary / S

	A	B	C
1	Qtr 1	£27,000	
2	Qtr 2	£33,000	
3	Qtr 3	£51,000	
4	Qtr 4	£39,000	
5	Total	£150,000	

91-93 Summary / Sheet5 /

A fourth Worksheet is used to summarise the data for the three years, producing quarterly totals for the three years. The results are shown on the left.

Displaying the formulas in place of the results illustrates how 3-D cell references have been used, as shown below.

3-D_NAME.XLS:4

	A	B	C
1	Qtr 1	=SUM('1991 Sales:1993 Sales'!A2)	
2	Qtr 2	=SUM('1991 Sales:1993 Sales'!B2)	
3	Qtr 3	=SUM('1991 Sales:1993 Sales'!C2)	
4	Qtr 4	=SUM('1991 Sales:1993 Sales'!D2)	
5	Total	=SUM(B1:B4)	

91-93 Summary / Sheet5 / Sheet6 /

Note
The convention used for these 3-D references is to specify the range of Worksheet names, in single quotes where spaces are employed, followed by '!' and the cell reference.

Advantages of 3-D References

To use such references, it is essential that the data sheets all have exactly the same format, in this example so that each quarterly amount lies in the same cell on each sheet. It is useful to picture the sheets as a set of layers with identical layouts.

You may better appreciate the advantage of such a reference by considering an alternative formula without the 3-D facility:
"=SUM('1991 SALES'!A2,...

    '1992 SALES'!A2,'1993 SALES'!A2,)".
Clearly, the advantage increases according to the number of sheets.

Entering 3_D Cell References

You can, if you wish, key in such references but it is much easier to point and click. For example if you were in the process of entering a formula and came to the position of the cell reference:

1 Click the tab of first sheet, e.g. Excel inserts '1991 SALES'
2 Press the Shift key for a range of adjacent sheets, and click the tab of last sheet so that Excel extends the reference to '1991 SALES:1993 SALES'.
3 Click the cell (or range of cells) which is the same for all the sheets and Excel will complete the reference for you to '1991 SALES:1993 SALES'!A2.

Using 3-D Names

Book Level 3-D Names may be applied as shown in the modified example on the right. Such names must be defined by using the **Insert** menu and the **Names** sub-menu and selecting the **Define...** command.

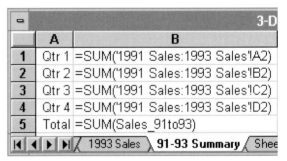

Name: The Name is keyed in as usual.

Refers to:
Unfortunately, it is not possible to select the cell reference before using the command. However to avoid keying this in, you may use the technique described above.

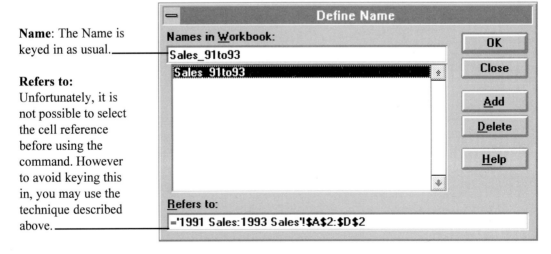

Formatting
Worksheets

Overview

Eventually the data and calculations on a spreadsheet need to be communicated more widely and this will probably be in the form of a printed report. Like most application programs operating under Windows, Excel can enable the user to produce the highest of standards in the presentation of such reports. So far we have concentrated on the techniques of developing spreadsheets, with only an occasional mention of formatting techniques where this has been unavoidable. Now we will consider Excel's extensive formatting facilities.

These techniques have the sophistication that you might expect only from a word processing or a desktop publishing application. The major difference is that whereas the latter types of program operate on paragraphs of text, which are limited to the width and length of the containing page or column, the data in Excel is constrained to the containing cell and therefore to the width of the column and the height of the row. Otherwise the features are remarkably similar. If you already have experience of these features, then the formatting and printing techniques should be fairly obvious. Either way they should be good fun.

The formatting and printing techniques provided by Excel requires quite a different expertise from that needed to produce a spreadsheet. Here we need aspects of graphic design which call for flair and creativity and, above all, subtlety. Under Excel you have an overwhelming range of choices for the formats and their combinations. If you are uncertain of what you are doing, keep the formatting simple!

Fortunately Excel helps the inexperienced by offering *AutoFormatting*. Also it provides the facility of using *Styles*, which can make formatting much easier and maintain a uniformity of style, which may well be required for a 'House Style' or a 'Corporate Image'.

This chapter will concentrate on comparing the different techniques of formatting rather than on the widely different ways of combining them.

Format Menu versus Formatting Toolbar

To format cells, you have a choice of using the Format Command Menu or the Formatting Toolbar. As usual the command menu gives you the widest range of choices but the selection of facilities packed into the toolbar will enable you to apply the majority of formats required.

The Format Menu

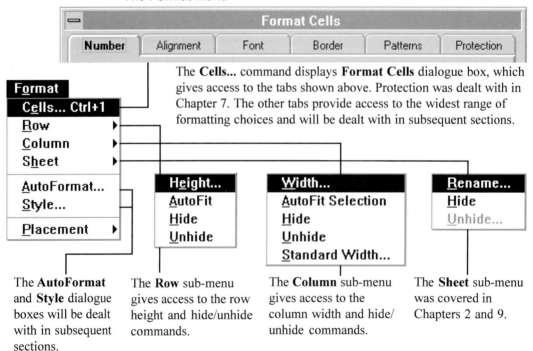

The **Cells...** command displays **Format Cells** dialogue box, which gives access to the tabs shown above. Protection was dealt with in Chapter 7. The other tabs provide access to the widest range of formatting choices and will be dealt with in subsequent sections.

The **AutoFormat** and **Style** dialogue boxes will be dealt with in subsequent sections.

The **Row** sub-menu gives access to the row height and hide/unhide commands.

The **Column** sub-menu gives access to the column width and hide/ unhide commands.

The **Sheet** sub-menu was covered in Chapters 2 and 9.

The Formatting Toolbar

Font, Font Size and Font Style   Alignment   Number Formats   Borders

Background and Font Colours

Using AutoFormat

The AutoFormat command is designed to be used for tables:

1   Select the area which requires formatting.

	A	B	C	D	E	F	G
1			Quarterly Sales				
2			1991 to 1993				
3							
4		Qtr 1	Qtr 2	Qtr 3	Qtr 4	Totals	
5	1991:	£8,000	£10,000	£15,000	£12,000	£45,000	
6	1992:	£9,000	£11,000	£17,000	£13,000	£50,000	
7	1993:	£10,000	£12,000	£19,000	£14,000	£55,000	
8	Totals:	£27,000	£33,000	£51,000	£39,000	£150,000	
9							

2   From the **Format** menu, select the **AutoFormat...** option.

3   In the **AutoFormat** dialogue box you may try various
     Table Formats until the Sample format is acceptable.

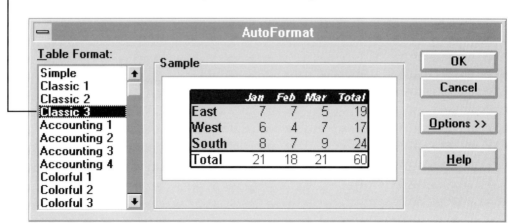

Note
If Excel fails to locate a table from your selection, an appropriate warning
will be displayed.

4   If in the AutoFormat dialogue box, you click the
     Options>> button, the box displays the following options.
     By Unchecking the check boxes, you can suppress some
     formats of the selected Table Format and see the effect in
     the Sample box.

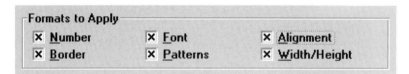

5   Clicking the OK button will format your selection...

	A	B	C	D	E	F
1		*Quarterly Sales*				
2		*1991 to 1993*				
3						
4		*Qtr 1*	*Qtr 2*	*Qtr 3*	*Qtr 4*	*Totals*
5	1991:	£8,000	£10,000	£15,000	£12,000	£45,000
6	1992:	£9,000	£11,000	£17,000	£13,000	£50,000
7	1993:	£10,000	£12,000	£19,000	£14,000	£55,000
8	Totals:	£27,000	£33,000	£51,000	£39,000	£150,000

6   Clearly, the above would require some additional
     formatting to make the last 'Totals' column appear the
     same as the 'Totals' row.

7   If you are unhappy with the results, then you can restore
     your original selection by selecting the **Undo AutoFormat**
     option from the **Edit** menu.

Tip
*Even if you find that the Table Formats supplied for AutoFormat are not
acceptable to you, they will give you some ideas of the different types of
appearance that can be applied to your data. Also it is useful to view some
of the Workbooks supplied with Excel.*

Alignment and Orientation

The **Formatting Toolbar** provides control only of horizontal alignment. For vertical alignment, fill, orientation, text wrap and justification, you must use the **Alignment Tab** of the **Format Cells** dialogue box:

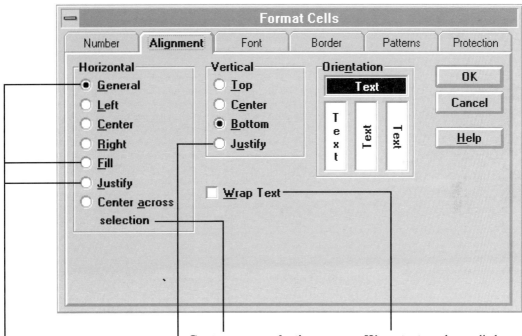

Horizontal Alignment: Left   Centre   Right   Centre across selection

General means left for text and right for numbers.

Fill means to repeat character(s) across the width of cell.

Justify means to wrap text and to increase inter word gaps to give alignment to the right as well as the left.

Centre across selection means centre the contents of the left hand cell of the selection across the width of the selection.

Vertical Justify means to wrap the text and to increase the inter line gaps (leading) so that the lines of text fill the row height.

Wrap text can be applied to both horizontal and vertical alignment. It constrains the text to the width of the cell, splitting it into lines. The height of the containing row is adjusted automatically to accommodate the extra lines.

Horizontal and Vertical Alignment

All text samples, to show differences in horizontal alignment, are stored in column E.

For centre across columns, E5:G5 were selected before using the Format Cells command.

All text, to show vertical alignment, is stored in row 11. Each case uses centre horizontal alignment.

The height of row 11 was made sufficiently large to show differences between vertical alignments.

	A	B	C	D	E	F	G	H	I
1	Horizontal Alignment								
2	Left:				Sample of Text				
3	Centre:				Sample of Text				
4	Right:				Sample of Text				
5	Centre Across Columns E to G:					Sample of Text			
6	Centre with Text Wrap:				Sample of Text				
7	Fill means repeat text (here full stop):				....				
8									
9	Vertical Alignment								
10		Top		Centre		Bottom		Centre with Text Wrap	
11	Sample of Text		Sample of Text		Sample of Text			Sample of Text	
12									

Comparison of Text Wrap and Justification

The example on the next page shows the difference between text wrap and justification. Two long samples of text have been used for these illustrations, so long that in the cells which were aligned left, the text has run off the display.

The first sample contains a complete paragraph with no line breaks. The second sample contains five separate lines and also illustrates the use of tabs. The keys required to do this are:

Remember
The Enter key alone or the Tab key alone will terminate the entry of data into a cell.

Newline: **Alt + Enter**

Tab: **Ctrl   +   Alt + Tab**

	A	B	C	D	E
1	Horizontal Alignment = Left				
2		To demonstrate text wrap and justification, it is necessary to show a few lines. Her			
3		First Line□Second Line with No Indent□		Tab Once□	Tab Twice□
4					
5	Horizontal Alignment = Left with Text Wrap			Horizontal Alignment = Left with Text Wrap	
6	Row Height is adjusted automatically			Row Height is adjusted automatically	
7		To demonstrate text wrap and justification, it is necessary to show a few lines. Here Excel is providing basic word processing techniques!		First Line Second Line with No Indent Tab Once Tab Twice Tab Three Times	
8					
9	Horizontal Alignment = Justify			Horizontal Alignment = Justify	
10	Row Height is adjusted automatically			Row Height is adjusted automatically	
11		To demonstrate text wrap and justification, it is necessary to show a few lines. Here Excel is providing basic word processing techniques!		First Line Second Line with No Indent Tab Once Tab Twice Tab Three Times	

Observe the difference between text wrap and justification. In each case Text Wrap is applied to subdivide the paragraph into lines so that maximum number of words are fitted on each line up to the limit imposed by the cell width. Justification also expands the inter word gaps.

For this sample of text, there is no difference between Text Wrap and Justification, since the text sample consists of five separate lines, each sufficiently short to fit the cell width. Note that special keyboard combinations are necessary to produce linefeeds and tabs (see previous page).

Orientation

The adjustment of orientation is indicated clearly from the graphic selection boxes but the application may not be so obvious. This screen shows one application where the column headings are longer than the abbreviated data entries.

	A	B	C	D	E	F	G
1							
2		Name				Personal	
3		Surname	Initials	Title	Sex	Marital Status	Religion
4		Brown	A.B	Ms	F		CE
5		Jones	C	Mr	M	M	RC
6		Smith	F.R.J	Miss	F	S	
7							
8							

Fonts, Font Styles and Sizes

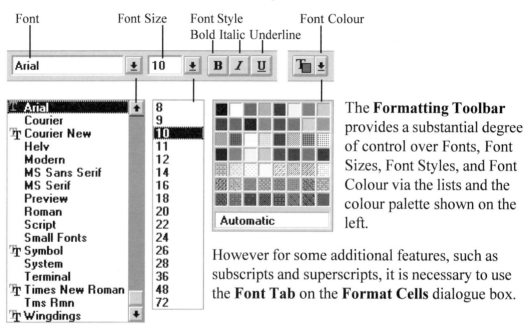

Font   Font Size   Font Style   Font Colour
                       Bold Italic Underline

The **Formatting Toolbar** provides a substantial degree of control over Fonts, Font Sizes, Font Styles, and Font Colour via the lists and the colour palette shown on the left.

However for some additional features, such as subscripts and superscripts, it is necessary to use the **Font Tab** on the **Format Cells** dialogue box.

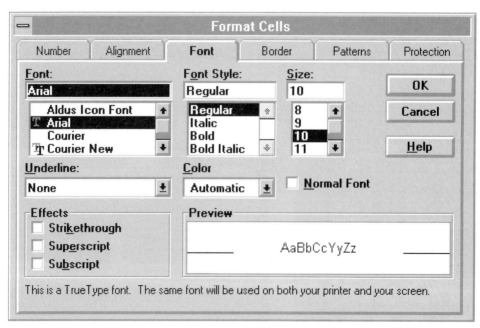

	A	B	C	D	E	F	G	H	I	J
1										
2	Fonts versus		Regular		Bold			Italic		
3	Font Styles									
4	Arial:		Sample of Text		**Sample of Text**			*Sample of Text*		
5										
6	Courier New:		Sample of Text		**Sample of Text**			*Sample of Text*		
7										
8	Times New Roman:		Sample of Text		**Sample of Text**			*Sample of Text*		
9										
10	Symbol:		Σαωπλε οφ Τεξτ		**Σαμπλε οφ Τεξτ**			*Σαμπλε οφ Τεξτ*		
11										
12	Wingdings:		♠☜○□◆ℜ □⊀		♠☜○□◆ℜ □⊀ ✿ℜ⊠◆			♠☜○□◆ℜ □⊀ ✿ℜ⊠◆		
13										
14										
15										
16			Single		Double		Single Accounting		Double Accounting	
17										
18	Underlines:		<u>Sample of Text</u>		<u>Sample of Text</u>		<u>Sample of</u> Text		<u>Sample of</u> Text	
19										

*Note: The above example compares five '**TruType**' fonts, which have the advantage of displaying on screen exactly what will be printed, whatever the printer type.*

*Note: The '**Accounting**' underlines give continuous underlines which are restricted to the width of the containing cell (and any overflow cells to its left).*

Tip
Try using as a toggle the keyboard short-cuts:
CTRL + B   *for Bold*
CTRL + I   *for Italic*
CTRL + U   *for Underline*

Formatting Characters within a Cell

To format individual characters, go into edit mode, either on the formula bar or directly at the cell. Select the character(s) to be formatted by clicking and dragging the mouse. Then apply the format required, such as font, style, size, ... using the Format Menu or the Formatting Toolbar.

	A	B	C	D	E
1	Character Formatting Within a Cell				
2					
3	Original:			FastPrint 24	
4					
5	Font Style:			FastPrint **24**	
6		*Note: the need for Kerning!*			
7	Font Size:			F$_{ast}$P$_{rint}$ 24	
8					
9	Subscripts and Superscripts:			H_2SO_4	
10				$18°C$	
11		$y = a_0 + a_1 x + a_2 x^2 + a_3 x^3 + ...$			

Cell Borders

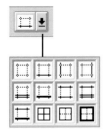

As usual, the **Formatting Toolbar** provides a substantial choice of borders but for the full range of options you have to use the **Format Cells** dialogue box **Borders Tab**, shown on the next page. For a clearer picture of the somewhat small icons on the **Border Button** list, the example below was prepared. Here the three by four format follows the order of the border icons. In each sample of two by two cells, the selection has been shaded in grey to identify the selection and the corresponding icon pressed.

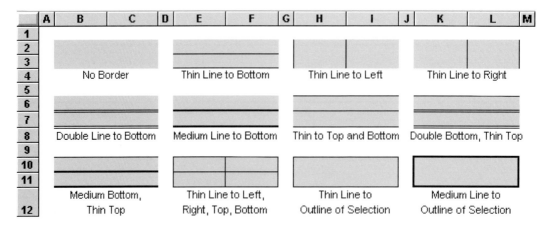

To apply these Border patterns, it is necessary to overwrite the patterns. For the example below, this was done by the following sequence:

1   Cells C2:G6 were selected and the 'Thin Line to Left' icon clicked

2   Cells C2:G2, B6:G6, B3:B6, G2:G6 were selected in turn and the 'Medium Line to Outline' icon was clicked.

Note
Once a Border Icon is selected from the list, this choice will be offered next in the Border button, ready for use.

	A	B	C	D	E	F	G
1							
2			Qtr 1	Qtr 2	Qtr 3	Qtr 4	Totals
3		1991:	£8,000	£10,000	£15,000	£12,000	£45,000
4		1992:	£9,000	£11,000	£17,000	£13,000	£50,000
5		1993:	£10,000	£12,000	£19,000	£14,000	£55,000
6		Totals:	£27,000	£33,000	£51,000	£39,000	£150,000

The Border tab gives better control and more choice but takes longer to use. Select the Border first and then the Style. Four line thicknesses, a double line and two dotted lines are available, as well as no line to clear a border. A combination of borders may be applied to a range of cells. A colour palette is also available.

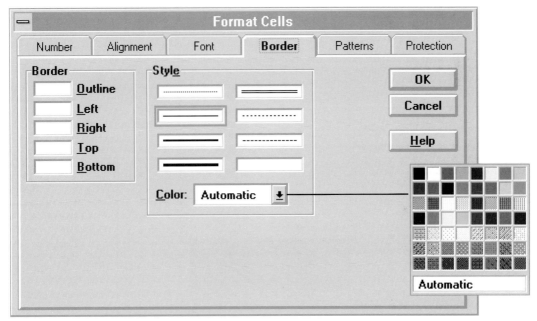

The following sequence was used on the example below:

1   Cells D3:F5 were selected and the left border was set to the thin line.

2   Cell ranges C2:G2 and B6:G6 were selected together (by pressing CTRL key) and the left border was set to thin line and the outline to double line.

3   Cell ranges B3:B6 and G2:G6 were selected together and the outline was set to double line.

	A	B	C	D	E	F	G
1							
2			Qtr 1	Qtr 2	Qtr 3	Qtr 4	Totals
3		1991:	£8,000	£10,000	£15,000	£12,000	£45,000
4		1992:	£9,000	£11,000	£17,000	£13,000	£50,000
5		1993:	£10,000	£12,000	£19,000	£14,000	£55,000
6		Totals:	£27,000	£33,000	£51,000	£39,000	£150,000

Background Colours and Patterns

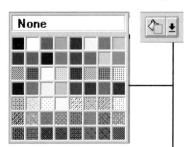

The **Colour Button** on the **Formatting Toolbar** gives access to the same colour palette as the **Patterns Tab** of the **Format Cells** dialogue box but it is more convenient to use. You only need to use the Patterns tab if you require the additional black and white patterns, provided in the Pattern palette.

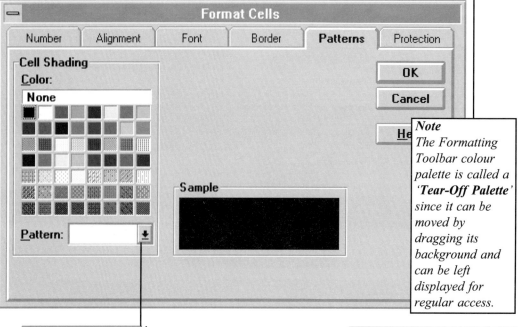

Note
The Formatting Toolbar colour palette is called a ***'Tear-Off Palette'*** *since it can be moved by dragging its background and can be left displayed for regular access.*

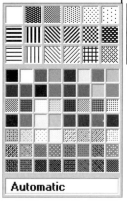

These are patterns supplied additionally to the colours in the Pattern palette.

The use of background colours has been illustrated in previous chapters by the reports produced automatically by Excel. This simple example illustrates another feature of reversing out text by changing the font colour.

	A	B	C
1			
2		*FastPrint 24*	
3			
4		*FastPrint 24*	
5			
6		*FastPrint 24*	
7			
8		*FastPrint 24*	

Using the Format Painter

The **Format Painter** button is located on the **Standard Toolbar**, being placed in the Cut, Copy and Paste group. Its action is very powerful for copying the formats of cells:

1 Suppose in the example below, you had experimented with the formatting for the cell B2, eventually settling for 'Times New Roman' 16 Point, Bold and Italic, Left Alignment with a light grey Background Colour. You can save time setting up the format again for other cells.

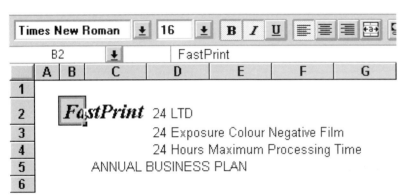

Tip

Although this technique is very fast for copying the formats of a single cell or of a range of cells with a uniform format, it can prove less efficient if the format has an outline border or strips of background colours.

Either...

2 With the cell selected, which contains the required format, click the Format Painter button. The 'paintbrush' icon will be attached to the pointer 'plus' icon.

3 Select cell or cell range to which copied format is to be applied, e.g. B2:I5.

4 Repeat steps 2 and 3 as many times as necessary.

Or keeping Format Painter pointer active...

2 With the cell selected, which contains the required format, *double* click the Format Painter button. The 'paintbrush' icon will be attached to the pointer 'plus' icon.

3 Select cells *and* cell ranges to which copied format is to be applied.

4 Click Format Painter button to cancel.

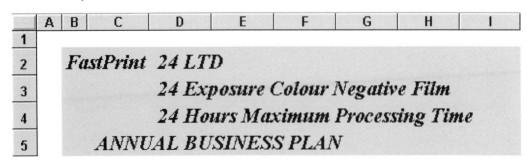

Number Formatting

Using the Formatting Toolbar

The Formatting of Numbers, Fractions, Percentages, Dates, etc. is more complex than the types of formatting covered so far. For most, the Formatting Toolbar will provide sufficient control:

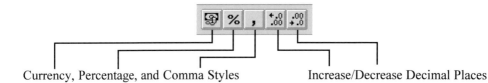

Currency, Percentage, and Comma Styles   Increase/Decrease Decimal Places

Tip
If the currency style does not appear as shown, you may have to adjust it:
*From **Format** menu, select **Style...** command. Click **Modify...** button. Select the 'Currency' category. Select format "#,##0.00; [Red]#,##0.00"*

It is not apparent from these toolbar icons that when you use them, you are applying three 'Format Styles'. (see next section.) This means that if one of the three styles is applied, then it will override whatever format was applied previously. The sequence for using these five icons is:

First: apply one of the three styles.
Second: if required adjust the decimal places.

The example below illustrates this. Here the number '1250.7' was keyed in and stored in the body of the table. Initially it was displayed in the 'General Format', i.e. '1250.7'. The two stage process was used to change the formats. The blank cells were left where it was not possible to reduce the decimal places.

	A	B	C	D	E	F	G	H
1								
2		(2) Second Adjust			(1) First Select Style:			
3		Decimal Places			General Format	Currency Style	Percentage Style	Comma Style
5		Decrease Twice:				£1,251		1,251
6		Decrease Once:			1251	£1,250.7		1,250.7
7		No Change:			1250.7	£1,250.70	125070%	1,250.70
8		Increase Once:			1250.70	£1,250.700	125070.0%	1,250.700
9		Increase Twice:			1250.700	£1,250.7000	125070.00%	1,250.7000

Using the Format Cells Number Tab

The Formatting Toolbar should provide sufficient control of number formats for most users. If this is not the case then you will need to familiarise yourself with the 'Format Codes' used in the Number Tab. The procedure to use these codes is:

1   Select the cell(s) to be formatted. In the example below, a cell containing the number '-1250.7' was selected.

2   Select the **Category**, in this case 'Number'.

3   Select the **Format Code**. In this example, '0'.

Note
*The **All** Category lists all the format codes. The other categories give more specialised groupings.*

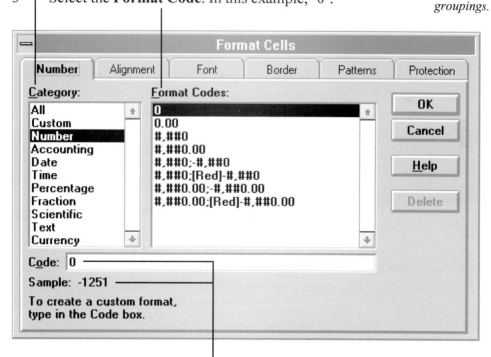

4   The **Code** applied will be displayed together with the **Sample** which shows the result of applying this code to selected cell.

Sections for Number Format Codes

Number format codes may have up to four sections separated by semicolons.

First Section gives format for positive numbers.	;	Second Section gives format for negative numbers.	;	Third Section gives format for zeros.	;	Last Section gives format for text.

e.g.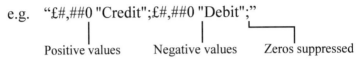

"£#,##0 "Credit";£#,##0 "Debit";"

Positive values   Negative values   Zeros suppressed

Symbols for Number Formats Codes

Since there is an extensive range of symbols, only the more important ones will be summarised here.

Digit Placeholders (# and **0**)

is used to allocate locations for digits. If situated before the decimal point, it will display any number of digits. If there are no digits before the point, then it will display none, as it suppresses non significant leading zeros. If situated after the decimal point, each # represents one digit, except that trailing zeros will be suppressed.

0   is used similarly except that all zeros, whether leading or trailing will be displayed.

Conventionally these two placeholders are used together so that "#0.00" would display a number rounded to two decimal places with at least one digit if only zero before the decimal point.

Commas (**,**) are used to display commas as thousand sub-divisions, e.g. "#,##0.00".

Colours may be displayed on monitor by starting the format with the colour in brackets, e.g. "[Green]£#,##0;[Red](£#.##0)".

Text can be displayed by inserting it in double quotes.

To understand these symbols better, you should investigate the codes provided. In the examples which follow, the top cell in each case is formatted in the Normal style, as keyed in. The rest are formatted in the order of the Format Codes for the Category.

Currency Category

The number '-1250.7' was keyed in and copied to other cells.

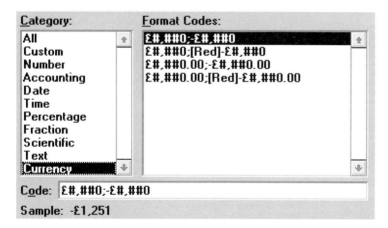

Note the rounding to nearest pound for the first and second format codes.

Note the grey of second and fourth codes, which indicates red on display.

Percentage Category

Here the fraction '0.175' was keyed in and copied to lower cells.

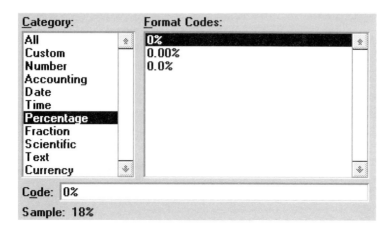

Note the rounding to nearest whole number for the first format code.

Note the trailing zero given by the second code.

Date Category

Here the date and time were keyed into the upper cell in the form "11-1-94 7:20" and copied to other cells below.

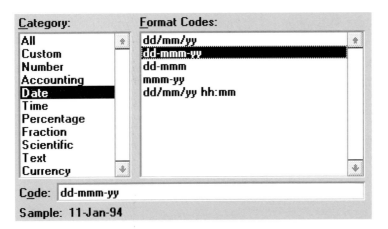

Note
*Code **mm** gives digit abbreviation for month, **mmm** gives three letter abbreviation and **mmmm** will give the full spelling.*

Customising a Format Code

To customise a format code, either key in the new code in the code box or edit an existing code as indicated below.

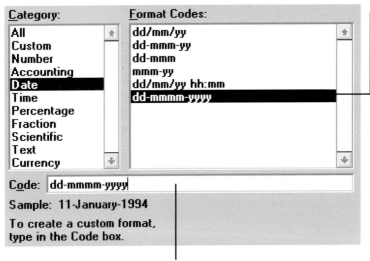

Note
*Subsequently your new code will be stored automatically in the current category, in the **All** category and in the **Custom** category.*

Note
*To remove custom format codes, highlight the code and click the **Delete** button.*

Tip *To key in or edit Format Code, point to code box and click to insert the I-beam and use the editing keys used for editing on the formula bar or for editing at a cell.*

Conditional Number Formats

By preceding the number format by a condition within square brackets, it is possible to set up more complex custom formats. Consider this example for very large sums of money. The left hand column contains a growth series in Normal style. The right hand column displays the same values using the custom format below. Observe the rounding of the displayed numbers. There are three formats separated by semicolons:

1.25	£1
12.5	£13
125	£125
1250	£1,250
12500	£12,500
125000	£125,000
1250000	£M1
12500000	£M13
125000000	£M125
1250000000	£B1
1.25E+10	£B13
1.25E+11	£B125
1.25E+12	£B1,250

Note
The Normal style reverts to scientific format for very large numbers.

 If the value exceeds one billion, then the first format is applied.

 If it exceeds one million, the second format is used.

 Otherwise the last format is applied.

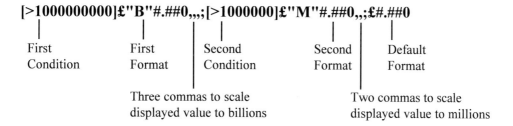

[>1000000000]£"B"#.##0,,,;[>1000000]£"M"#.##0,,;£#.##0

First Condition	First Format	Second Condition	Second Format	Default Format

Three commas to scale displayed value to billions

Two commas to scale displayed value to millions

The above example should give you some idea of the power of customised number formats. However there are far more format symbols for use in these codes than it has been possible to illustrate here. To find out more about these, use the Help system.

Note
The definition used here for a billion was a thousand million (not a million million)!

Also it is worthwhile looking at the number codes in the more specialised categories such as time, fractions, accounting and scientific.

Using Format Styles

It has been seen that considerable time and effort may be used in setting up the various combinations of formats for a spreadsheet. It is advantageous to store these specifications in 'Styles' which can be applied easily and quickly to selections of cells. This is similar to the style facility used in word processing and desktop publishing where combinations of formats are applied to paragraphs.

Tip
Keep the style simple! Select only single cells or cells which have identical formatting. Styles are not suitable for ranges of cells with different outline borders.

Note
Initially, the Style Name list box will contain only the default 'Normal' style and the 'Comma', 'Currency' and 'Percent' styles available on the Formatting Toolbar.

Creating New Styles

1   Select the formatted cell for which you wish to create the style.

2   From the **Format** menu, select the **Style...** option.

3   The **Style** dialogue box will be displayed.

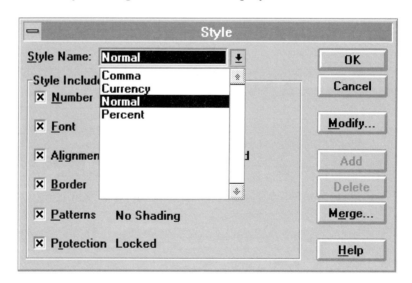

4   Key in the name of the new style. The **Style** dialogue box will list the format specification of the selected cell, as shown on the next page.

5   Complete the **Style** dialogue box.

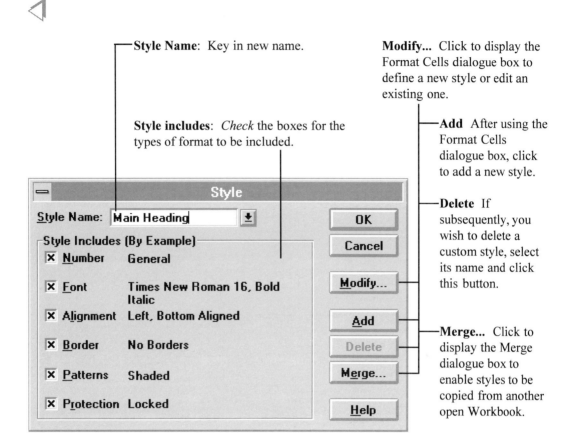

Style Name: Key in new name.

Style includes: *Check* the boxes for the types of format to be included.

Modify... Click to display the Format Cells dialogue box to define a new style or edit an existing one.

Add After using the Format Cells dialogue box, click to add a new style.

Delete If subsequently, you wish to delete a custom style, select its name and click this button.

Merge... Click to display the Merge dialogue box to enable styles to be copied from another open Workbook.

Applying Styles

1   Select the cell or range of cells to be formatted.

2   From the **Format** menu, select the **Style...** command.

3   In the **Style** dialogue box, select the name required and click the OK button or press Enter.

Remember
If you apply a style to previously formatted cells, the formatting of newly applied style will override the original format.

If you edit a style, then all cells previously formatted with that style name will have their formats updated.

Formatting and the Edit Menu

Certain commands and sub-menus on the **Edit** menu are particularly relevant to formatting:

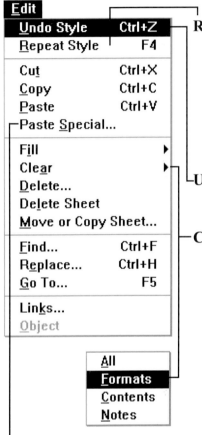

Repeat Style: If you have just used the Format Style command to apply a style to format cells, then the Repeat Style command becomes available. If you need to apply the same style to several ranges of cells, this can save you time in using the Style dialogue box and locating the style name.

Undo Style: Correspondingly, the Undo command becomes replaced by the Undo Style command.

Clear: The Clear sub-menu allows you to specify what is cleared from the selected cell(s), i.e. 'Contents', 'Formats', 'Notes' or 'All' three.

To clear 'All', it is easier to use the 'Delete' key. Unfortunately this causes confusion with the 'Delete' command, which removes the containing cells as well, replacing them with surrounding cells!

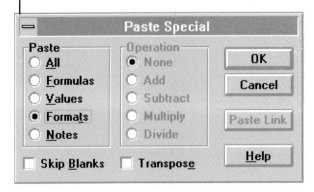

Paste Special... This command becomes available when you have selected a cell and used the Copy (but not Cut) command . The dialogue box enables you to specify 'Formats' only, although it is easier to use the Formatting Toolbar Format Painter.

Printing
Worksheets

In easy steps

Overview

Just as Formatting enables you to style your spreadsheets to the same standards that can be achieved by word processing and desktop publishing programs, Printing enables you to exploit the full potential of your printer, just as these other programs do. Ideally, a Postscript printer is best, but remarkably high quality output can be achieved on much cheaper bubble jet printers!

However for spreadsheets, there is an additional objective. For desktop publishing and word processing, the document is made to fit a target page size as the text and graphics are introduced. Many users of spreadsheets concentrate on the calculations and only think about subdividing them into the pages of a report at a later stage. Invariably the resulting spreadsheet will not fit on a single (say A4) page. Although more of a spreadsheet can be accommodated on a printed page than can be viewed in a window on a screen, you are faced with subdividing either a long or a wide spreadsheet, or a spreadsheet, which is both wide and long, into several pages. Also it must convey the information clearly when subdivided into the separated pages of a report.

The technique of achieving this is usually by trial and error. Fortunately an excellent Print Preview is provided which facilitates such tests and avoids outputting to the printer until you are satisfied. Typically you will allow Excel initially to subdivide the spreadsheet automatically inserting its own page breaks. You will then progressively adjust these sub-divisions by introducing manual page breaks, repeating row or column headings from page to page, and adjusting the magnification of the printout to fit the page.

Although this Chapter cannot show the full trial and error process, it will illustrate a typical sequence. It will use the 'FastPrint 24' Monthly and Annual Plans as examples of long and wide spreadsheets. Both plans have been given a very simple format to emphasize their main results.

Selecting Printer via Windows

You should first make sure that a printer is selected which is capable of supporting graphics. This is usually done from the Windows operating system:

1   From the Windows' **Program Manager** screen, *double-click* the **Main** group icon to display its window.

2   On the **Main** window, *double click* the **Control Panel** icon.

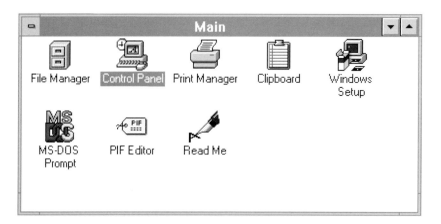

3   On the **Control Panel** window, click the **Printers** icon.

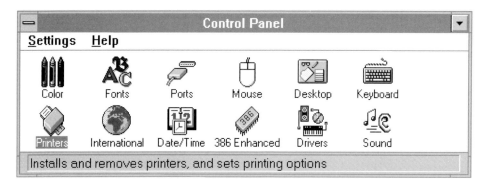

4   In the **Printers** dialogue box, select the Printer required or click the Add>> button if its driver is not already installed.

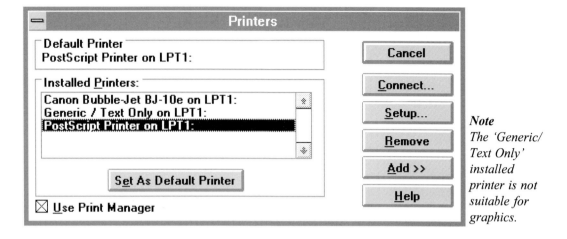

Note
The 'Generic/
Text Only'
installed
printer is not
suitable for
graphics.

File Menu versus Standard Toolbar

Most of the commands required to set up the Worksheet within
Excel are available from the Command Menus, mainly under
File. Only two commands are available from the **Standard
Toolbar**.

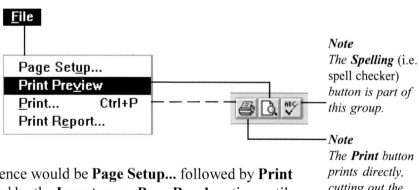

Note
*The **Spelling** (i.e.*
spell checker)
button is part of
this group.

Note
*The **Print** button*
prints directly,
cutting out the
Print dialogue
box.

The usual sequence would be **Page Setup...** followed by **Print
Preview** assisted by the **Insert** menu **Page Break** option until
the preview is satisfactory. Finally **Print...** would be used.
Examples follow to illustrate their use...

Setting Up the Printed Page

The **File** menu **Page Setup...** option displays the Page Setup dialogue box, which has four tabs. The **Page** and **Sheet** tabs require some initial settings. The **Margins** and **Header/Footer** defaults will be accepted for now but we will return to these in later sections.

Page Setup 'Page' Tab

Complete the dialogue box.

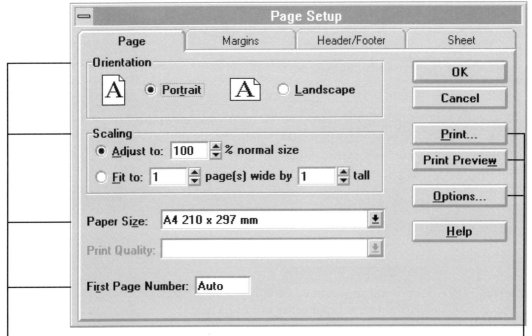

Orientation: Normally Portrait is required although for wide spreadsheets and charts Landscape can be useful.

Scaling: We will return to this.

Paper Size: Select from list.

First Page Number: Accept 'Auto' default or key in starting page number if this printout is to form part of a report.

All the Tabs in this dialogue box give the set of commands on the right hand side.

Print and **Print Preview...** gives you direct access to these commands. The latter facilitates testing, enabling you to switch between Page Setup and Print Preview.

Options... displays a printer Options dialogue box.

Page Setup 'Sheet' Tab

Here the dialogue box has been completed for the 'FastPrint 24'
'Monthly Plan' worksheet.

Page Setup

| Page | Margins | Header/Footer | **Sheet** |

Print Area: $A$1:$I$75

Print Titles
Rows to Repeat at Top: $1:$5

Columns to Repeat at Left:

Print
☐ Gridlines   ☒ Black and White
☐ Notes   ☐ Row and Column Headings
☐ Draft Quality

Page Order
○ Down, then Across
● Across, then Down

OK

Cancel

Print...

Print Preview

Options...

Help

Print Area: Although not strictly required, it is good practice to specify the area to which printing is to be restricted. This is because there may be some peripheral calculations which have been made to one side and are not appropriate in a final report. You simply key in the cell range.

Print Titles: There is an option to repeat a set of rows at the top of each page or to repeat a set of columns on the left of each page. To illustrate this the first five rows, which contain the main heading, have been keyed in.

Print: Various options may be checked/unchecked. Here Gridlines, Notes, Draft Quality, Row and Column Headings have been suppressed. The **Black and White** option is normally required to convert a colour display to greys.

Page Order: This makes no difference for these examples, but generally for wide spreadsheets, it seems more appropriate to print across first.

Inspection of the 'Monthly Plan' Worksheet will show that, as a result of Page Setup, it is now intersected by dashed lines.

	A	B	C	D	E	F	G	H	I	J
51				Monthly Average =				£33.33		
52		Maintenance		Annual Average =		£500.00				
53				Monthly Average =				£41.67		
54		Telephone		Annual Average =		£300.00				
55				Monthly Average =				£25.00		
56		Rent/Rates		Annual Average =		£6,000.00				
57				Monthly Average =				£500.00		
58		Capital Costs								
59			Processing Equipment =			£35,000.00				
60			Fitting out Shop =			£5,000.00				
61			Total Capital Costs =			£40,000.00				
62										
63		Monthly Lease Rates per £1000 borrowed								
64		Years	Rates							
65			1	£89.08						
66			2	£47.31						
67			3	£33.45						
68			4	£26.58		Lease Term in Years =		5		
69			5	£22.50		Monthly Lease Costs =		£900.00		
70										
71		Average Monthly Expenses =							£1,616.67	
72										
73	Net Profit									
74		Average Monthly Net Profit =							£1,325.28	
75		Percentage of Sales =							19.2%	
76										

Scenario Summary \ **Monthly Plan** / Annual Plan / Sh

The Bold Dashed Lines indicate the extent of the Print Area that was selected in the Page Setup dialogue box, i.e. $A$1:$I$75.

The Fine Dashed Lines show the position of the Automatic Page Breaks which have been inserted by Excel.

The above indicates that Excel has subdivided the Worksheet into four pages. Two pages down were expected to cover the length of the spreadsheet. Two pages across are less desirable because it makes the report difficult to follow and only the final column of monthly totals appear on the right hand pages.

The Print Preview command shows the overall layout more clearly, although the fine detail is less distinct. (see opposite page of 4 Print Preview views.)

Note: Heading repeated from first five rows.

Note: Automatic page breaks are placed between columns H and I and between rows 55 and 56.

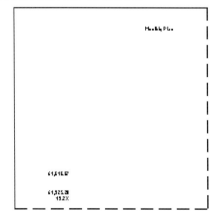

Inserting Manual Page Breaks

Often it will be necessary for you to override the automatic page breaks inserted by Excel. For the 'FastPrint 24' example, the section on the 'Expenses' starts at the bottom of one page and continues on another. There is sufficient room to move the whole section onto the next page. The procedure for inserting page breaks manually is simple:

1   Select the *row* or *column* or *cell* at which the new page is to start as follows...

Row:	Select the row which is to form the top line of next page.
Column:	Select the column which is to form the left most column of next page.
Cell:	Select the cell which is to form the top left cell of next page.

In this example row 45 is selected.

2   From the **Insert** menu select the **Page Break** option. A course dashed line will show the new page break position, which will override Excel's automatic page break.

	A	B	C	D	E	F	G	H	I	J
40										
41	Gross Profit									
42		Average Monthly Gross Profit =							£2,941.95	
43		Percentage of Sales =							42.7%	
44										
45	Expenses									
46		Accountancy		Annual Average =		£400.00				
47				Monthly Average =				£33.33		
48		Advertising		Annual Average =		£1,000.00				
49				Monthly Average =				£83.33		
50		Insurance		Annual Average =		£400.00				
51				Monthly Average =				£33.33		

Note
*To remove manual page breaks, either make the individual selections described above (or select the whole worksheet by clicking the **Select All** button) and apply the **Insert** menu **Remove Page Break** command.*

Adjusting Margins and Page Alignment

The **Page Setup** dialogue box **Margins** Tab enables you to set the margins and choose the alignment on the page.

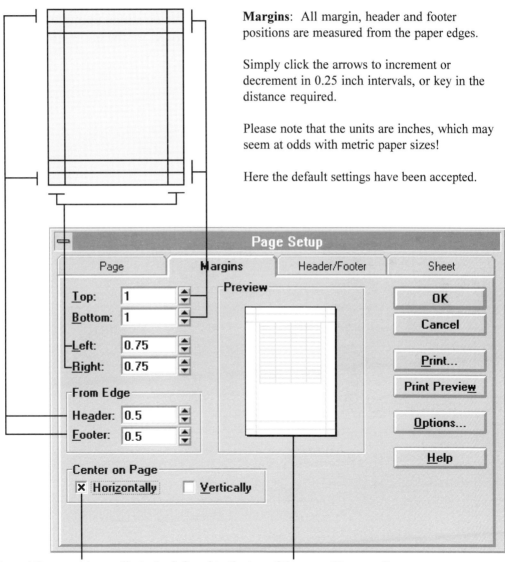

Margins: All margin, header and footer positions are measured from the paper edges.

Simply click the arrows to increment or decrement in 0.25 inch intervals, or key in the distance required.

Please note that the units are inches, which may seem at odds with metric paper sizes!

Here the default settings have been accepted.

Page Alignment is usually to the left and to the top of the page. However it can be centred either horizontally or vertically or both by checking the appropriate box(es). The sample gives a convenient indication of the effect. In this case Horizontal Centring is chosen.

Fitting Worksheet to Page

It is possible to incorporate the final column of 'FastPrint 24' 'Monthly Plan' into the left hand pages. In much earlier versions of Excel, you would have been obliged to try increasing the left and right margins, reducing the width of any columns which could be compressed and would still display the full information, or by reducing the type size used in cells. This took skill and time. The **Page** Tab of the **Page Setup** dialogue box enables you to *scale* the worksheet directly to the page size.

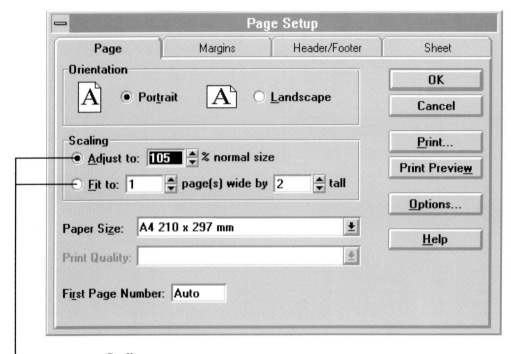

Scaling:

Either **Adjust To**: Click button and try increasing the percentage size of Worksheet to be fitted to the paper size less margins. Here 105% was found to be sufficient to accommodate the final column, reducing the number of pages by half.

Or **Fit to**: Click button and select the number of pages into which you wish the worksheet to be fitted.

After this adjustment, click the Print Preview button to display the results of the scaling.

Using Print Preview

The effect of all these adjustments can be constantly monitored by using the **Print Preview** command. The Print Preview window shows each page as it will be printed with margin settings, with manual and automatic page breaks, with scaling, with page alignment and with headers and footers in place. It can save time paper!

The disadvantage with Print Preview is apparent here! The display of an A4 page makes the fine detail un-readable. Only headings and any graphics enable you to locate the main sections of the report. Fortunately, the excellent Zoom facility enables you to view the fine detail and move about the page very easily.

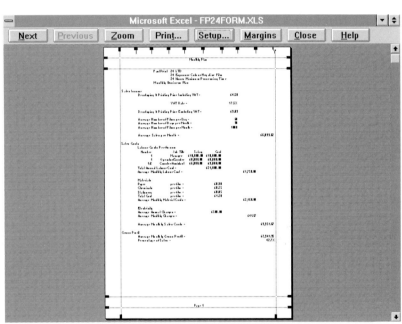

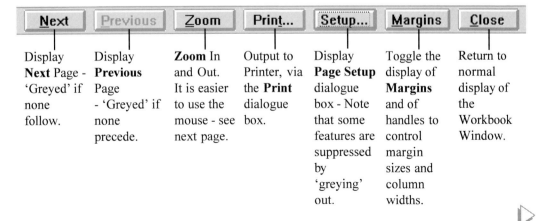

Next	**Previous**	**Zoom**	**Print...**	**Setup...**	**Margins**	**Close**
Display **Next** Page - 'Greyed' if none follow.	Display **Previous** Page - 'Greyed' if none precede.	**Zoom** In and Out. It is easier to use the mouse - see next page.	Output to Printer, via the **Print** dialogue box.	Display **Page Setup** dialogue box - Note that some features are suppressed by 'greying' out.	Toggle the display of **Margins** and of handles to control margin sizes and column widths.	Return to normal display of the Workbook Window.

Mouse Zoom Control

On the page, the pointer changes to a 'magnifying glass' icon. Position this and click to zoom in. Click the magnified view to zoom out again.

Margin Lines and Size Handles

The Margin button is used to toggle the display of margin lines and size handles. If mouse pointer is located at a handle or at intersections of columns, the icon changes to a line crossed with double headed arrow. You may drag to resize visually, although Setup gives better control.

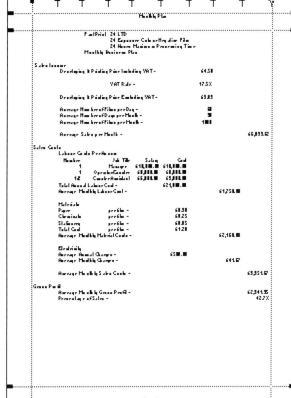

Summary so far

105% scaling has fitted the 'Monthly Plan' on two pages. The manual page break has moved the whole of the 'Expenses' section to the second page. The horizontal page alignment to centre has made little difference in this case. The repeat of first five lines has put the general heading at the top of each page. The automatic header gives the sheet name and the automatic footer gives the page numbers.

Editing Headers and Footers

To edit headers and footers, you must use the **Header/Footer Tab** on the **Page Setup** dialogue box.

Header:

- **List**: You may select a header from Excel's comprehensive list of built-in headers.
- **Sample**: Resulting header will be displayed in its format and location.
- **Custom Header...** Alternatively edit or create your own header. (See next page)

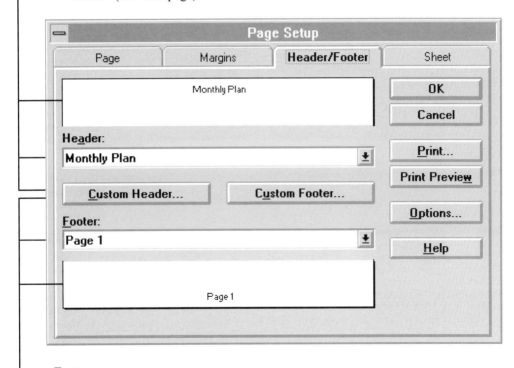

Footer:

- **List**: You may select a footer from Excel's comprehensive list of built-in footers.
- **Sample**: Resulting footer will be displayed in its format and location.
- **Custom Footer...** Alternatively edit or create your own footer. (See next page)

Both Header and Footer dialogue boxes have three boxes for storing information:
The Left has left alignment,
the Centre has centre,
and the Right box right.

To enter data or edit, simply point and click to place the text insertion point. A series of codes may be entered by clicking the buttons. The examples which follow use all the buttons.

Font Button displays Font dialogue box.

Page Number Button inserts code for page number.

Total Pages Button inserts code for total number of pages in Worksheet.

Date Button inserts code for current date.

Time Button inserts code for current time.

Filename Button inserts code for name of Workbook file.

Sheet Button inserts code for name of Worksheet.

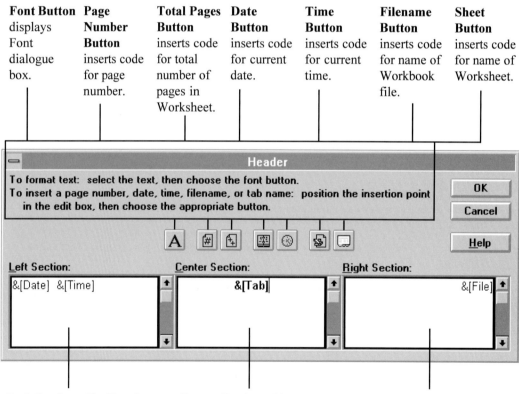

Left Section: The Date button is clicked, the space bar is pressed twice to introduce spacing and the Time button is clicked.

Centre Section: The Name button default is accepted but the line is selected and is made bold from the Font dialogue box, displayed by clicking the Font button.

Right Section: The File button is clicked.

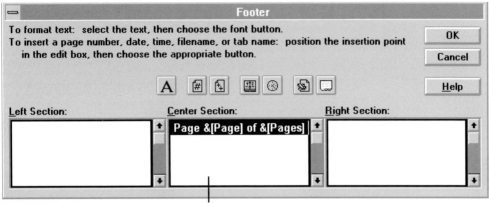

Centre Section only: The Default of the text "Page " and the Page code are accepted. To this is added the text " of " and the code for total number of pages in report. For this example the footer will show "Page 1 of 2". The line is selected and is made bold.

Page Setup dialogue box Header/Footer tab displays samples of headers and footers showing three sections with content, alignment and font formatting.

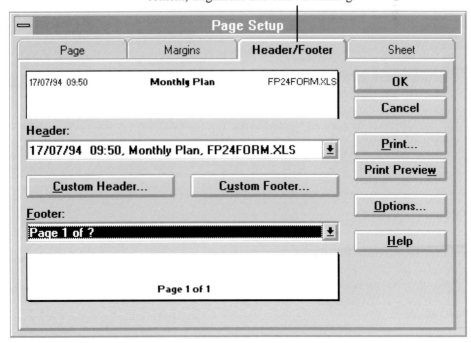

Using the File Print Command

Using the **File** menu **Print...** option displays the **Print** dialogue box, which should be completed as follows:

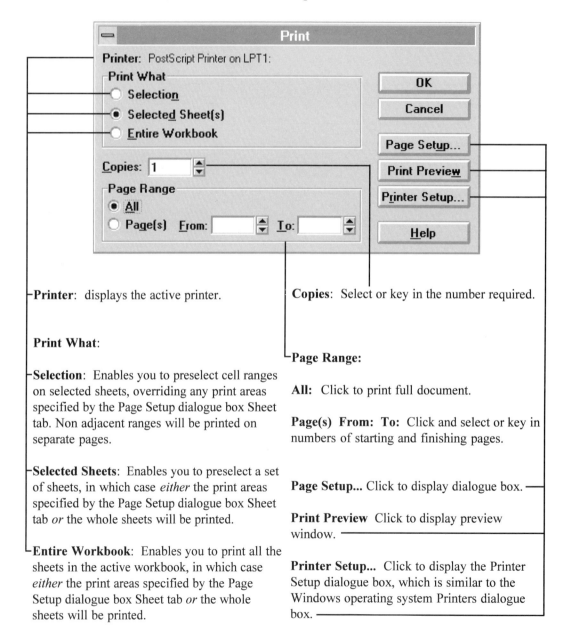

Printer: displays the active printer.

Print What:

Selection: Enables you to preselect cell ranges on selected sheets, overriding any print areas specified by the Page Setup dialogue box Sheet tab. Non adjacent ranges will be printed on separate pages.

Selected Sheets: Enables you to preselect a set of sheets, in which case *either* the print areas specified by the Page Setup dialogue box Sheet tab *or* the whole sheets will be printed.

Entire Workbook: Enables you to print all the sheets in the active workbook, in which case *either* the print areas specified by the Page Setup dialogue box Sheet tab *or* the whole sheets will be printed.

Copies: Select or key in the number required.

Page Range:

All: Click to print full document.

Page(s) From: To: Click and select or key in numbers of starting and finishing pages.

Page Setup... Click to display dialogue box.

Print Preview Click to display preview window.

Printer Setup... Click to display the Printer Setup dialogue box, which is similar to the Windows operating system Printers dialogue box.

Page Setup for 'Annual Plan'

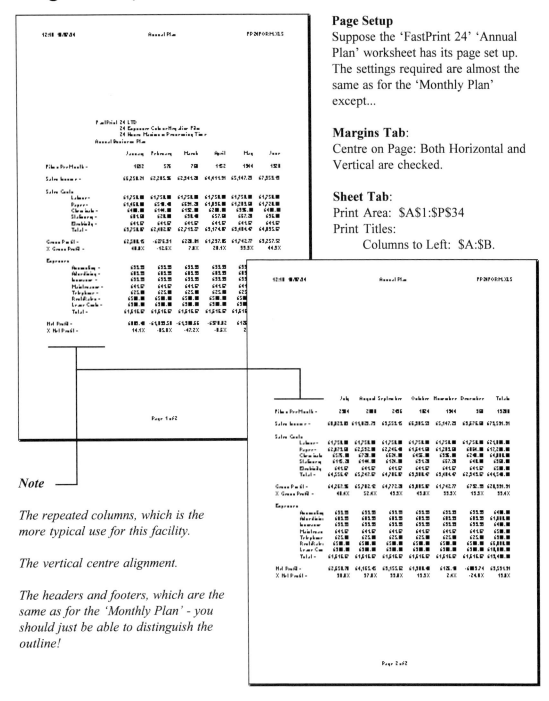

Page Setup

Suppose the 'FastPrint 24' 'Annual Plan' worksheet has its page set up. The settings required are almost the same as for the 'Monthly Plan' except...

Margins Tab:

Centre on Page: Both Horizontal and Vertical are checked.

Sheet Tab:

Print Area: $A$1:$P$34
Print Titles:
    Columns to Left: $A:$B.

Note

The repeated columns, which is the more typical use for this facility.

The vertical centre alignment.

The headers and footers, which are the same as for the 'Monthly Plan' - you should just be able to distinguish the outline!

Using View Manager

Tip
*Since the view
names apply to
worksheets it is
advisable to
include the sheet
name in the view
name as shown
here.*

The View Manager enables you to save different sets of
worksheet displays and print settings as named views:

1   Select the worksheet and set up its viewing and printing
     conditions. For this example the fully detailed views and
     the print settings used in previous sections for the
     'Monthly' and 'Annual' Plans of 'FastPrint 24' will be
     named.

Note
*The view manager
lists views only for
active worksheet.*

2   From the **View** menu select the **View Manager...** option.

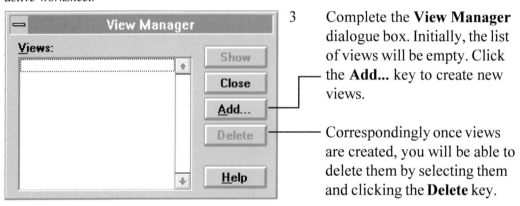

3   Complete the **View Manager**
     dialogue box. Initially, the list
     of views will be empty. Click
     the **Add...** key to create new
     views.

     Correspondingly once views
     are created, you will be able to
     delete them by selecting them
     and clicking the **Delete** key.

4   Key in the name of the
     view. In this case there
     are no **Hidden Rows
     & Columns** but this is
     normally checked.
     Print Settings must be
     checked.

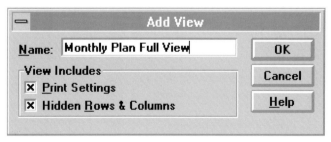

Correspondingly for this
example, the 'Annual Plan'
Worksheet is named
'Annual Plan Full View'.

*Note: If the view names were being used to store view
specifications, including hidden columns and formatting
information, more than one view would be named for each
sheet. To display such views, the name would be selected in
the View Manager dialogue box and the **Show** button
clicked.*

Using Print Report

The Print Report command combines several Worksheets into one report:

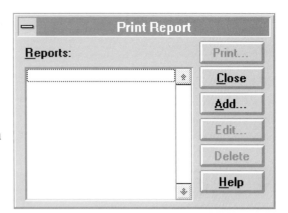

1   From the **File** menu, select the **Print Report...** option.

2   At first no reports will be listed in the **Print Report** dialogue box. Click the **Add...** key to create one.

3   Complete the **Add Report** dialogue box.

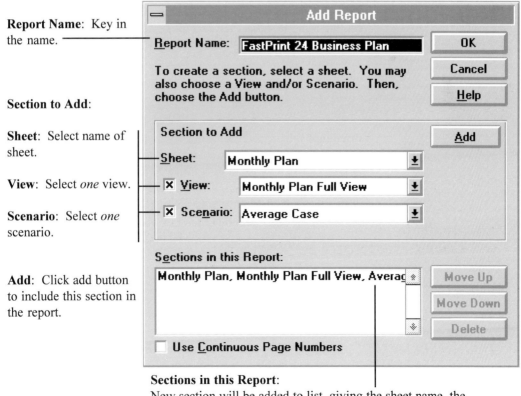

Report Name: Key in the name.

Section to Add:

Sheet: Select name of sheet.

View: Select *one* view.

Scenario: Select *one* scenario.

Add: Click add button to include this section in the report.

Sections in this Report:
New section will be added to list, giving the sheet name, the view name (if any) and the scenario name (if any).

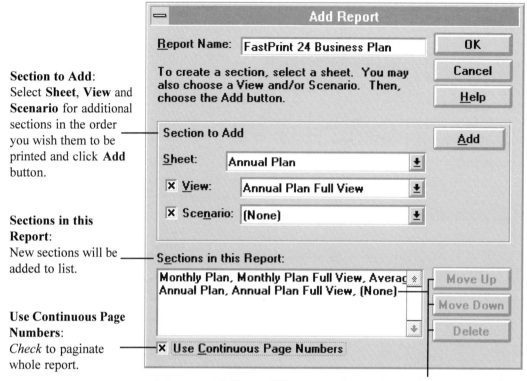

Section to Add:
Select **Sheet**, **View** and **Scenario** for additional sections in the order you wish them to be printed and click **Add** button.

Sections in this Report:
New sections will be added to list.

Use Continuous Page Numbers:
Check to paginate whole report.

Subsequent Editing: If later you wish to change the contents or the order of the sections, select a section and click **the Move Up, Move Down** or **Delete** buttons, as appropriate.

4   Click OK button to return to Print Report dialogue box.

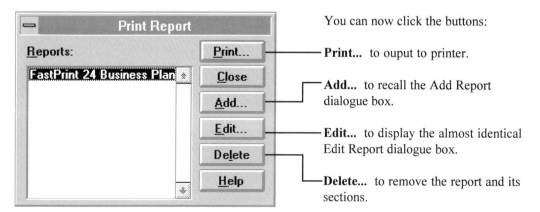

You can now click the buttons:

Print... to ouput to printer.

Add... to recall the Add Report dialogue box.

Edit... to display the almost identical Edit Report dialogue box.

Delete... to remove the report and its sections.

CHAPTER

12

Charts and Graphics

In easy Steps

Overview

Excel enables you to create charts and graphs to summarise or to further analyse your worksheet data. It also provides a comprehensive range of graphic objects to enhance presentation. This is done very easily and quickly to very high graphic standards. To achieve equivalent standards using pen and paper would take many hours of painstaking and skilful work.

To use these facilities successfully, it is necessary to understand that Excel provides two forms of chart.

> *An Embedded Chart* is produced on the worksheet which contains the data, so that it is displayed with its associated data. Like any other graphic objects, they are inserted on a transparent layer above the worksheet.

> *A Chart Sheet* is a chart on a separate sheet in the workbook devoted to displaying the chart, possibly because the information is too detailed to be compressed into part of a worksheet.

In either case the chart is directly linked to its data, just as dependent worksheets are linked to their source worksheets, so that when the source data is changed, the changes are reflected in the dependent chart almost instantaneously.

A distinction has also been made here between a Chart and a Graph. *A scientific graph* requires values for both the X and Y Axes. Excel uses the term 'XY (Scatter) Chart' for such cases. *A commercial chart* usually requires values only for the Y-Axis. The X-Axis is usually used to name the categories of data. The order of the categories may be significant, but the position isn't.

As usual there is a variety of ways of creating charts under your control or automatically, and of changing, editing and enhancing charts. This chapter will concentrate mainly on the commands and techniques available, using relatively few examples, rather than attempt to cover the large variety of combinations available.

Creating an Embedded Chart

Tip
Remember how to display the Chart Toolbar:
*From the **View** menu, select the **Toolbars...** command. In the dialogue box list check **Chart**.*

To illustrate the simplicity of creating an embedded chart, the simple data on quarterly sales over three years will be used again:

1   Carefully select the cells which contain the data required in the chart. In this case the range $B$2:$F$5 encloses the quarterly sales, the column headings for the four quarters and the row headings for the three years. The totals for the rows and columns have been excluded deliberately.

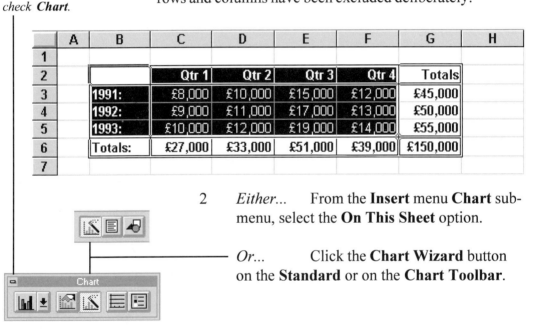

2   *Either...*   From the **Insert** menu **Chart** sub-menu, select the **On This Sheet** option.

Or...   Click the **Chart Wizard** button on the **Standard** or on the **Chart Toolbar**.

Tip
Alternatively just click the location of the top left hand corner of the containing rectangle if you wish Excel to size the chart. Either way, it is easy to adjust the size and position later.

3   The worksheet pointer will change to fine cross-hairs with a small chart icon attached. Point it to one corner of the chart's containing rectangle and **drag** it to the opposite corner. An **outline rectangle** will appear as you do this. Here the cross-hairs are dragged from the top left corner of cell $B$8 to the bottom right corner of cell $G$18.

4   On releasing the mouse button, the first dialogue box of a sequence of five **Chart Wizard** dialogue boxes will appear. Complete this as shown on the next page.

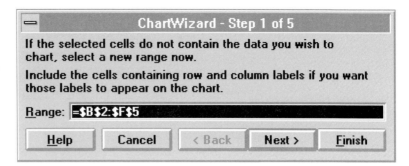

Range: You are asked to confirm that the selected range is correct. If this is not so, you can re-select the area of the worksheet or you may type in the correct range.

Next>: Since in this case the range is correct, the Next button is clicked to advance to next dialogue box.

Finish: This would be clicked only if you wished to complete the chart with all the default settings.

5   The Chart Wizard's second dialogue box enables you to select the Type of Chart.

Excel offers you 14 chart types together with the fifteenth alternative of a combination of certain types. Each chart type has several sub-types, which are offered at the next stage in the next dialogue box.

Here the default column chart, as highlighted, is accepted. In practice, it is useful to try the various options.

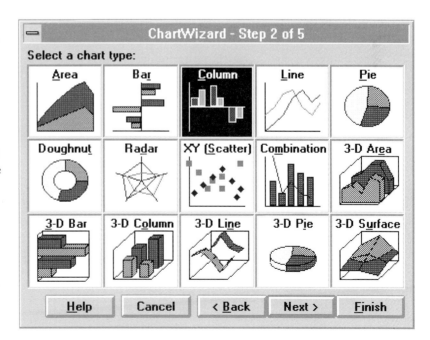

Next>: The Next button is clicked to advance to the next dialogue box.

◁

6   The Chart Wizard's third dialogue box enables you to
     select the Chart's sub-type or format.

Depending on the
type of chart, various
formats are offered.
Again in this case,
the default format is
accepted.

In practice, it is useful
to try the various
alternatives to
establish the clearest
format for your data.

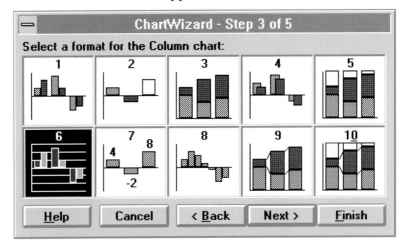

<Back: The Back button may be clicked to
return to the previous dialogue box.

Next>: The Next button is clicked to advance to
the next dialogue box.

7   The Chart Wizard's fourth dialogue box enables you to decide the order in
     which the selected data will be plotted and which rows or columns (if any)
     will be used for X-axis or for legend text. A proposed sample chart is given.

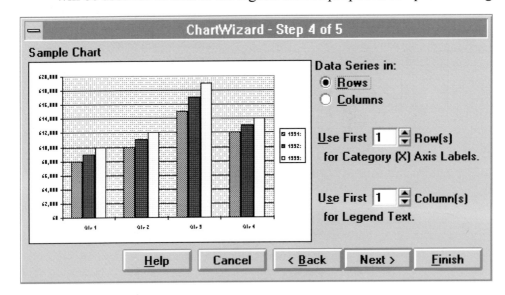

Data Series in: Here this is changed to columns to produce modified graph shown.

Use First Columns/Rows: Here the defaults are correct but zero could be needed.

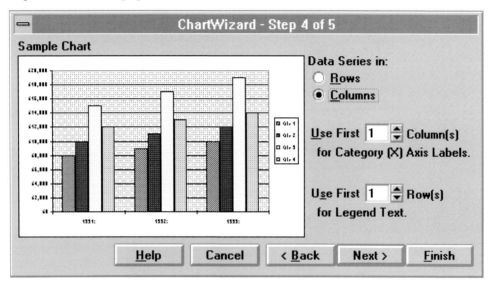

8   The Chart Wizard's fifth and final dialogue box enables you to insert supporting text.

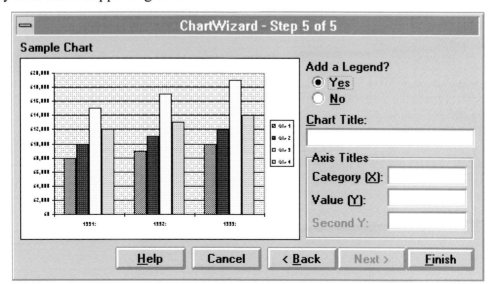

Add a Legend? Here the default 'Yes' is accepted.

Titles: The various titles may be keyed in or the cells selected which contain the text.

9   Finally clicking the **Finish** button, will produce the
     embedded chart as specified in the chosen location.

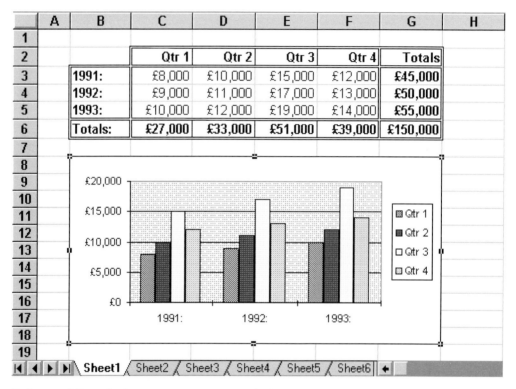

	A	B	C	D	E	F	G	H
1								
2			Qtr 1	Qtr 2	Qtr 3	Qtr 4	Totals	
3		1991:	£8,000	£10,000	£15,000	£12,000	£45,000	
4		1992:	£9,000	£11,000	£17,000	£13,000	£50,000	
5		1993:	£10,000	£12,000	£19,000	£14,000	£55,000	
6		Totals:	£27,000	£33,000	£51,000	£39,000	£150,000	

Sheet1 / Sheet2 / Sheet3 / Sheet4 / Sheet5 / Sheet6

Data Points and Data Series
A Data Point is a single value from worksheet, e.g. the value for Quarter 3 in 1992, i.e. £17,000.

A Data Series is a set of ordered data points, e.g. the values for Quarter 3 in the years 1991 to 1993 inclusive, i.e. £15,000, £17,000 and £19,000. This is why it was so critical to change the order to **columns**.

The column chart above contains four data series, corresponding to the four quarters. Each series is identified by the shading shown in the Legend.

Sizing and Moving an Embedded Chart
Since the embedded chart has sizing handles (small black boxes on the containing rectangle), it is said to be 'selected'.

As for any graphic object, it can be **sized**: Drag the middle handles on the horizontals or verticals to adjust the height or width respectively. Drag any corner handle to adjust the overall size. Hold down the **Shift** key to maintain the aspect ratio.

As for any graphic object, it can be **moved**: Point to anywhere inside the containing rectangle and drag to move the chart.

Creating a Chart Sheet

Chart sheets are slightly more simple to create than embedded charts. To illustrate this another almost identical chart will be produced for the quarterly sales:

1   Make the same data selection as for the embedded chart, i.e. the range $B$2:$F$5.

2   From the **Insert** menu **Chart** sub-menu, select the **As New Sheet** option. (No equivalent button on Toolbars)

[3   The third step to size the containing rectangle is omitted, since Excel will automatically size the chart on new sheet.]

4   Chart Wizard Step 1   )   Repeat all
5   Chart Wizard Step 2   )   five steps
6   Chart Wizard Step 3   )   exactly
7   Chart Wizard Step 4   )   as for
8   Chart Wizard Step 5   )   embedded chart.

In this case Excel will open a new sheet, which it names 'Chart 1'. The column chart alone will appear on the new sheet as shown on the next page. Apart from minor formatting differences reflecting its different scale, it will be almost identical to the chart embedded on the worksheet which contains the source data.

Linking of Charts to Data

Remember that both embedded charts and chart sheets are dependent on the data in the source sheet. If any data point values are changed, the charts are automatically reconstructed to reflect these changes. Quite apart from the saving in time in drawing such charts by hand, there are further savings should the data need updating. Also this feature can be further exploited in investigating spreadsheets, e.g. in What-if tests.

Tip
Which type of chart is the more appropriate - Embedded or Chart Sheet? Embedded charts are used where it is better to display the chart close to the data. Chart sheets are better for greater detail or for isolating charts.

By opening a second window to view both 'Sheet1' and 'Chart1', and arranging the two sheets, the Embedded Chart and the Chart Sheet can be compared.

With the 'Chart1' Window active, there is a change to the Command Menu structure. All that is apparent here is the absence of the 'Data' menu but there are more significant changes - see next section.

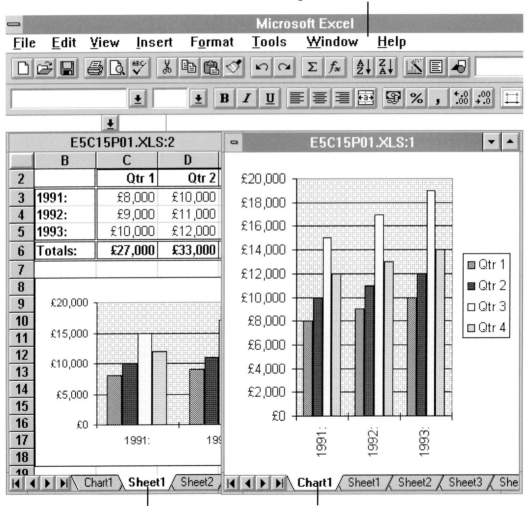

Sheet1 contains both the source data and the **embedded** column **chart**. Any changes made to the source data will immediately ripple through both charts.

Chart1 was created and named by Excel. Apart from the greater detail in the Y-axis, reflecting the larger size, and the distortion from the window arrangement, it is almost identical to the embedded chart.

Command Structure for Charts

It was indicated on the previous page that the Command Menu structure is different for Worksheets and Charts. Superficially the main menu bars appear the same, since only the Data menu is omitted from the Chart Menu Bar. However the **Insert** and **Format** menus contain major differences in the choice of command, offering powerful techniques of enhancing and editing charts. Also the Chart Menu Format option can be circumvented by double clicking a part on a chart. For these reasons the Chart Toolbar provision is relatively lacking in scope.

For the remainder of this chapter, the two menus will be clearly distinguished by the terms *Worksheet Command Menu* and *Chart Command Menu*.

Worksheet Insert Chart Command versus Chart Toolbar

We have seen that Embedded or Sheet Charts can be created by using the Worksheet **Insert** menu **Chart** sub-menu to select the command **On This Sheet** or **As New Sheet**, respectively.

To create an Embedded Chart only, the **Chart Wizard** button is provided both on the **Chart Toolbar** and on the **Standard Toolbar**.

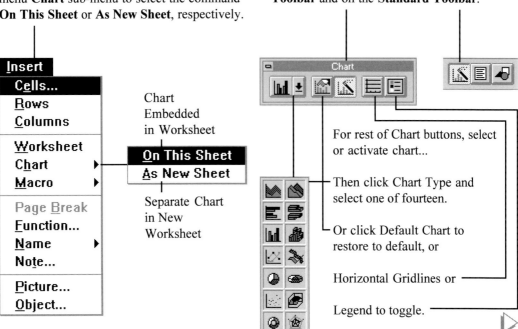

Insert

Cells...
Rows
Columns

Worksheet
Chart ▶
Macro ▶

Page Break
Function...
Name ▶
Note...

Picture...
Object...

Chart Embedded in Worksheet

On This Sheet
As New Sheet

Separate Chart in New Worksheet

For rest of Chart buttons, select or activate chart...

Then click Chart Type and select one of fourteen.

Or click Default Chart to restore to default, or

Horizontal Gridlines or

Legend to toggle.

Worksheet Command versus Chart Command Menus

The Chart Command menu structure is very similar to the
Worksheet Command menu structure, apart from the Insert and
Format menus, which contain many new commands relating to
charts. The purpose of some is indicated below.

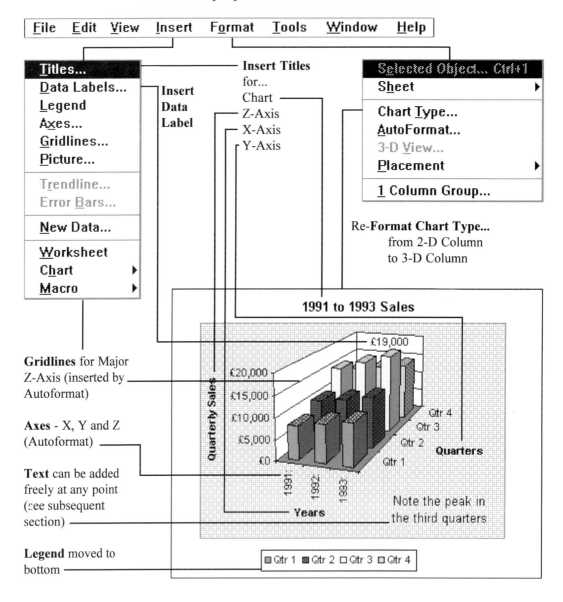

Activating versus Selecting Charts

Chart Sheets are always activated, which means that the Chart Command Menu bar is always displayed for a Chart Sheet.

Embedded Charts lie on Worksheets to which the Worksheet Command Menu bar normally applies. To display the Chart Command Menu bar, you must first activate the chart. Since the chart is a graphic object, it is also possible to select it...

Note that Worksheet Command Menu is active.

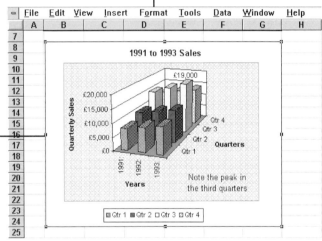

To Select an Embedded Chart, *click it (once)* anywhere within the chart so that Sizing Handles appear on its border.

Note that Chart Command Menu is active.

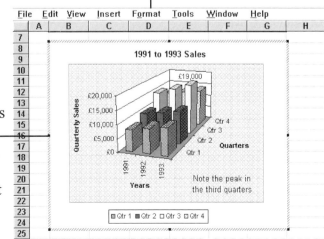

To Activate an Embedded Chart, *double click it* so that its border changes to a thick grey line and Sizing Handles appear.

To De-activate or to De-select Chart, click anywhere on worksheet, away from chart.

Inserting Extra Data

To insert extra data points or extra data series:

1   Introduce extra rows/columns and extra data into the
     worksheet, e.g. extra data points for 1994 quarterly sales.

2   Select the range of new cells, i.e. $B$6:$F$6.

	A	B	C	D	E	F	G	H
1								
2			Qtr 1	Qtr 2	Qtr 3	Qtr 4	Totals	
3		1991:	£8,000	£10,000	£15,000	£12,000	£45,000	
4		1992:	£9,000	£11,000	£17,000	£13,000	£50,000	
5		1993:	£10,000	£12,000	£19,000	£14,000	£55,000	
6		1994:	£11,000	£13,000	£21,000	£15,000	£60,000	
7		Totals:	£27,000	£33,000	£51,000	£39,000	£150,000	

3   Point to boundary of selected cells so that pointer changes
     to an arrow and drag onto the chart area, where the pointer
     will have a small plus sign attached.

4   On releasing the mouse button, the chart will be
     reconstructed with the data points for 1994.

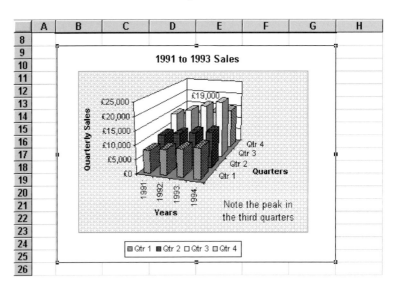

Selecting Parts of a Chart

It is necessary for you to select precisely the various parts of an activated chart prior to editing or formatting them. You may use the mouse or the keyboard:

> **Selection with Mouse**: With the mouse, you keep **pointing and clicking** to select items of finer detail.

> **Selection with Keyboard**: Use the **arrow keys**, generally **up** and **down** to move between groups and **left** and **right** to move between items within a group.

By both techniques the selection is monitored on the formula bar.

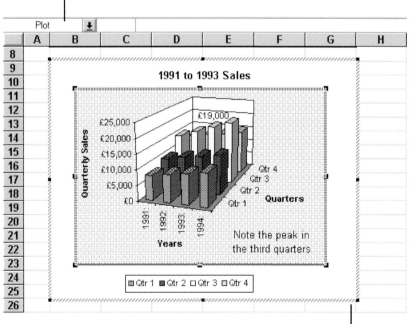

Tip
Although the mouse is more intuitive, the keyboard is more positive and faster.

Note
Although the X-axis label has been changed, the title needs editing.

Plot Area selected.

Formula Bar

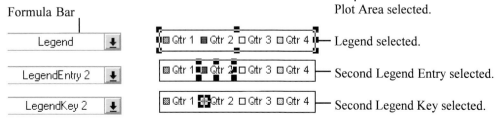

Legend selected.

Second Legend Entry selected.

Second Legend Key selected.

The Series Function

Note
If generally you only require commercial charts then you may not need to read this section.

If you select a series on a chart, you will see on the formula bar an abbreviation such as 'S2' and a formula of the form "=SERIES(   )". Its arguments provides Excel with the information it requires to build a chart for that particular series. Some knowledge of this function can help you understand how Excel builds up charts and in particular how the Chart Wizard must interpret the selection of cells you have made. The Series function has four arguments, separated by commas:

=SERIES(Series Name, X-Axis Names or Values, Series Values, Plot Order Integer)

If supplied, this text is used in the Legend to identify the series. If omitted, Excel substitutes the text, 'Series #' where # is the series number.	If supplied, this will be a list of text or numbers. If it is text, Excel uses it to name the X-axis or Category values. If it is a number, Excel uses it for the X-Axis values. If omitted, Excel merely counts the number of values in the series to form the Y-Axis values and doesn't name the categories.	This must be supplied. It gives the list of values to be plotted. These provide the Y-Axis values for a 2-D chart or the Z-Axis values for a 3-D chart.	This is just a digit which gives the series number.

Note
Normally the first three arguments will be in the form of cell references or cell names. However text or lists of numbers can be supplied.

When you make a selection of cells, and call up the Chart Wizard, it must try to sort your data into sections which can be used for one or more series and must be further separated to supply the cell references for the first three arguments above. This is why at step one, the Chart Wizard asks you to confirm the range of cells selected and in particular at step four it asks you to say whether the data series are in rows or columns, and which rows/columns, if any, have been used to store the X-Axis labels/values and/or Legend text.

▷

The example below gives some simple typical scientific data and shows how Excel would plot the charts according to the amount of information supplied for the Series function arguments. The graphs were constructed using the chart type 'XY (Scatter)'.

Note cell ranges:
X:$C$1:$K$1
Y1:$C$2:$K$2
Y2:$C$3:$K$3
Legends:$B$2,$B$3

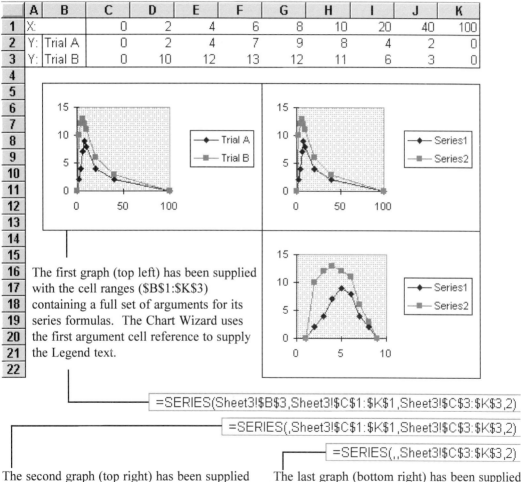

	A	B	C	D	E	F	G	H	I	J	K
1	X:		0	2	4	6	8	10	20	40	100
2	Y:	Trial A	0	2	4	7	9	8	4	2	0
3	Y:	Trial B	0	10	12	13	12	11	6	3	0

The first graph (top left) has been supplied with the cell ranges ($B$1:$K$3) containing a full set of arguments for its series formulas. The Chart Wizard uses the first argument cell reference to supply the Legend text.

=SERIES(Sheet3!$B$3,Sheet3!$C$1:$K$1,Sheet3!$C$3:$K$3,2)

=SERIES(,Sheet3!$C$1:$K$1,Sheet3!$C$3:$K$3,2)

=SERIES(,,Sheet3!$C$3:$K$3,2)

The second graph (top right) has been supplied with the cell ranges ($C$1:$K$3) which does not contain the first argument. Excel still constructs a Legend but uses the general text, e.g. 'Series 2'.

The last graph (bottom right) has been supplied with the cell ranges ($C$2:$K$2) which does not contain the first and second arguments. The Chart Wizard does not have access to the X-Values and does its best by substituting a linear series from 1 to 9, which totally distorts the plotted graph.

Plotting Non-Adjacent Cell Ranges

The data required for the construction of charts and graphs is not usually placed conveniently in adjacent blocks of cells. Excel still handles this easily. As an example consider the creation of a chart sheet for the 'FastPrint 24 Annual Plan'. Suppose a comparison is required over the twelve months of the Sales, the Gross and the Net Profits:

1   Select the ranges as shown below by clicking and dragging with the mouse, whilst holding down the Control key...

Months of the year: $D$6:$O$6   Gross Profit: $D$20:$O$20

Sales Income: $D$10:$O$10   Net Profit: $D$33:$O$33

	A	B	C	D	N	O	P
1			FastPrint 24 LTD				
2			24 Exposu				
3			24 Hours I				
4			Annual Business Pla				
5							
6				January	November	December	Totals
7							
8	Films Per Month =			1632	1344	960	19200
9							
10	Sales Income =			£6,250.21	£5,147.23	£3,676.60	£73,531.91
11							
12	Sales Costs						
18		Total =		£3,750.07	£3,404.47	£2,943.67	£44,540.00
19							
20	Gross Profit =			£2,500.15	£1,742.77	£732.93	£28,991.91
21	% Gross Profit =			40.0%	33.9%	19.9%	39.4%
22							
23	Expenses						
31		Total =		£1,616.67	£1,616.67	£1,616.67	£19,400.00
32							
33	Net Profit =			£883.48	£126.10	-£883.74	£9,591.91
34	% Net Profit =			14.1%	2.4%	-24.0%	13.0%
35							

Annual Plan / Sh

2   From the **Insert** menu **Chart** sub-menu, select the **As New Sheet** option.

3   Complete the Chart Wizard's five dialogue boxes...

Step 1 of 5:   Confirm the list of selected cell ranges.
Step 2 of 5:   Select the **Line Type** of chart.
Step 3 of 5:   Select the **Line Sub-type** which has straight lines joining the markers and horizontal gridlines.
Step 4 of 5:   Accept that the **data series** is in **Rows** and Use First **1 Row** for Category Axis Labels and Use First **0 Column** for Legend Text.
Step 5 of 5:   Add a **Legend**: select **Yes. Chart Title**: key in 'FastPrint 24 Annual Plan'. **Y-Axis Title**: key in 'Sales, Gross & Net Profits'.

4   On clicking the Finish button the chart will be created on a new sheet, which is named 'Annual Plan Chart'.

Tip
*To improve view of chart, from the Chart **View** menu, select the **Sized With Window** option.*

Note
The automatic placement and formatting of the Chart Title and of the Y-Axis Title. This is done by AutoFormatting, part of the chosen Chart Type and Sub-Type (see pages 320-321).

However, not all features, e.g. the clarity for Series 3, are entirely satisfactory. The chart can be improved by further formatting.

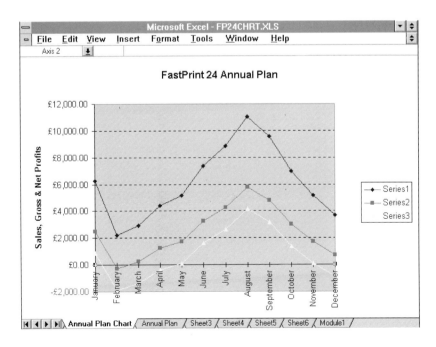

Formatting Charts

The procedure for formatting a chart follows:

1   Select the part of chart to be formatted, either by clicking once with the mouse or by changing the selected part by using the keyboard arrow keys. Select from the chart **Format** menu the '**Selected Object...**' option.

Or... Double click the part with mouse.

Tip
Instead of keying in Legend names, you may click the cells on source worksheet in which labels have been stored. Alternatively, you may supply the cell names.

2   The appropriate dialogue box will be displayed. Select the required tab and complete it.

The number of such dialogue boxes and tabs is so extensive that only a few will be shown to indicate how the 'Chart of Annual Plan' was improved.

The indistinct series 3 is selected for formatting and the **Line** and **Marker** Colours are changed to Black. The **Weight** of the **Line** is increased for all three series.

The Names for Legend are keyed in on the **Name and Values** tab...
Series 1 'Sales', Series 2 'Gross Profit', Series 3 'Net Profit'.

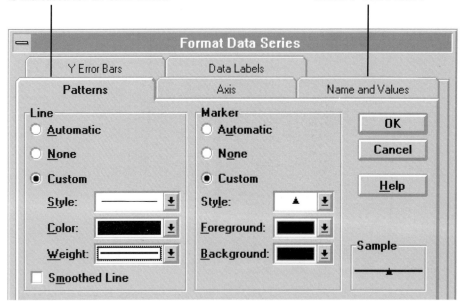

Both the axes are selected in turn and the **Font** is changed to **Bold**. The **Pattern** of axis lines is increased in **Weight**.

The Y-Axis **Number** format is changed so that no decimal places are displayed. The X-Axis label **Alignment** is altered to the vertical.

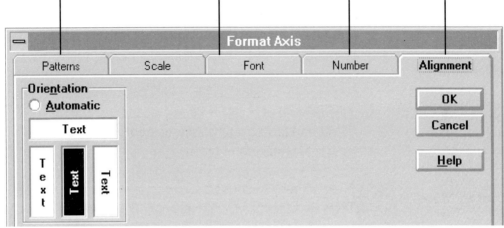

The Legend was selected and dragged to top right hand corner of the chart.

To accommodate the new text, the Legend was stretched in width, by dragging a sizing handle.

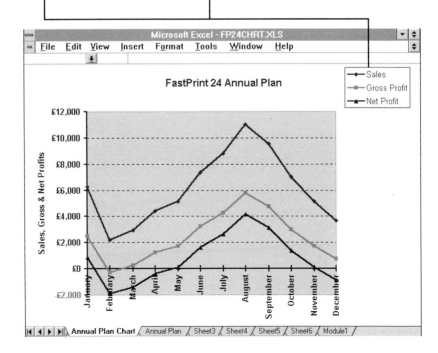

Adding a Secondary Axis

Note
*You cannot first select the data on the worksheet and drag it to a chart sheet because you cannot copy in this way between sheets. Alternatively you can use the worksheet menu command **Edit Copy** together with the chart menu command **Edit Paste**.*

Sometimes it is necessary to plot mixed data series which require different scales. This requires a Secondary Axis. As an example, extra data will be added to the 'Chart of Annual Plan', which requires a Secondary Axis:

1   From the Chart **Insert** menu, select the **New Data...** option.

2   Complete the **New Data** dialogue box by clicking the 'Annual Plan' sheet tab and selecting by dragging with the mouse the cell range for the 12 monthly 'Gross % Profits'.

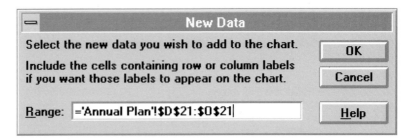

3   'Series 4' will appear on the chart, plotted very close to the X-Axis because the £1000s scale for the Y-Axis is too large for the fractions stored for percentage values.

4   Double click 'Series 4' on the chart and the **Format Data Series** dialogue box will appear as on the next page. Complete it as shown.

Patterns Tab
Line and **Marker**: change colour to dark grey.
Line Weight: select medium.

Name and Values Tab
Key in the series name as '% Gross Profit'.

Axis Tab
Plot Series On: Select **Secondary Axis**.
The sample will show the modified chart with 'Series 4' re-scaled to the new secondary axis on the right. Excel extends the new scale from -10% to –60% to cover the data range. It can still be improved by choosing a scale which corresponds to the existing horizontal gridlines.

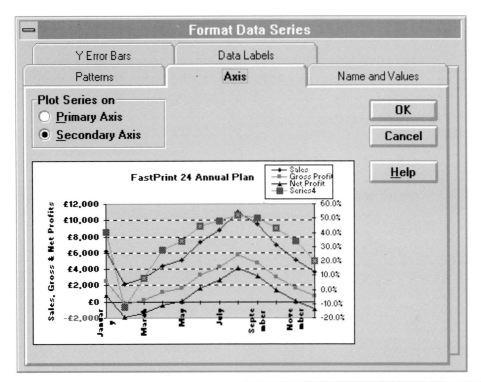

5   Double click the secondary axis on the chart and complete the Format Axis dialogue box.

Patterns Tab:
Axis Weight: Select medium.

Font Tab: Select Bold.

Number Tab: Remove decimal place.

Scale Tab: Edit Minimum, Maximum and Major Unit. —————

The resultant chart is shown on the next but one page.

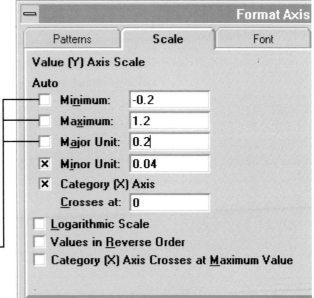

Adding Extra Text to a Chart

The procedure for adding any extra elements to a chart follows:

1   From the Chart **Insert** menu, select the option for the
     element to be inserted, e.g. Titles..., Data Labels...,
     Legend..., Axes..., Gridlines..., Picture..., Trendline...,
     Error Bars..., New Data...

2   The appropriate dialogue box will be displayed.

Inserting a Secondary Axis Title

1   From the Chart **Insert** menu, select the **Titles...** option.

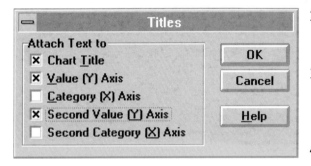

2   In **Titles** dialogue box, *check*
     the **Second Value (Y) Axis**.

3   A title, containing the text
     'Y2' will appear against the
     secondary axis.

4   If not selected, then select it.

5   Click it again and the existing text should reappear with the
     text insertion point. Edit it so that it is replaced by the new
     title, 'Percentage Gross Profit'.

6   Click away from title text and new title will be realigned
     alongside the axis. See the next page.

Inserting Text

The easiest element to insert in a chart is text. Since it doesn't
appear in the Insert menu, it is possibly the least obvious:

1   Make sure the Chart or the Plot area is selected.

2   Just key in the text, e.g. 'Note the small Christmas peak'.

3   The text will appear in the middle of the chart area.

4   By dragging its border, it can be moved to its preferred position. By dragging its handles its size can be adjusted. The text will be automatically wrapped to the width of containing box.

5   By double clicking it, it can be reformatted as shown to Bold Italic.

6   To edit such text subsequently, click it once to select it and click it again to put it in editing mode with the text insertion point in place.

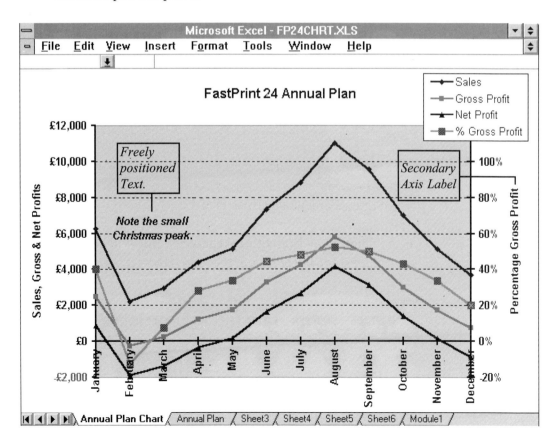

Built-in versus Custom AutoFormats

When you use the Chart Wizard to choose a Chart Type and a
Sub-Type, you are actually applying a Built-in AutoFormat
which as well as giving you the chart type also provides chart
formatting. You can create Custom AutoFormats:

1   First create a chart and format it. As an example, we will
     use the 'Annual Plan Chart'.

2   From the **Chart Format** menu, select the **AutoFormat...**
     option. The **AutoFormat** dialogue box will display the
     built in formats. For **Formats Used**, click **User-Defined**.

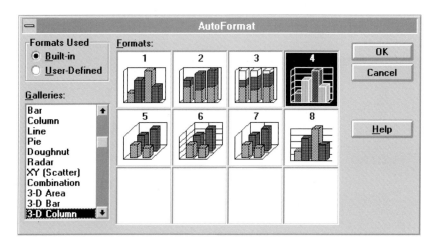

3   Click the **Customize...** button and in the **User-Defined**
     AutoFormats dialogue box, click the **Add...** button.
     Complete the **Add Custom AutoFormat** dialogue box.

Key in the
Format Name
and its
Description.

Warning
Don't exceed 32
characters!

4   The **User-Defined AutoFormats** dialogue box displays
     the new format name, description and a sample chart.

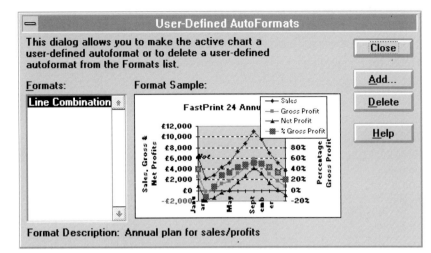

Note
*This dialogue box
enables additional
AutoFormats to be
added or existing
custom
AutoFormats to be
deleted. You are
not allowed to
delete the Built-in
AutoFormats.*

5   When subsequently you apply to an activated chart the
     AutoFormat command **User-Defined** option, your
     Custom AutoFormat will be displayed.

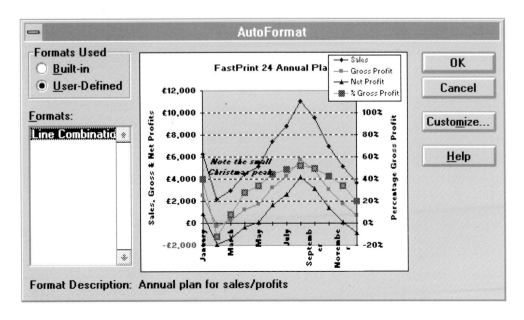

Using Graphic Objects

You may construct graphic objects on your worksheets and charts to further annotate and improve the presentation. A substantial range of objects and features are available on the **Drawing Toolbar**, which can be displayed most conveniently from the Standard Toolbar. You *must* employ the mouse to use these tools.

Click the **Drawing Button** on the **Standard Toolbar** to display or to remove the **Drawing Toolbar**.

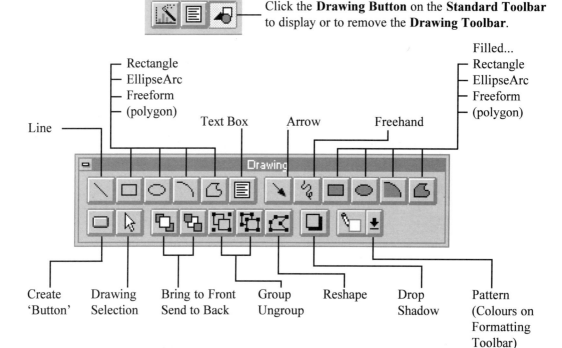

Line

Rectangle
EllipseArc
Freeform
(polygon)

Text Box   Arrow   Freehand

Filled...
Rectangle
EllipseArc
Freeform
(polygon)

Create 'Button'   Drawing Selection   Bring to Front Send to Back   Group Ungroup   Reshape   Drop Shadow   Pattern (Colours on Formatting Toolbar)

To draw an object the procedure is almost always the same. For rectangles, ellipses, arcs and text boxes, drag the containing rectangle from one corner to the opposite corner. For lines and arrows drag from one end to the other. Holding down the **Shift** key at the same time constrains the former objects to symmetry within a containing square, and the line and arrow to angles at 45 degree increments. Holding down the **Alt** key will attach corners or ends to the nearest worksheet gridlines.

Once Text Boxes are inserted, the text insertion point will appear within the box awaiting text. The text can be formatted as for cells.

Possible confusion may be caused by pre-setting the pattern and colour for filled objects. This is because the pattern is set by the **Drawing Toolbar Pattern Button** and the colour of the pattern by the **Formatting Toolbar Colour Button**. Objects may also be filled later.

To use a drawing tool once, click its button once. To use repeatedly, double click and cancel by clicking button.

The straight parts of a **Feeform** polygon are constructed by clicking the end nodes; the curves by dragging the mouse.

If the **Reshape Button** is selected, a node can be dragged to adjust its shape.

The **Create 'Button' Button** draws buttons for macros. See Chapter 13.

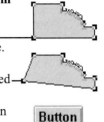

Tip
*Even better control is afforded by clicking the object with the **mouse right button** to display the short-cut menu.*

	A	B	C	D	E	F	G	H	I	J	K
1		Object		Object		Object		Object		Object	
2		Name		Drawn		with Shift		Filled with		with Drop	
3				Normally		Key		Colour		Shadow	
4											
5		Rectangle									
6		(Square)									
7											
8		Ellipse									
9		(Circle)									
10											
11		Ellipse Arc								No Effect!	
12		(Circle Arc)									
13											
14		Freeform									
15		Polygon									
16											
17		Text Box		Text is		No Effect!		Text is		Text is	
18				wrapped.				wrapped.		wrapped.	
19											
20		Line						No Effect!		No Effect!	
21		(45degrees)									
22											
23		Arrow						No Effect!		No Effect!	
24		(45degrees)									
25											
26		Freehand						No Effect!			
27											
28											

Cut
Copy
Paste
Clear
Edit Object...
Format Object...
Bring to Front
Send to Back
Group
Assign Macro...

In particular the s... command gives control of line thickness and fill colour.

This example shows the combination of a spreadsheet, an embedded chart and several types of graphic object. The graphic objects can also be used on chart sheets.

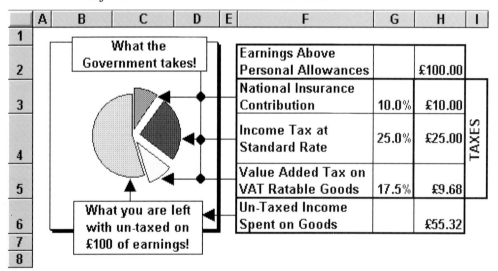

If accidentally the chart was moved above the graphic objects, then the **Move to Back** key would rectify the fault.

Suppose it was decided to move the piechart and the supporting graphics to a new location. To select them, the **Drawing Selection** button would be clicked and a containing rectangle dragged around them.

It would be even better to use the **Group** button to prevent the parts being separated.

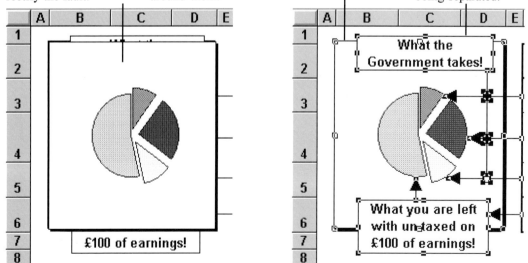

Using Charts in What-If Tests

An example is now given of using a 3-D chart to aid What-If tests. It investigates the 'FastPrint 24 Model', introduced in the earlier chapter on 'What_If Tests':

1   A two-input data table is first created on the 'Monthly Plan' sheet.

Data is first entered into the shaded cells, retail prices into the row and annual advertising expenditure into the column. Cell K50 is linked to cell I74, which contains the 'Net_Profit'.

From the **Data** menu, select the **Table...** option. For the **Row Input Cell**, key in 'Retail_Price'. For the **Column Input Value**, key in 'Annual_Advertising'.

K50	↓	=I74							

	J	K	L	M	N	O	P	Q	R	S	T
49											
50		£2,849	£3.00	£3.25	£3.50	£3.75	£4.00	£4.25	£4.50	£4.75	£5.00
51		£1,000	-£1,216	-£817	-£728	-£695	-£712	-£772	-£868	-£993	-£1,141
52		£2,000	-£28	£239	£398	£457	£1,094	£987	£1,064	£839	£574
53		£3,000	£1,175	£1,536	£1,751	£2,082	£2,041	£1,896	£2,330	£2,026	£1,917
54		£4,000	£1,645	£2,080	£3,006	£3,103	£3,305	£3,130	£2,849	£2,482	£2,716
55		£5,000	£2,279	£2,774	£3,318	£4,095	£4,040	£3,841	£3,772	£3,355	£2,864
66		£16,000	£3,869	£4,573	£5,908	£6,064	£5,986	£5,954	£6,166	£5,574	£5,125
67		£17,000	£3,846	£4,553	£5,891	£6,048	£5,969	£5,935	£6,146	£5,550	£5,098
68		£18,000	£3,811	£4,521	£5,860	£6,018	£5,939	£5,904	£6,112	£5,514	£5,059
69		£19,000	£3,765	£4,477	£4,901	£5,976	£5,897	£5,861	£6,068	£5,468	£5,011
70		£20,000	£3,712	£4,426	£4,851	£5,926	£5,847	£5,810	£6,016	£5,414	£4,955

2   The complete range of cells above, i.e. $K$50:$T$70 is selected.

3   From the **Insert** menu **Chart** sub-menu, the **As New Sheet...** option is selected. The Chart Wizard dialogue boxes are completed.

Step 1 of 5: The area is checked and accepted.

Step 2 of 5: The chart type **'3-D Surface'** is selected.

Step 3 of 5: The first default format is selected.

Step 4 of 5:
Data Series In: Select **Rows**.
Use First **1** Row for X-Axis.
Use First **1** Column for Y-Axis.

Step 5 of 5:
Add a Legend: Select **No**.
Chart Title: 'FastPrint 24 Advertising Model'.
X-Axis Title: 'Retail Price'.
Y-Axis Title: 'Annual Advertising Expenditure'.
Z-Axis Title: 'Net Monthly Profit'.

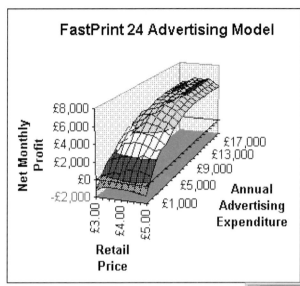

According to the *theoretical advertising model*, this graph shows that as the expenditure on advertising is increased, the net monthly profit rises and levels off reaching a value where any further increase is a waste of money. Correspondingly it shows that if the retail price is raised too much, sales will decline or if it is lowered too much, profits will decline. Of particular interest are the three maximum ridges. It was these optimum regions that Solver was trying to locate in Chapter 8, 'What-If Tests'. In particular the smaller nearer region explains the final solution that was located.

To adjust the 3-D view of the model, click the surface with the **mouse right button** to display the **short-cut menu** and select the **3_D View...** command. Adjust the settings in the **Format 3-D View** dialogue box and see the effect of the changes as you do so. To revert to the original, click on **Default.**

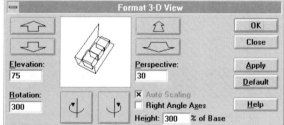

Note the default values are:

Elevation   15 degrees,
Rotation   20 degrees,
Perspective   30%,
Height   100 %.

Alternatively, you can select the walls or floor of the graph and use the mouse to drag the corners. The graph will change into a wire frame model of the walls and floor to speed up the display as you twist it to its new position. On releasing the mouse, the graph will be redrawn in its new position.

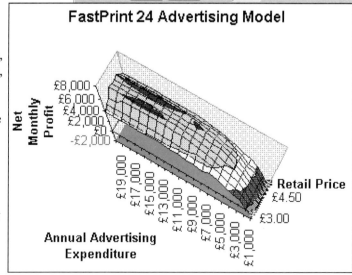

Macros and
Customizing

Overview

A Macro is a pre-specified sequence of commands, which Excel executes automatically. Why should you ever need to use macros? As soon as you start routinely carrying out repetitive sequences of commands, you will realise that you need a macro to store the sequence so that it can be replaced by a single command. Excel makes it easy for you to record and store such sequences and to recall them subsequently...

> by selecting the macro name,
> by using a short-cut keyboard control key,
> by selecting a new menu bar command,
> by clicking a customized sheet button
> or by clicking a customized button on a toolbar.

Excel allows you to **Customize Toolbars**, which means that you are allowed to change the buttons on the built-in toolbars and you can make new toolbars to display the buttons you most often use. Excel provides many more buttons than those used on the built-in toolbars and it is also possible to create your own.

A new feature of Excel 5 is that macros are automatically recorded in **Visual Basic**. Many users will be content to use macros quite happily without being aware of this. However if you can program in BASIC and you are willing to learn about Visual Basic, then the further possibilities of customizing and enhancing applications are extensive, for example, creating your own dialogue boxes to interact with the user.

There are so many customizing features and they are so extensive that it is possible to change substantially the usual Excel interface of command menus and in-built toolbars for very powerful and specialised applications. The only problem is that Excel could appear less familiar to other users and particularly to new users.

This chapter will concentrate on using macros and customizing toolbars. In a short section, it will provide an insight into the power of Visual Basic.

Recording a Macro

In earlier chapters, the example worksheets on 'FastPrint 24' contained sub-headings in capitals for emphasis. In later chapters following formatting, such sub-headings were converted to bold but the letters were changed to the more subtle style as for 'Proper Nouns', i.e. the first letter of a word in caps, the rest in lower case. Instead of re-keying all the sub-headings, a simple macro was developed. This was done in two stages:

1   A macro was recorded to convert selected cell to bold

2   Visual Basic was used to alter the words to 'Proper' style.

To record, follow the precise sequence:

1   Select the cell to be processed.

2   **Start** the **Macro Recorder**...

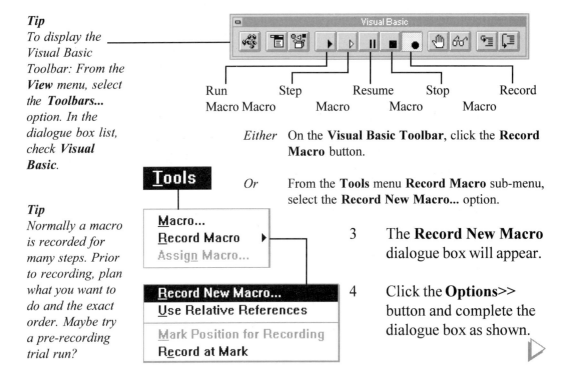

Run   Step   Resume   Stop   Record
Macro Macro   Macro   Macro   Macro

Tip
To display the Visual Basic Toolbar: From the **View** *menu, select the* **Toolbars...** *option. In the dialogue box list, check* **Visual Basic**.

Either On the **Visual Basic Toolbar**, click the **Record Macro** button.

Or From the **Tools** menu **Record Macro** sub-menu, select the **Record New Macro...** option.

Tip
Normally a macro is recorded for many steps. Prior to recording, plan what you want to do and the exact order. Maybe try a pre-recording trial run?

3   The **Record New Macro** dialogue box will appear.

4   Click the **Options**>> button and complete the dialogue box as shown.

▷

Macro Name:
Either accept the default
name, 'Macro1' or key
in your own name. ———

Description:
Here the default is ———
accepted.

Assign to Menu Item:
This is optional but here
a new command is ———
introduced. Note the
ampersand precedes the
character to be
underlined on the
command menu.

Short-cut Key: Again
optional but here the ———
lower case letter 'w' is
entered.

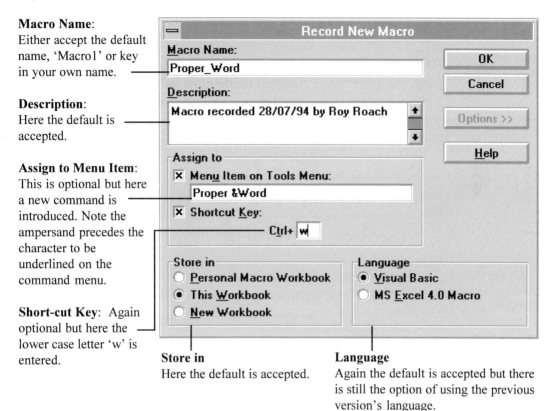

Store in
Here the default is accepted.

Language
Again the default is accepted but there
is still the option of using the previous
version's language.

5   On clicking the OK button, the **Stop Macro Record** sheet ———
     button will appear somewhere on the screen. This acts as a
     reminder that you are in record mode and that everything
     you do will be recorded! (Don't even move this button!)

6   Carefully in the correct sequence, carry out the commands
     you require to record. For this oversimplified example this
     consists only of clicking the **Bold** button on the
     Formatting Toolbar.

7   Stop the macro recording by clicking the **Stop Record** ———
     Button on the screen or the **Stop Macro** button on the
     Visual Basic Toolbar.

Running a Macro

There are several alternative ways of running a macro:

1   Select the cell to be processed. (At this stage only to be changed to Bold!)

2   Run the macro...

> *Either*   From the **Tools** menu,
>   select the **Macro...** option.
> *Or*   Click the **Run Macro** button
>   on the **Visual Basic Toolbar**.
> *And*   Complete the **Macro** dialogue box.

Macro Name/ Reference:
Select the name of the required macro. Click the **Run** button.

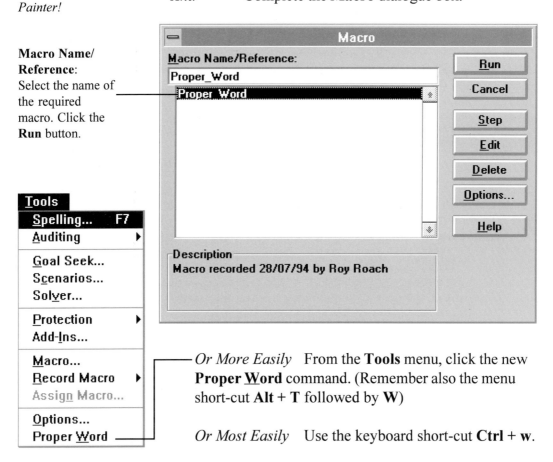

Or More Easily   From the **Tools** menu, click the new **Proper Word** command. (Remember also the menu short-cut **Alt + T** followed by **W**)

Or Most Easily   Use the keyboard short-cut **Ctrl + w**.

Extending a Macro with Visual Basic

If you examine the sheet tabs, you will find that Excel has inserted a new sheet named by default 'Module1'. This contains the Visual Basic code for your macro.

```
'
'   Proper_Word Macro
'   Macro recorded 28/07/94 by Roy Roach
'
'   Keyboard Shortcut: Ctrl+w
'
Sub Proper_Word()
    Selection.Font.Bold = True
End Sub
```
`|◄|◄|►|►|/ Sheet5 / Sheet6 \ Module1 / || ◄ |`

Comments start with single quotes.

The main code is relatively short.

Tip

If you make a mistake in recording a macro and you want to start again, delete the last addition to this 'Module' sheet, i.e. the last procedure starting with 'Sub' and finishing with 'End Sub'. Here the whole sheet could be deleted, as it contains only one procedure.

The code can be extended as shown below. It is beyond the scope of this book to explain or teach Visual Basic. However, you may be able to follow it by reading the comment lines:

```
'   Proper_Word Macro
'   Macro recorded 28/07/94 by Roy Roach
'   and extended in Visual Basic.
'   Keyboard Shortcut: Ctrl+w
Sub Proper_Word()
    Cell_Value = ActiveCell.Value
    ' Check that the selected cell contains text.
    If TypeName(Cell_Value) = "String" Then
        ' If it contains text, then
        ' first convert it to "Proper" style.
        ActiveCell.FormulaR1C1 = Application.Proper(Cell_Value)
        ' Next change it to Bold.
        Selection.Font.Bold = True
    Else
        ' If the cell contains a number or a formula,
        ' then do not attempt to process it.
        ' Just send a warning message to the user.
        MsgBox "You must select a cell containing text!"
    End If
End Sub
```
`|◄|◄|►|►|/ Sheet5 / Sheet6 \ Module1 / || ◄ |`

Excel function called from Basic.

If the extended Macro is applied to
a single cell containing text, then it
converts it as shown.

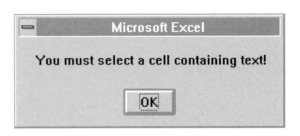

If the cell contains
a number, formula
or is empty, then
this error message
will appear.

It is hoped that
this simple example of Visual Basic may give you some insight
into the considerable scope for developing and customizing
Excel for specific applications.

Assigning Macros to Buttons

Excel's in-built customizing features allow you to create buttons
to execute your macros, either on a particular worksheet or chart
or, more conventionally, on a toolbar, which makes the macro
available to the containing workbook.

Assigning a Macro to a Sheet Button

1   On the **Drawing Toolbar**, click the '**Create Button**'
     button and construct the button on the sheet to the
     required size by dragging the mouse from corner to corner.

2   The **Assign Macro** dialogue box will be displayed. Select
     your macro name and click the **OK** button.

3   Edit and format the text on the button.

Assigning a Macro to a Toolbar

The next section shows you how to assign your macro to a
button on a customised (or in-built) toolbar.

Creating Custom Toolbars

To create your own toolbar:

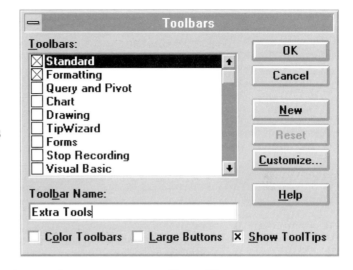

1 From the **View** menu, select the **Toolbars...** option.

2 Complete the **Toolbars** dialogue box.

> **Toolbar Name**:
> Key in new name.

> Click **Customize...** button.

3 The **Customize** dialogue box and a new empty toolbar will be displayed. Use the dialogue box to place buttons onto the toolbar.

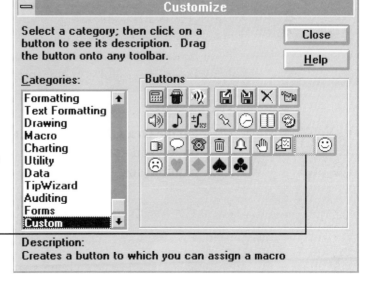

Categories:
Select the **Custom** category.

Buttons:
Select the **empty** button.

With the mouse, **drag** the empty button into place on the toolbar.

Note This dialogue box contains many more buttons than are available on the built-in toolbars. Some may have been mentioned by the Tip Wizard. You can use this technique to alter the in-built toolbars. Subsequently to revert to the original contents, use the **Reset** command in **Toolbars** dialogue box.

◁

You could also add three useful buttons from the **Utility** category: **Increase Magnification**, **Decrease Magnification** and **Toggle Full Screen**. Finally click the **Close** button.

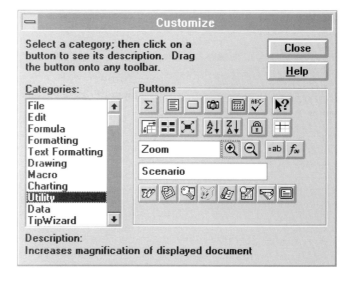

4   To edit the button image, click the new toolbar with mouse right button and from short-cut menu, select **Customize...** Then click empty button with mouse right button and from short-cut menu, select **Edit Button Image...**

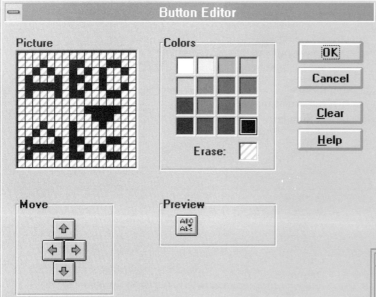

Edit the empty button image as shown and finally click the **OK** button.

There are now six ways to run the macro:
1   Tools Macro option.
2   Visual Basic Toolbar Macro Run button.
3   Tools Proper Word option.
4   CTRL + w.
5   Sheet button.
6   Toolbar button.

Index

Symbols

A

B

C

Other in easy steps Books

by Harshad Kotecha 1-874029-18-0 128pp £9.95

by Scott Basham 1-874029-16-4 306pp £14.95

by Harshad Kotecha 1-874029-12-1 180pp £14.95

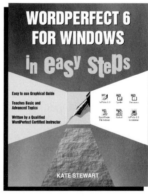

by Kate Stewart 1-874029-11-3 331pp £14.95

by Scott Basham 1-874029-19-9 220pp £14.95

For further information please contact:

COMPUTER STEP

5c Southfield Road Southam
Warwickshire CV33 OJH
England
Tel 01926 817999 Fax 01926 817005